TARGET
LEIPZIG

TARGET LEIPZIG

The RAF's Disastrous Raid of
19/20 February 1944

ALAN COOPER

Pen & Sword
AVIATION

First published in Great Britain in 2009
By Pen and Sword Aviation
an imprint of
Pen and Sword Books Ltd
47 Church Street
Barnsley
South Yorkshire S70 2AS

ISBN 978 1 84415 906 2

A CIP record for this book is available from the British Library

Printed and bound in England
by the MPG Books Group

Typeset by S L Menzies-Earl

Pen and Sword Books Ltd incorporates the imprints of
Pen and Sword Aviation, Pen and Sword Maritime, Pen and Sword Military,
Wharncliffe Local History, Pen and Sword Select,
Pen and Sword Military Classics and Leo Cooper.

For a complete list of Pen and Sword titles please contact
Pen and Sword Books Limited
47 Church Street, Barnsley, South Yorkshire, S70 2AS, England
E-mail: enquiries@pen-and-sword.co.uk
Website: www.pen-and-sword.co.uk

Acknowledgements

Nick Knilans
Norman Storey
Leslie Burton
Gordon Carter
Freddie Brown
Steve Bethell
Len Young
Ernest Windeatt
Robert Trett
John Carter
Paul Zorner
Ray Shield
Leslie Bartlett
Tony Sherwin
Bernard Downs
Patrick Turner
Alan Morgan
Victor Southwell
Ken Watkins
Marshal of the Royal Air Force Sir Michael Beetham
Bob Baxter
Mike King
My wife Hilda for her patience and help whenever it was needed

Contents

Introduction 9

Missing Failed to Return...10

Chapter 1   Aerial Warfare...11

Chapter 2   Between the Wars.......................................23

Chapter 3   Bomber Command......................................26

Chapter 4   Bomber Offensive......................................35

Chapter 5   The German Defenses 51

Chapter 6   The German Aircraft Industries 65

Chapter 7   Leipzig 81

Chapter 8   Target Leipzig 87

Chapter 9   The Second Attack 92

Chapter 10   The Third Attack 98

Chapter 11   To the Target 103

Chapter 12   Combat with the Enemy...........................109

Chapter 13   Over the Target 117

Chapter 14   The Home Run 122

Chapter 15   Casualties 128

Chapter 16   The Outcome 140

Chapter 17   The Aftermath...145

Chapter 18   US 8th/15th American Army Air Force 152

Chapter 19   The Last Operations 173

Chapter 20   Post-war...176

Appendix   Losses at Leipzig 181

Bibliography 217

Index 219

Introduction

What did happen at Leipzig on 19/20 February 1994, the third major attack on the German city in WWII? The first two attacks were quite successful, and, with modest casualties – thirty-eight aircraft were missing in two operations.

The third and last major raid on the city took place at the latter end of the Battle of Berlin and proved to involve, at that time, the heaviest losses suffered by Bomber Command in WWII and double the losses of the two previous raids put together.

As proved in other books such as *The Nuremberg Raid* by Martin Middlebrook, there has to be a reason for these great losses. Perhaps there was a leak in information to the enemy, or other such reasons. By examining the now available material and by talking to the crews involved one can come up with a sound, logical reason why this attack on Leipzig went sadly wrong and many fine men were lost.

Along with the last raid on Berlin by heavy bombers, plus the Nuremberg raid, this raid made the casualties for the first three months of 1944 seem rather high, and in retrospect slightly distorted.

This book is an account of what happened on this operation over sixty years ago and on the two previous raids on the German city of Leipzig, plus the subsequent attacks by the US Army Air Force.

Missing
Failed to Return

Missing, Failed to Return was the terminology in the RAF during WWII for aircraft and men that failed to return from an operation. Some squadrons used 'missing' in their operations record book, officially known as the 540/541, others 'failed to return'. It matters little as they both meant the same thing – that a crew and a fighting machine of Bomber Command were out of action. The crew may not be dead of course, a percentage having been taken prisoner and an even small percentage evading capture. But, the facts are there, sixty years later, that the greater percentage would be casualties.

Chapter 1

Aerial Warfare

—⁓—

It was in 1909 that Lord Montague of Beaulieu outlined the effects of a raid on London by a fleet of airships. He was adamant that in future wars the enemy would not hesitate to use air bombardment to achieve a possible victory.

At this time the Italian Giulio Douhet became involved in the Italian Air Force. He had also written books on mechanised war. He said that in the future war would not only be on the land and at sea but also in the air and would become the third part of any future wars.

In 1910 there were signs that Great Britain would be subject to attack from the air in a future war.

With the use of the machine-gun, tanks and U-Boats also came the aeroplane. This opened the battlefield from the sea and the trenches. It also meant that not only soldiers were involved but also civilians. It also meant that technology would play an important part in all future wars.

This would be based on the accuracy of the bombs dropped from the air and in the early days of aerial warfare this was very hit and miss.

There were a number of factors, two vital:

1. Was supremacy in the air really of such great importance?
2. Could supremacy be attained?

It was considered that such air attacks would considerably harm morale and material damage could be achieved.

In 1909 a meeting was held by Lord Montague and the National Defence Association that outlined the possible effects of a raid on London by a fleet of airships directed on the main government buildings and concluded that this could paralyse the nation. Montague developed an early and important theory about strategic bombing, in which cities such as London were national 'nerve centres' that could be incapacitated by an air attack.

The first bombs were dropped on 1 November 1911 by the Italians during the Italian–Turkish war. A Lieutenant Gavotti carried four bombs in a leather bag and dropped one on a Turkish encampment. Following on from the success of the first drop he then dropped the remainder in a second run over the target. In those days the bombs were more like grenades than bombs and weighed only four and half pounds.

Giulio Douhet first served in the Italian army as an artillery officer but between 1912 and 1915 he commanded Italy's first aviation unit, known as the Aeronautical Battalion. He had become involved with the Italian Air Force from about 1909, during which time he had written books on the mechanical side of war. During WWI, having criticised the way the war was being conducted and managed, and saying so in public, he was court-martialled. He was found guilty and imprisoned until 1917. When what he had been saying was found to be true his conviction was retracted and he was put in charge of the Italian air service with the rank of general. But in 1921 he left the services and set out to write books on the theory of air warfare. His book *Command of the Air* was published in 1922. That same year Benito Mussolini made him head of Italy's aviation programme. But he again resigned this post to concentrate on writing.

His theory was that the essence of air power was the offensive and the only good defence was a good offence. The air force who could command the air by bombing the enemy air arm into extinction would doom its enemy to perpetual bombardment, and so command of the air meant victory.

In WWI he had called for a massive build up of the Italian Air Force and proposed a force of 500 bombers that could drop 125 tons of bombs daily. This was completely ignored.

Douhet advocated that the offensive use of aircraft would cut off an opponent's army and navy from their bases and that it was much more important to destroy a railroad station, bakery, a war plant or to machine-gun a supply column, moving trains, or other targets than to strafe or bomb a trench. (This we would see in 1944 when the German Army was on the retreat and coming under constant air attacks.)

Douhet believed in the effects on morale of bombing. He said air power could break people's will by destroying country's 'vital centres'. Armies would become superfluous because aircraft could overfly them and attack these centres of the government, military and industry with impunity. He identified five targets: industry, transport infrastructure, communications, government and 'the will of the people'. He believed in the principle of Total War.

Not all his predictions came true but some did. For instance, gaining command of the air, terror bombing and attacking vital centres did occur in

WWII. What did not come true was Douhet's argument that in the future war would be become so terrible that common people would rise against their government, overthrow it with revolution, then sue for peace.

As far as bombers were concerned he felt one had to have the greatest possible number so as to be able to launch major offensives whenever the opportunity arose.

He continued his writing up to his death in 1930. Today his theories of air war are still popular and well read and he is known as the father of air power.

In 1912 a German naval officer gave a lecture on bombing and claimed that an attack on England would cause serious material damage and affect the morale of the people. So, two years before WWI an attack and war with England was being considered in Germany. In Germany, airships were being armed with machine-guns and bomb racks were introduced.

Also in 1912 the possibility of an attack on London was taken seriously and steps were made to take precautions against such an attack using guns and searchlights.

A memorandum from the British government in 1912 stated:

> In the case of a European war between two countries, both sides would be equipped with large corps of aeroplanes, each trying to obtain information about the other, and to hide its own movements. The efforts which each would exert, in order to hinder or prevent the enemy from obtaining information, would lead to the inevitable result of a war in the air, for the supremacy of the air, by armed aeroplanes operating against each other. This fight for the supremacy of the air in future wars will be of the first and greatest importance, and when it has been won, the land and sea forces of the loser will be at such a disadvantage that the war will certainly have to terminate at a much smaller loss in men and money to both sides.

In 1913 in Germany more experiments were carried out carrying larger bombs and from a height of 350 feet. In the future strategic bombing was meant to attack not only the airfields but also the airfield factories and the enemy's industries. It would be long range, which would be the purpose of a main bomber force.

In August 1914, attacks were made on Antwerp by German Zeppelin airships.

In September 1914 war was declared by Germany. Elements of the aerial warlords in Germany wanted to attack England by air from the outset but when the Kaiser opposed this it was a year before this came to fruition, and then with some strict conditions. No attacks were to be made on many of the buildings in London such as Buckingham Palace and other Government buildings but there were no restrictions about hospitals, schools and civilian homes.

There were in Germany prominent people who were against indiscriminate bombing.

The first raid on England came in January 1915 and the first attack on London in May 1915.

In 1916, Lord Trenchard, commander of the Royal Flying Corps, said:

> The aeroplane is not a defence against the aeroplane. But the opinion
> of those more competent to judge is that the aeroplane, as a weapon
> of attack, cannot be too highly estimated.

In France, Trenchard was later the first Chief of Air Staff in the newly formed RAF and ended his service with the rank of Marshal of the Royal Air Force.

The raids by airships continued throughout WWI until the first aeroplane attack on 25 May 1917 when twenty-three Gotha aircraft set out to attack London but only got as far as Gravesend. They did, however, drop their bombs before turning back owing to cloud and killed ninety-five people. This new aeroplane could carry 3,000-lb bombs and fly for five hours without refuelling.

The first daylight raid on London was in June 1917 with over 162 people killed and 432 injured. All but eleven casualties were civilians, one bomb hitting a school and killing sixteen and injuring thirty. This caused an outcry in England and 500 aircraft were sent to bomb Berlin.

As in WWII the clergy in the UK were against reprisals, considering them to be wrong and immoral. But also as in WWII there was no alternative to a bombing offensive.

In 1917 General Jan (Manny) Smuts was asked to investigate 'Air Organisation and the direction of aerial operations'. In his report of August 1917 he said 'Air power can be used as an independent means of war operations'. His report was thought to be the most important paper in the history of the creation of the Royal Air Force.

A study was made of the industrial area in Germany around the cities of Düsseldorf, Cologne, and Mannheim and the steel industry of the Saar Valley. Night and day bombing was discussed. The preference was for day bombing and the reasoning was that during the day at work or in the streets, people were vulnerable to air attacks whereas as night they had a roof over their head. Night time bombing also depended on good weather and moonlight.

The first of what was an early Blitz period started in September 1917, when in two raids twenty-three people were killed and 107 injured in Britain.

It's strange we often think of the Underground stations being used in WWII as air raid shelters but in WWI in September 1917, 300,000 people used them as shelters from air attacks too.

An air offensive from Flanders against Germany as a reprisal was considered.

In another raid in October 1917 thirty-three people were killed and forty-nine were injured. Churchill wrote after this raid about the effects of such raids on the civilian population.

In November a further study and paper was written on targets and selection and it suggested a bomber force of 2,000, of which 1,000 would be available to attack any specific targets.

In April 1917 the USA entered the war and a Lt/Col William Mitchell of the US Army Air Service was sent out to France to liaise with the British and French Air Force leaders. In September 1918 he led a force of 1,476 Allied aircraft on an attack on St Mihiel, a salient on the Western Front in France. It was about 35 miles wide at its base and 15 at its apex. It had been formed in September 1914 in an attempt to envelope the fortress of Verdun. Over four years all attempts to eliminate it had been foiled. This was to be the greatest air battle of the Great War. The battle was over 12–16 September 1918.

The objectives of the attack were: the destruction of German air forces to prevent them flying over Allied lines; reconnaissance of enemy positions, including direction of artillery fire; and lastly destruction of enemy ground forces through bombardment and strafing. In the case of the bombers the objectives were simply to hinder enemy concentration by railroads and destruct enemy aircraft on its airfields.

Air superiority was essential by a large force on the enemy's air force wherever it was found. Of the 1,476 aircraft over a 1,000 would be used for the destruction of the German Air Force. The most important element was providing air cover for Allied ground forces.

The attack on St Mihiel was a great success with the salient being reduced in four days and the German army given a mauling.

One of the things that came out of this operation was that although destroying enemy aircraft was the main objective there was no attempt to destroy the German aircraft industry.

Colonel Mitchell was one who did not believe that WWI would be the War to End All Wars.

Plans were being made to make reprisal raids on Germany. Further raids were made in 1918, including the first dropping of a one-ton bomb.

It was May 1918 when the last attack came. Forty-three Gotha bombers took off but only thirteen reached London. Nevertheless, the bombs they dropped killed forty-nine people and 177 were injured. In eight daylight raids and nineteen night raids by the Gothas 435 people were killed and 997 injured.

Between 1914/18 103 raids by airships and aeroplanes dropped 8,000 bombs, killing 1,414 and injuring 3,416, which included 670 killed and 960 injured in London.

In Great Britain there were 469 anti-aircraft guns, 622 searchlights, 259 height-finders and ten sound locators manned by 6,136 officers and men. At this time, May 1918, the Air Council in the UK decided to form an Independent Force for large-scale bombing attacks on Germany. Trenchard wrote a paper entitled 'Long Distance Bombing'.

Some 210 targets were highlighted for attack in Germany. This would be carried out by the Super Handley Page bomber capable of carrying 230-lb bombs. But as the Armistice came in November 1918 and with it the end of WWI, so these attacks never took place.

In 1921 Colonel Mitchell, now the deputy director of the Air Service in the USA, was trying to get over his theory of ships being destroyed by aerial bombing. They worked on the theory of aiming bombs near the target ship so that expanding water pressure from underwater blasts would stave in and open the ship's plates.

In July 1921 this theory was put into practice and a former German battleship was attacked from the air with 2,000-lb bombs – the ship sank in twenty-two minutes. It was shown that there were no direct hits but three bombs landed nearby and as predicted blew out the ship's plates.

In 1921, the Italian General Giulio Douhet published a paper entitled 'The Theory of Air War in the Future'. His main argument was that it was important 'To eliminate the enemy air force's operations by attacks on the opposing ground organisations, and the destruction of enemy flying units in the air.' He was an artillery officer and later in command of airship battalions in Italy. He recognised the sky as the main battle area.

In 1922 Colonel Mitchell met Giulio Douhet in Europe and shortly after a translation of Douhet's *Command of the Air* began to circulate around the Air Service.

At the end of WWI, in 1918, the RAF had the largest air force in the world with 300 squadrons, 233,000 officers and men, 23,000 aircraft and 700 airfields. Three years later this had been reduced to only twenty-one squadrons.

In November 1932 the then Prime Minister of the UK, and also Chairman of the Committee of Imperial Defence, Stanley Baldwin declared in the House of Commons that 'the bomber will always get through'. This was in a speech he made about war and disarmament at that time. He went on to say that the greatest fear of future wars was in the air. An air force's speed of attack in comparison with an army on the ground was much greater and up to WWI civilians were exempt from the effects of war. He argued that any town near or within reach of an aerodrome could be bombed within the first five minutes of war being declared. He went on to say that that no power on earth could protect people from being bombed and that the bomber will always get through and that bombing would be from 20,000 feet and perhaps even higher.

He went on to say that munitions being made could play a big part in future wars (more so than ever before) and it was essential to knock these out. and in no other way could this be stopped than by bombing from the air. What he was saying was, deny the production of the bombs to be dropped so that they cannot be dropped.

The only defence he said was offence, which meant you had to kill more of the enemy (even women and children) quicker than the enemy could kill your people if you were to win or save yourself. He said he mentioned this so that people may realise what was waiting for them when the next war came. This was seven years before the Second World War began and how his words rang true when that war began and continued for six years.

In 1933 Hitler reformed the German Air Force and steps were taken to design a four-engine bomber with a range of 1,800 to 2,000 miles with a ceiling of 20,000 feet and a speed of 250 mph. Added to this, it was to be capable of carrying a bomb load of 12,000 lb.

On 14 July 1936 Bomber Command was formed in Britain along with Fighter and Coastal Command and the twin-engine Wellington bomber made its maiden flight.

But still in 1937 nothing had been done about a four-engine bomber in Britain on the lines the Germans had suggested three years previously and in hindsight the British were glad that they didn't.

The training of bomber crews was also in limbo. And although the plans were laid down in 1936 it was 1942 before the four-engine bomber was seen. To hit the target a bomber with the range and bomb capacity was needed. It must be also able to resist or evade enemy defences, navigate successfully to the target and, having arrived there, be able to release its bomb accurately.

In 1937 a Mr Alfred H.R. Fedden MBE, Chief Engineer with the Bristol Engine Division of the Bristol Aeroplane Co. Ltd, was sent to Germany by the Secretary of State for Air Lord Weir. He was accompanied by Captain Bartlett, the Continental representative of the Bristol Company, and Baron de Ropp, the German agent of the Bristol Company. On the second visit he was accompanied by Mr Devereus, Managing Director of High Duty Alloys Ltd, and Mr Evans of the Bristol Company's Experimental Department. During this visit they were guests of the *Reichsparteitag*, the Annual National Socialist Party Gathering, at Nuremberg.

These two visits were at the invitation of General Milch, the German Secretary of State for Air, and had for their objective a first-hand investigation of the technical and productive progress that had been made by the German aero engine and aircraft industry under the new regime. It was believed that Fedden was the first British engineer to have been given a comprehensive insight into the newly created German aircraft and allied material industries.

The visits were possible, it was considered by Fedden, because of his contacts in past years with General Milch, and a number of the executive managements of the various aircraft and aero engine contractors. Also, once the German Air Ministry policy of 'opening their doors' to a foreigner had been defined, they went out of their way to show what a great deal had been accomplished in so relatively short a period.

The first and perhaps most important deduction to be made from these visits was that the declared British plan of having an Air Force that was based on parity with Germany by April 1939 was out of the question. With regard to engines, it was considered that Germany would have produced a greater number of them by April 1939 than in Britain and that they would be of sound design and excellent workmanship.

However, there was hope that Britain could hold its own in a present expansion programme. The production complex was already in place for the manufacturing of aero engines but if we were not careful Germany would in five years time surpass us in design and technique.

The position between British and German aircraft was, however, a far more serious matter. The present and proposed production organisation of Britain was completely inadequate, and the British people were being kept in the dark as to the real situation.

The majority of aircraft plants involved in military aircraft were unsuitable and too restricted in comparison with the German factories. Unless this was faced up to by the Government there was no chance of ever achieving parity with Germany.

The report from this visit was discussed at a meeting in London on 2 November 1937. It was divided into three parts based on two reports by Mr Fedden and also reports by Major Bulman and members of the Rolls-Royce firm. The meeting was intended to cover the development of technique and materials in Germany, secondly the deductions made by Mr Fedden relating particularly to output, thirdly the suggestions of changes that should be made in organisation in the UK. Fedden suggested that the meeting should confine itself to the first of these. The second point was under constant review.

Lord Weir said how impressed he was by the great development that had occurred in Germany not so much by the conditions or organisation but by a few individuals. He asked if the people who had made the visit shared his opinion.

The reply was that what had impressed them in Germany was not so much that the individuals were outstanding but the very large number of people in what might be called the second rung who appeared to be capable of developing into leaders whenever leaders were required. Another who had been there, a Wing Commander Goddard, added that a number of people commented on the way in which the personality of the present leaders of the aircraft industry had developed in Germany since they had been advanced to positions of great responsibility.

With regard light alloy castings, Lord Weir said the report suggested that the Germans had made great strides in the new technique of aluminium and magnesium castings.

Two years before, in 1935, Mr Fedden had found the technique unreliable with the opinion that aluminium was most useful for forgings but not castings. But during these two years Reutenburg had gone ahead with development in Germany and Lord Weir was under the opinion that what had been done in Germany should have been done in the UK.

Plans were afoot in the UK for building a new factory for airframes.

Lord Weir's attention was brought to the German Dornier 17 bomber, which in Mr Fedden's opinion was superior to the Wellington bomber. But the Deputy Director of Technical Development said that the information he had received indicated that it had not been a great success in Spain. Even with BWW 750-hp engines it proved very vulnerable in the air, and there were frequent cases of engine failure and of difficulty taking off with the exception of from large airfields.

On the question of power-operated turrets it was reported that these were under development in Germany but the Germans were behind the UK and the Italians in this respect.

In March 1938 the first report to Bomber Command was made by the Air Targets Intelligence Committee in which the possibilities of crippling the German war industry by attacking coking plants and power stations in the Ruhr area of Germany were mentioned. It emphasised that by paralysing the Ruhr region it could prevent Germany waging war on a large scale in less than thee months. But in September 1938 the then Prime Minister returned from Munich with his now famous (or infamous) 'Peace for our time' speech. In fact, all it actually meant was you have twelve months to prepare for war with Germany. At this time Bomber Command had been given low priority and was in no way ready for war.

However, in 1938 a bombing programme as such was laid down in the event of war with Germany. It meant they would in effect operate with their hands tied behind their backs, only being able to attack a very small number of targets – mainly those at sea or near the sea.

On 15 September 1938 the AOC of Bomber Command was sent a letter from the Air Council. This was in reply to a letter the AOC had sent to the Council concerning attacking German aircraft factories as bombs aimed at these factories would fall outside the limits of the target, causing casualties to the civilian population.

The Prime Minister had three principles regarding the selection and attack of objectives by air forces:

(a) It's against international law to bomb civilians as such and to make deliberate attacks on the civil population.

(b) Targets which are aimed at from the air must be legitimate military objectives and must be capable of identification.

(c) Reasonable care must be taken in attacking these military objectives so that by carelessness the civilian population in the neighbourhood is not bombed.

The letter went on to say that the most probable roles for the air force in the event of war arising out of a German attack on Czechoslovakia were likely to be on the general lines of plan W1 and W4.

The letter continued that attacks on aircraft factories should be excluded from operational orders until further directives from the Air Ministry. Attacks should be under W4, confined to troops and transport and railway embankments, cuttings, sidings, road and rail bridges etc.

In August 1939 it was considered that attacks on the Ruhr in the early stage of the war would be effective. But the French objected, saying this should be done later, fearing retaliation raids on factories in France that were defenceless.

Prior to WWII, *Luftwaffe* General Walther Wever wanted to create a strategic bombing capacity for the German armed forces. Out of this desire came the design of the four-engined bomber the Dornier Do 19 and the adaptation of Junkers Ju 89s into four-engined bombers. His idea was cancelled when he died in 1936 and instead medium bomber production was implemented on the basis that for every one heavy bomber two medium bombers could be built.

In September 1939 the Germans had 1,500 bombers, all capable of attacking targets in Holland, Belgium and Northern France.

The German aerial bombing of civilians began on 1 September when the Polish town of Wielun was targeted. This was followed by great raids on Polish cities such as the city of Frampol when 90% of the city was destroyed. Attacks on Rotterdam followed in 1940. A flight of three Ju 87 *Stuka* aircraft took off to bomb the approaches to a railway bridge over the River Vistula at Dirschau with the invasion of Poland. This was the start of a non-stop campaign lasting twenty-six days and the loss of 100,000 civilians killed or hurt. The bombing of the Polish Air Force airfields reduced the effect of their air force in the early stages of the war.

On 1 September President Roosevelt in the USA appealed that civilian targets should not be bombed and he received a reply reassuring him that this would be the case. In Berlin Hitler said he would not wage war on women and children and had ordered his air force to restrict its attacks to military targets only. That same day his air force attacked over sixty towns and villages in Poland, including the capital Warsaw.

Two days later at 11 am on the 3rd the UK was at war with Germany. The Treaty of Versailles was dead and buried with all offers of peace refused by the Germans.

After twenty-seven days of bombing and nineteen of shelling the city Warsaw surrendered, but not before 16,000 people had become casualties. One day, 24 September, it was attacked by 1,150 German aircraft, which started 137 fires.

This was the first city to lay in ruins and was the first to suffer under the 'Blitz' or in German the *Blitzkrieg*.

The Germans never developed a heavy strategic bomber force and in the invasion of Russia the bomber's role was to support the army on the Eastern Front.

In 1940 in the UK the Bombing Restriction Committee was formed to determine between non-combatants pursuing purely civilian occupations and military objectives.

On 14 May 1940 Rotterdam was bombed with 1,000 people killed, 7,000 injured and 78,000 homeless. The next day the Dutch Army surrendered.

On 19 August 1940 an attack on Liverpool was made. Already a raid had been made on London and when Croydon was bombed sixty civilians were killed. In August 1,000 civilians were killed in the UK. But it was not until 25/6 August that the first raid on Berlin was made when Tempelhof airfield was attacked and the Siemens factories in Siemenstadt.

This spurred the Germans to make more raids and by September 8,430 Londoners had been killed. This was followed by raids on Birmingham, Liverpool, Bristol, Belfast, Cardiff, Kingston upon Hull and Coventry.

The RAF's bombing campaign began in 1940 and built up to massive proportions by the time it ended in 1945. The first raid on a German town was Mannheim on 16 December 1940.

But in 1941 the Butt Report showed that many of the attacks were way off target and the bombing very scattered.

Chapter 2

Between the Wars

—◆—

Under the Treaty of Versailles signed in June 1919, the Germans had to disband their air force. Over 15,000 aircraft and 25,000 aero engines were handed over to the Allies. Only civilian aircraft were permitted in Germany but in 1922 the size of these aircraft was limited.

In 1918 the UK's inventory of 300 squadrons was reduced to twenty-four. In the future the only defence and hope for victory was a powerful bomber force. The Air Staff thought the bomb was the offensive weapon of the Air Force. The then Sqn Ldr Arthur Harris, later the C-in-C Bomber Command, was convinced that bombing was the main task of the RAF. And it was he who developed a prone position for the bomb aimer to have the best position to obtain a good view of the target. At the time Harris was commanding 45 Squadron. The Air Staff estimated that in future wars, bombing casualties would be fifty per ton of explosives dropped on Britain.

In 1928 a system of air control under the Air Force was set up in the UK, whilst in Germany it would appear memories were short and limitations on the size and number of aircraft were withdrawn by the German Government. This without a shadow of a doubt was an error. All the major German military aircraft of WWII, particularly bombers, began life as civilian aircraft.

In 1931 because of the financial crisis all stocks of bombs, ammunition and spare parts had been allowed to fall to a very low level in Germany.

In 1933, Hitler and the Nazi party came to power. By 1932 the German Sporting Flying Club, which had been founded in 1920, already had a membership of 60,000 and in 1935 the German air force the *Luftwaffe* was re-established in Germany. Conscription was introduced and the first tanks seen. It was obvious with conscription having been instituted in Germany that war in the future was on the cards.

Many visits were made to the UK by the German airliner Lufthansa in

1936. This was said to have been the time when many photographs were taken of the UK and in particular the south coast.

In France they were still very much clinging to WWI technology. The French were still using horses for transport, although they had been very much involved in the development of the tank and aeroplanes. Those involved at the time feel that because of their victory in WWI the French became complacent.

In France in 1933 and after the depression of 1929 there were great divisions in the French Government and as a result many movements had sprung up. It was not until 1934 that the Popular Front was formed but it was 1936 before things began to get better.

In 1934 France needed to re-arm but didn't.

The French did build the Maginot Line which used twentieth century technology and was known as the 'Shield of France'. It was 87 miles long but stopped 250 miles short of the coast. It had tank obstacles, artillery casements, machine-gun posts etc. It was the idea of André Maginot, the Minister of War in the 1920s, and its construction began in 1930.

In 1936 Belgium declared itself neutral.

Also in 1936 three Commands were formed in the RAF, including Bomber Command, and plans were implemented for four-engine bombers, the Stirling, Halifax and the ill-fated Manchester.

The Germans had no fewer than 1,500 aeroplanes in up to 140 squadrons whereas the RAF had only seventy-eight. Many people in the UK including Churchill and Harris saw that Germany was preparing for war with England.

Harris served on a committee with Captain Phillips from the Royal Navy and Colonel Forbes from the Army, their task to compile a report entitled 'Appreciation of the Situation in the Event of War Against Germany in 1939'. This they did and submitted it to the Chiefs of Staff in October 1936. The bomber had prominence in this report. Harris recommended that a build-up of aircraft be made – a total of 2,204 by 1939.

Before the outbreak of WWII, General Walther Wever of the *Luftwaffe* had made a point of wanting to create a strategic bombing capability for the German forces. It was called the Ural-Bomber project and resulted in the design of the four-engine Dornier Do 19, and the adaptation of the Junkers Ju 89, another four-engine bomber. However, on his death in 1936 this project was cancelled and medium bomber production advocated in its place; this was on the basis that two medium bombers could be built instead of one heavy bomber.

In 1938 Harris decreed that all aircraft on bomber stations were to be used for flying practice.

The Spanish Civil War showed the part modern aeroplanes could play in future wars.

In the UK the Cabinet approved the production of 12,000 aircraft by 1 April 1940.

Hitler, on 1 September 1939, said he had ordered his Air Force not to wage war against women and children and to keep to attacking military targets.

That same day his bombers attacked sixty towns and villages in Poland, including Warsaw.

On 1 September targets such as Wielun in Poland were attacked by Ju 87 (*Stuka*) dive bombers. This began a twenty-six-day onslaught in which 100,000 civilians were killed or injured. The city of Frampol was bombed by the *Luftwaffe* and 90% destroyed as a form of experiment – probably a rehearsal for London and other cities in the UK.

In this attack on Poland 700 bombers were involved. But the first bomb dropped in WWII was by a single Polish PZL.23 Karas of the 21st Squadron on a factory in the Silesian town of Ohlau. At this time as with other countries such as America there was a reluctance by the Polish Air Force to begin attacking targets in Germany. The *Luftwaffe* attacks on civilians soon dispelled the reluctance of the Polish Air Force making such attacks on civilian targets in Germany but the moment had been lost and it was now too late to carry them out.

On 3 September 1939 the UK announced it was at war with Germany.

On 21 September Warsaw was bombarded and the whole of Poland swamped by Germany and Russia.

Little was done to take on the Germans by the French Army. No bombing of the Ruhr took place by the French Air Force who feared retaliation. All the while in Germany they forged on. It is now felt that if the French had attacked rather than prepared to defend, the German Army would have only lasted one or two weeks.

The Maginot Line did not cover the Ardennes, which is the way the Germans came through by flanking the defensive line.

Chapter 3

Bomber Command

———⚍———

It was in 1915 during the First World War that one saw the beginning of tactical bombing. The Royal Flying Corps on the Western Front in France first put it into action. The first VC was awarded to the RFC for such an attack on the Courtrai railway station with a 100-lb bomb by Lt Rhodes Moorhouse.

In 1916 attacks on enemy airfield, billets and ammunition dumps were carried out. In 1917, bridges became the target to prevent German troops at the front receiving supplies via the bridges. They were attacked by a special unit that had been formed, known as the 8th Brigade. They used DH 4 day bombers or Handley Page night bombers.

In October 1917 the then Secretary of State for Air, Winston Churchill, was very aware of the need to get to a target, identify and attack it. He wrote:

> The dominating and immediate interests of the Army and the Navy have overlaid air warfare and prevented many promising lines of investigation from being pursued with the necessary science and authority. As a result, it remained true even at the end of the war that aerial warfare had never been practised except in miniature; that bombing had never been studied as a science; that the hitting of targets from great heights, by day or night is worthy of as intense volume of scientific study, as for instance, is brought to bear upon perfecting the gunnery of the fleet; that much of the unfavourable, accumulated data showing the comparative ineffectiveness of bombing, were the results of unscientific action. For instance, dropping bombs without proper sighting apparatus, trained 'Bomb' droppers (the equivalent of 'gun layers'), instead of dropping them in regulated salvos by specially trained men, so as to 'straddle' the targets properly. It is believed by the sanguine school that a very high degree of accuracy similar to that which had been attained at sea

under extraordinary difficult circumstances, could be achieved if something like the same scientific knowledge and intense determination were brought to bear.

In 1918, a unit consisting of bombers was entitled the Independent Force with Major General Hugh (Boom) Trenchard as its commander. Its role was to carry out a sustained offensive against the German industries. This was carried out and a noticeable reduction in German production was evident.

In October 1918, Handley Page bombers capable of carrying 1,650 lbs were to be used in the bombing of Berlin. This was because the Armistice in November 1918 never materialised.

On 11 November 1918, at the end of WWI, the RAF had the largest air force in the world – 23,000 aircraft and 700 airfields. In 1925 came a pledge to build up the RAF once again, but after the disarmament conference this was put on hold and financial crisis in 1931 made it impossible go through with the plan to order modern bombers.

By 1931 all expansion and progress had come to a halt because of the financial crisis.

Since 1925, with the formation known as the Air Defence of Great Britain, a bomber force had been in existence with the idea that in the time of war it would be used for strategic bombing.

On 14 July 1936, Bomber Command was formed along with Fighter and Coastal Commands. It began with 1, and 3 Groups of 20 Squadrons. In April 1937 came 4 Group and in July 5 Group.

In September 1937 Air Chief Marshal Sir Edgar Ludlow-Hewitt was posted in as AOC in C Bomber Command. He soon visited all the bomber stations in the UK but although he found the crews in good spirits he also found that Bomber Command was completely unprepared for war. He asked for a number of things to improve the situation such as navigation aids, safety devices, and the ability to train in all weathers.

The Air Staff compiled a list of targets in Germany for Bomber Command, which was working on targets for the bombers to attack in the event of war. This became known as the Western Air Plans and included attacks on German industry and the German Air Force and even setting fire to the German forests with incendiaries. Some of the predictions were to say the least a little far reaching. To attack nineteen power plants and twenty-six coking plants was thought by Bomber Command to be able to bring the German war production to a standstill in two weeks. Furthermore, it would require 3,000 aircraft and would result in the loss of 176 aircraft.

In 1936/7 Harris had prophesied that France would attain a aircraft strength of 2,000, of which 775 were bombers. But by September 1939 the bombers they had were of no use at all.

In March 1938 Harris again asked for all aircraft on bomber stations to be used for flying practice. When Prime Minister Chamberlain came back from Munich in September 1938 it was thought he had arranged with Hitler a peace deal. Bomber Command was therefore put on a low priority and was in no state for the war that lay ahead.

A report from the Air Targets Intelligence Committee who dealt with power, fuel, chemical, engineering, metallurgy and transportation in Germany mentioned the possibilities of crippling German war industry by attacking coking plants and power stations in the Ruhr area; this became plan WA5 and was sent to the Air Ministry on 28 July 1938. It emphasised the Ruhr's importance as the industrial centre of Germany. Attacks on this area could slow up and shorten a future war with Germany.

Although in 1938 a bombing programme was decided upon in the event of war it was very much restricted. Any targets in which civilians were likely to be killed or hurt were out. All targets were of a direct military standing.

At the end of August 1939 it was assumed at the Air Ministry that targets in the Ruhr would be of some strategic value. It was thought they could strike before the German defences were at full strength and well established. However, the French were not keen on this and asked that the Ruhr be left for a later date. Their view was that the Germans would retaliate against their factories, which at that time were undefended.

In September 1939, the outbreak of the Second World War, Bomber Command had thirty-three squadrons and only 638 aircraft. Of these, 398 were twin-engine aircraft. The Germans had 1,600 long-range bombers, 355 dive-bombers and 50,000 aircrew.

On 3 September 1939, His Majesty the King made a broadcast to the nation saying that the UK was at war with Germany.

On 4 September he sent a message to the RAF. He said that although behind the other two services the RAF would have to assume much greater responsibilities than the RFC/RAF had had to undertake in the First World War. The safeguarding of the UK would the RAF's role.

On 6 September South Africa joined the war and Canada on the 10th. Both would play a big part in the RAF's role in WWII.

When the war began the Germans had 900,000 men involved in the defence of Germany, or the *Reich* as it was known.

In September 1939, the Western Air Plans had fifteen possible targets for Bomber Command.

WA1   Attacks on the German Air Force.
WA2   Reconnaissance in co-operation with the Navy.
WA3   Close co-operation with the Navy in convoy
        protection in home waters.
WA4   Attacks on German military rail, canal and road
        communications.
WA5   Attacks on German manufacturing resources.
WA6   Attacks on Italian manufacturing resources.
WA7   Counter-offensive action in defence of sea borne
        trade in co-operation with the Navy.
WA8   Attacks on specially important depots.
WA9   Putting the Kiel Canal out of action.
WA10   Destruction of enemy shipping and facilities in
        German mercantile ports.
WA11   Attacks on forests.
WA12   Attacks on the German Fleet.
WA13   Attacks on the enemy's headquarters and
        administrative offices in Berlin and elsewhere.
WA14   Dropping propaganda leaflets.
WA15   Operations against enemy shipping by magnetic
        mines in concert with the Navy.

On 3 September aircraft of Bomber Command were in the air seeking out the German warships. The aircraft included Blenheim N6215 of 139 Squadron flown by Flying Officer A. McPherson and eighteen Hampden and nine Wellington bombers. The same night leaflets were dropped over Hamburg, Bremen and the Ruhr.

On 4 September came the first of many Bomber Command casualties when a Blenheim of 107 Squadron was shot down whilst attacking enemy shipping.

On 27 September 1939, it was announced that 18,000,000 leaflets had been dropped over Germany since the war began.

This type of operation continued until 10 May 1940, when Mr Winston Churchill became Prime Minister and the Germans invaded France and the Low Countries. Fifty airfields in France were attacked from the air.

One bridge was left standing over the Meuse and this was where Rommel and his forces came over into France. At this time the French Army was concentrating its forces on Holland and Belgium.

On 13 May the German infantry crossed over the Meuse. The British troops in France had not seen any serious fighting.

On 10 May the RAF fighters in France had suffered the greatest losses ever recorded in its history.

On 15/16 May 1940, eighty-three bombers, a mixture of Wellingtons, Whitleys and Hampdens, set out for the first attack on the Ruhr in WWII. The Ruhr Valley and the Krupp's factory at Essen became a common target for the crews of Bomber Command. The Ruhr soon became known as 'Happy Valley' or 'The Valley of Death' or finally 'The Land of No Future'.

On 17 May Brussels fell.

As one French General said at the time, the French troops did not show the same spirit and dedication as they did in WWI. This was put down to the long 'Phoney War' and their belief that there would not be another war as in WWI. After all, WWI was said to be the war that ended all wars.

On 20 May the German troops moved 200 miles in seven days.

On 25 May Boulogne fell and on the 26th Calais and Belgium capitulated.

The number of casualties had become so high that on 30 May 1940 a new bombing directive came out that No. 2 Group was to reduce its operations and to re-group with aircraft and crews.

On 4 June Dunkirk fell. Hitler asked for all the bells to ring in Germany.

On 10 June the French Government left Paris and Italy entered the war.

On 20 August 1940, Winston Churchill made a speech in the House of Commons.

> British airmen who, undaunted by odds, unwearied in their constant challenge and mortal danger, are turning the tide of world war by their prowess and by their devotion. Never in the field of human conflict was so much owed by so many to so few. All hearts go out to the fighter pilots, whose brilliant actions we see with our own eyes day after day, but we must never forget that all the time, night after night, month after month, our bomber squadrons travel far into Germany, find their targets in the darkness by the navigational skill, aim their attacks, often under the heaviest fire, often with serious loss, with deliberate, careful discrimination, and inflict shattering blows upon the whole of the technical and war-making structure of the Nazi power. On no part of the Royal Air Force does the weight of the war fall more heavily than on the daylight bombers who will play an invaluable part in the case of invasion and whose unflinching zeal it has been necessary in the meanwhile on numerous occasions to restrain.

He followed this with another speech on 3 September 1940.

The Navy can lose us the war, but only the Royal Air Force can win it.

Therefore our supreme effort must be to gain overwhelming mastery in the air. The fighters are our salvation, but the bombers alone can provide the means of victory. We therefore develop the power to carry on an ever-increasing volume of explosives to Germany, so as to pulverise the entire industry, and scientific structure on which the war effort and economic life of the enemy depends, while holding him at arm's length in our island.

On 22 June 1941, Germany invaded Russia and that evening Churchill made a speech in which he said '...any man or state who fights against Nazism will have our aid. Any man or state who marches with Hitler is our enemy'. He went on to say:

We shall bomb Germany by day and night in ever-increasing measures, casting on them month by month, a heavier discharge of bombs and making the German people taste and gulp each month a sharper dose of the misery that they have showered upon mankind.

On 14 July 1941, Churchill said: 'We shall have now intensified for a month past our systematic, scientific, methodical bombing on a large scale over the cities, seaports, industries and other objectives in Germany. But it is only the beginning.'

The hub of any bomber station was the Control or Watch Tower set in the middle of the airfield and surrounded by runways. It was manned twenty-four hours a day and each station had its own call sign. The Operations Room was also manned round the clock.

Before each operation a briefing was held and all matters concerning the operation were discussed (weather, defences and so on) to help the crews get to the target and also return safely. Those that did return were debriefed and from these debriefs information was stored and used in future operations.

The ground crew, without whom the aircrew could not operate, also worked around the clock making sure the aircraft were serviceable again to give the crews the best chance of survival.

They worked in all manner of weather conditions and in the main in the open. They only worked indoors on an aircraft that needed a major overhaul. At all other times it was out on the hard standing. To have some idea of what it was like in the winter of 1944, think about when you have been working on your car engine and you hit your knuckles with a spanner. On a Lancaster there were ninety-six spark plugs, forty-eight on each side and twenty-four in each engine. It would take three hours to check the electrics, the controls, instruments, radio, auto–pilot, hydraulics, guns and the ammunition feed to the guns. On the ground the engines were given a maximum 'run up' and had a final check on the hydraulics system servicing the flaps and gun turrets to make sure they were in perfect order for the crew who may have a an eight-hour journey ahead of them.

Only after this was the aircraft handed over to the pilot and his crew for an air test.

The men in the bomb dump would make up and load the required bomb loads onto the standard bomb trolleys and the armourers would do the fusing. The belts of ammunition were often belted up by WAAFs with 10,000 rounds for the rear gunner and 2,000 for the mid-upper gunner. For a station possibly putting up a maximum effort of say thirty-six Lancasters this would require no fewer than 432,000 rounds.

The crew of the fuel bowsers would put something like 2,000 gallons of petrol into a Lancaster. Medical and rescue crews stood by when the aircraft returned.

The parachute store was manned by WAAFs. Their task was to look after not only the parachutes issued to crews each time but also the Mae West worn in the vent of ditching in the sea and also the dinghies carried in each aircraft. They all had to be checked to make sure they were in good order and had no signs of wear.

Here the parachutes were hung on long pulleys for twenty-four hours before being packed. Each chute had its own flying log book in which all re-packing was entered by the packer.

The WAAFs on a bomber station played a varied role, including taking the crews to their aircraft in all manner of vehicles. In the officers' and sergeants' messes they made sure the crews had the famous 'operational supper of egg and bacon' and on return the same for breakfast.

The 'Map Queen' had the job of looking after thousands of maps and at a moment's notice had to be able to produce an appropriate map. These maps were known by the navigators as 'gen'. On occasions they were returned to her blood stained, evidence that it had been a hard trip and maybe for some a fatal one. She also kept quiet about the target for that night, although she would be one of the first to know. There were as well as the 'Map Queen' many others working in the background to make sure crews knew as much as possible before setting out.

The Station Intelligence Officer would plot the routes to and from the target using every scrap of information that had been gathered from previous debriefings, such as where flak was heavy on the previous night. He would then change the route slightly to avoid the flak and so on. It was very much a cat and mouse game – always trying to outwit your enemy.

If the 'Met Man' gave a good forecast it was known as 'pukka gen'. If he gave a bad one leading the crews to meet weather that had not been forecast it was known as 'duff gen'.

The briefings each time would cover all aspects of the operation and a groan would go up when the curtain was pulled back and the target was seen to be Berlin or Essen – all heavily defended. The Ruhr was know as 'The Valley of Death Or No Return' and Berlin 'The Big City'.

They were the unsung heroes of Bomber Command, all working on one cause – getting as many bombers into the air night after night and taking the fight to the enemy. Their motto was 'Keep Them Flying at All Costs'.

In a bomber crew there were seven men. The pilot was the captain, sometimes known as Skipper. The flight engineer assisted the pilot and in some cases could fly the aircraft if necessary. Many pilots gave the flight engineer a chance at the controls in the event he was hit etc. He was also an important man when the aircraft was short of fuel as he somehow could get every gallon possible out of the aircraft and in some cases was responsible for the aircraft getting back or not. They all relied on the navigator to get them there and back. The wireless operator was the man who kept them in touch with base. The bomb aimer controlled the aircraft over the target and was the man who on occasions uttered the words the crew did not want to hear – that they had to go around again. And last but not least there were the two air gunners, rear and mid-upper. They were the eyes of the aircraft with the rear gunner facing in the opposite direction to the rest of the crew. Many an aircraft owes its return to its gunners. On the other hand many air gunners never fired their guns in anger but if they had to you could be sure with the excellent training they had they were ready and more than capable.

How did bomber crews crew up? It was a bizarre system but seemed to work. At an Operational Training Unit the prospective crews were assembled in an aircraft hanger. A pilot would find a navigator, and the gunners would know other gunners from gunnery schools and so on it went until a crew was formed. Many stayed together for a full tour of operations, but of course sadly some also died and are now buried together in War Graves cemeteries all over Europe.

On a large bomber station would be up to 2,000 men and women. It resembled a hotel with people booking in and sadly and in many cases for a very short stay beforebooking out.

Once the pilot received the signal to take off from the Control Tower he would open the throttle and roar down the runway with the Lancaster's four Merlin engines at full power. To ensure the throttle stayed open at the crucial time of take-off the flight engineer would put his hand under the pilot's hand; if power was lost at this stage with an aircraft loaded with petrol and oil plus a full bomb load, the result would be fatal. As soon as they were airborne the navigator would give the course to the pilot. Over the sea the bomb aimer would arm the bombs and the gunners test their guns.

Over the target area the pilot would say 'Bomb doors open'. The bomb aimer would then take over and direct the pilot left or right or stay centre. When he was satisfied all was well he gave the words the crew wanted to hear and their reason for being there, 'Bombs gone'. Then came the eternal thirty seconds of flying straight and level while the bombing photograph was taken – the only method of determining the accuracy and success of the bombing.

The next day all the bombing photographs, developed by the photographic section, were published for all to see.

On return to base the Control Tower, mainly staffed by WAAFs, would receive from the wireless operator a request for landing instructions. She would reply, for example, 'Parsnip answering E-Edward, I am receiving you loud and clear'. Each station had its own call sign. The pilot would be given landing instructions from the Control Tower. If an aircraft was in trouble then it would be given a priority landing and the others told to circle and await their turn. It was her voice they last heard on take-off and hers would be the first voice they would hear on return.

All over the UK telegram boys would be on red bikes delivering small yellow envelopes that normally contained bad news. 'I am sorry to inform you that your son Sgt — is missing as a result of operations last night etc.'

Each commanding officer on many stations would be writing letters to next of kin.

It is important to remember that all RAF aircrew were volunteers. Whether volunteering or being conscripted into the RAF no one was forced to fly. One wonders over sixty years later what would have happened if they had not done so. Only thirteen out of every 100 of these brave and dedicated airmen in Bomber Command survived the war.

Their training was carried out in the USA, Canada, and South Africa and then in the UK on return. An RAF tour was twenty-five to thirty operations as opposed to the US 8th Air Force who had a limit of twenty-five.

Of course, many of the crews who flew in Bomber Command were from Australia, Canada, New Zealand, the West Indies and of course from the USA (men who before America entered the war in 1941 joined the RCAF). They came from all walks of life but as a crew it worked.

One day in the life of Bomber Command: there would be many more days, many more operations, many letters to write and many telegrams delivered before victory and peace would be achieved.

Chapter 4

Bomber Offensive

—ⵠ—

In April 1938 the British Cabinet approved Scheme L, under which 12,000 aircraft would be provided by 1 April 1940. But by September 1939 none of the heavy bombers, the ideal four-engine bomber, had been delivered and the total aircraft available was 488, many being obsolete. Of this total only sixty were Wellingtons. It would appear that despite the warnings signs from Germany little as far as the bomber offensive had been heeded.

On 4 September 1939, fifteen Blenheims of No. 2 Group and fourteen Wellingtons of No. 3 Group took off to attack German warships that were seen in the Schillig Roads and Wilhelmshaven and off Brunsbuttelkoog. It was not a great success because of the weather conditions. The Danish town Esbjerg was bombed in error, for which the British Government had to apologise and pay compensation for the deaths and damage incurred. The German battleship *Admiral Scheer* was hit by at least three bombs which, however, did not explode. The cruiser *Emden* was also hit. The losses were severe: five Blenheims and two Wellingtons were shot down by either anti-aircraft fire or by fighter attacks and the first RAF aircraft was shot down by the *Luftwaffe* in WWII. On 18 December 1939, the losses were even greater when an operation was mounted against German shipping in the Heligoland Bight area. However, the German fighters were waiting for them and a number of the Wellington force of 38, 115, and 149 Squadrons were shot down. This was a stark warning of what the men of Bomber Command were to face in the coming years of WWII.

On 4 April 1940, a new Commander-in-Chief of Bomber Command was appointed, Sir Charles Portal, later to be the Chief of the Air Staff. On 9 April Germany invaded Norway and Denmark. On 10 May 1940, after Germany had invaded France and the Low Countries, Winston Churchill became Prime Minister. Holland and Belgium fell a few days afterwards. Up to this time Bomber Command had flown 990 night operations, lost twenty-eight aircraft and in 393 daytime operations lost forty-five aircraft. Because the percentage of losses was lower during night operations Bomber Command's role for the rest of the war was at night. On 10 May 1940 the restrictions on attacks on Germany were lifted. After Rotterdam had been bombed on 14 May Bomber Command attacked industrial targets in the Ruhr for the first time. On 31 May it became necessary to review Plan WA1.

(i) Operations will take place only at night.

(ii) During the night period now prevailing, deep penetration will be possible.

The aircraft industry is highly dispersed. Both on the airframes and engine sides, great numbers of component factories contribute to the finished part. There are, however, certain factories specialising in assembling components: thirteen principal bomber airframe-assembling factories and thirteen principal bomber engine factories.

For reasons given in the plan it is clear that it would be far easier to destroy the airframe factories than the engine factories. Moreover, engines are installed at airframe assembly factories so that destruction of the latter would involve a certain loss in engine reserves.

All the German airframe assembly factories are on aerodromes; some are near rivers. Their identification on moonlit nights might be possible, although they are not self-illuminating targets.

Six airframe factories are close enough to the Dutch coast or to the French frontier to allow operations against them to be carried out under the cover of summer darkness. One of these six also produces Me 110 fighters.

The effect of these attacks would be a loss of output of the factories over the period required to rebuild and re-equip them either on the original site or elsewhere.

On 8 July Churchill wrote that the one thing that could bring the enemy down was an absolute, devastating, exterminating attack by a very heavy bomber from this country upon the Nazi homeland. He added in his own hand 'We cannot accept any lower aim than air mastery. When can it be obtained?' In July 1940 he had laid down a plan to bomb Berlin if London was attacked. When in August London was attacked an operation was made the next day on Berlin. On 3 September 1940, Churchill made another speech in which he said that the Navy could lose the war and only the RAF could win it. He went on to say that the fighters were the UK's salvation but the bombers alone could provide the means of victory. On 4 September 1940, he said that if Germany attacked our cities he would raze theirs to the ground.

Bomber Command played a big part in preventing Germany's planned invasion of the UK in 1940 by destroying many transport ships, tugs and barges – all intended to bring German troops and equipment to the UK. It was after this that Hitler postponed the invasion of the UK indefinitely. In October 1940, the newly appointed CinC of Bomber Command sent a special message of the day to all ranks of Bomber Command. In it he said that the achievement of victory fell to the RAF and Bomber Command in particular.

It became clear that the success of Bomber Command operations would depend on the ability or failure to solve the three main problems that confronted Bomber Command.

(i) Expansion of the Command and its re-equipment with more suitable types of aircraft, while at the same time attacking the enemy on every favourable opportunity.

(ii) Finding and hitting our targets in the difficult conditions with which we were faced.

(iii) Countering the growing strength and effectiveness of the enemy's defences.

In order to expand, the Command needed a substantial investment of national resources.

Apart from aircraft and aerodromes there was a need for a training organisation to turn out trained crews to address expansion and casualties. The Empire Training Scheme and Operational Training Units were doing this whereas in Germany they did not have such schemes, thinking that the war would be won rapidly by *Blitzkrieg* methods.

This training scheme would mean that it would be 1942 before the bombing of Germany would show potential as the more men you put into training schemes the fewer you have to fight at the same time and until the foundations of this scheme are set the outcome will be small.

Once the men arrived back in the UK they were trained in their respective crew positions but not yet operating as a crew. This was where the Operational Training Units came in and men were crewed up. Here they learned team work and operating on twin-engine bombers. Their instructors all had a tour of operations under their belt and could pass on this experience. The course at these training units was a long one but its length and content were most important if crews were to have a chance on operations. From this they went on Heavy Conversion Units where they learned to fly four-engine bombers. And from there to a main force squadron. Again, the instructors had returned from operations and could teach tactics that they had picked up during their tour.

However, in 1941 an investigation found that many of the bombs dropped were no nearer than 5 miles to the target.

On 8 January 1942 Air Marshal Sir Richard Peirse, the CinC of Bomber Command, was relieved of his command. This came after in November 1941, thirty-seven aircraft failed to return from an operation to Berlin. After twice submitting an explanation for the losses to Portal, the Chief of the Air Staff, both not being accepted, it was on the cards that a replacement was being sought.

On 16 January 1942 a letter was sent by the Air Ministry to the Deputy of Director of Bomber Operations reporting on the vulnerability of the aircraft industry in the UK. In particular it highlighted the Bristol Aircraft Company, which had been heavily damaged from German bombing.

It went on to say that the weight of the attack necessary to damage an aircraft factory was surprisingly high. With a 600-yard aiming error and accurate identification of the works it would be necessary to drop about 100 tons of bombs to 'write it off'.

However, another point made in this letter was that in recent attacks on the factory the building itself was not hit but the surrounding area was. Also, many of the men who worked at the factory houses were hit and absenteeism was high. One bomb destroyed 450 houses, of which 15% were occupied by the aircraft company workmen.

On 14 February 1942 came Directive No. 22 issued to Bomber Command.

On 22 February 1942, the leadership of Bomber Command was taken over by Air Chief Marshal Sir Arthur Harris. He had commanded No. 4 Group before the war and No. 5 Group in the early part of the war, and so had the experience to know what was required if the bomber force was to make an impact on the war. However, he found the Command strength no better in 1942 than in 1939 when the war began. Over three years, the bomber crews, with great dedication and courage, had in the main made very little difference to the way the war was going. They had, however, kept things going while the bomber force was developed and given hope to the people on the continent and in the occupied countries that Britain had not been invaded and was still fighting back. As long as they heard the bombers coming over night after night they knew they could ignore the German propaganda machine that was telling them England had been invaded. There was a great need for more bombers, aircraft that could carry greater bomb loads. The great problem Harris faced in 1942 was that aircraft that were coming off the production lines were being sent to Coastal Command and the campaign against the U-Boat, and Commands abroad. Bomber Command was at the bottom of the list and in great danger of being lost altogether. Harris had to think of a way to convince the powers that be that a large, well equipped bomber force, a force that could swamp a target to such an extent that the defences and rescue services could not cope, would have a great effect on the winning of the war in Europe.

During 1942 twenty-three squadrons were formed but the majority were sent to the Mediterranean and India or, as already mentioned, Coastal Command to combat the 'Battle of the Atlantic'.

During these first few months the question of what was the most effective way to use the nation's resources was addressed. Professor Lindeman, a government leading scientific advisor, wrote a paper in favour of the use of area bombing with the view of making the German workforce homeless, reducing morale and the enemy work production.

Mr Justice Singleton, a High Court judge, was asked by the War Cabinet to look into the various cases put forward by the three services. After deliberation, and thanks to Lindeman's paper, he came down on the side of Bomber Command, saying that the Command would be an important factor in the British war effort up to the end of the war.

On 20 February 1942, Bomber Command had only twenty-six medium bomber squadrons, consisting of Hampdens, Wellingtons and Whitleys, but only seven heavy bomber squadrons consisting of Manchesters, Stirlings, and Halifaxes, but as yet no Lancasters.

The introduction of 'Gee' meant a major move away from the sextant for navigators to navigate at night, permitting blind bombing and identifying targets at night and under operational conditions. This was used for the first time on 8/9 March 1942 against Essen, the chief target in the Ruhr, but because of industries in this area the haze made it difficult to identify the target.

On 9 March Harris despatched 235 aircraft to attack the Renault factory at Billancourt, which was making trucks for the German Army. This was the start of a target marking pattern with 470 tons of bombs being dropped on Billancourt and the bombing photographs showed that it had been a great success with two months' production being lost at the factory.

On 28/29 March 1942 the port of Lubeck was attacked by 234 aircraft; it was said that it was being used as a supply base for the German occupying forces in Norway. The operation was a success and the port was out of action for three weeks and its capabilities much longer.

This was followed by an operation on Rostock, which had a ring of Heinkel aircraft factories. It was after this raid that the Germans used the

word *Terroranggriff* (Terror Raid) and called the British aircrew *Terrorflieger*
or 'Terror Flyers'.

Photographic reconnaissance showed much damage to the Heinkel
bomber fuselage assembly sheds, three bombs having gone through the main
assembly shed. One hole was 70 foot across and the other 250 feet across.
Photographs showed that more than seventy fuselages had been destroyed
and also showed damaged Heinkel bomber fuselages, which the Germans
had dragged out of the assembly sheds. The experimental assembly sheds
and other aircraft factories suffered direct hits and the main offices,
including the drawing office, were damage by fire.

This was the first of four successive attacks on this town and 500 sorties
in which 305 tons of incendiaries and 442 tons of high explosives were
dropped. The Heinkel factory was severely hit and the report from Berlin
was that it had been completely destroyed end to end.

It was then that the idea of a 1,000 bomber raid was developed. Although
the Admiralty were happy about the concept of a strategic bombing
offensive Harris had to demonstrate that a large bomber force, targeted on
one target, was a success before it would give its support to Bomber
Command. The Admiralty wanted the aircraft for Coastal Command and
others wanted them in the Middle East.

With this in mind Harris, helped greatly by his Senior Air Staff Officer
and later Deputy Commander in Chief Robert Saunby, began to work on a
1,000-bomber raid to Hamburg. To achieve what was in 1942 an
astronomical number of aircraft would mean every aircraft and crew being
made available, including the crews and instructors in Operational Training
Units all over the UK.

On 20 May Harris wrote to all units in Bomber Command, Coastal
Command, Flying Training Command and Army Co-operation Command
outlining his plan and asking for their support and help. Coastal Command
originally promised 250 aircraft but this was overruled by the Royal Navy
under whose control Coastal Command came on 13 May 1942.

Despite this Harris was able to assemble 1,047 aircraft. The original
target was to be Hamburg on 27/28 May but because of the weather in that
area it was changed to Cologne, a heavily defended target with 120
searchlights and 500 anti-aircraft guns. This operation to deliver 1,500 tons
of bombs would take 2,000,000 gallons of petrol, 70,000 gallons of oil and
10,000,000 rounds of ammunition.

The date of the Cologne raid, now known as the 1,000 bomber raid, was
30/31 May.

Harris sent a message to AVM Coryton AOC of 5 Group marked personnel and most secret.

> Please convey the following message from me during their briefing to all crews taking part in this operation.
>
> The force of which you form a part tonight is at least twice the size and has more than four times the carrying capacity of the largest Air Force ever before concentrated on one objective.
>
> You have an opportunity therefore to strike a blow at the enemy which will resound, not only throughout Germany, but throughout the world. Next to London, New York and Liverpool, Hamburg is the most important commercial and industrial port in the world. It is, however the main centre of Germany's submarine building and manning activities, the very focus of German nautical tradition, and a vast hive of general war industry. In your hands lies the means of destroying a major part of the resources by which the enemy's war effort is maintained. It depends, however, upon each individual crew whether full concentration is achieved. Press home your attack to your precise objective with the utmost determination and resolution, in the fore-knowledge that if you individually succeed the most shattering and devastating blow will have been delivered against the very vitals of the enemy. Let him have it right on the chin.

So this could have been the first raid on Hamburg, whereas it was in August 1943 before this happened.

The ARP were swamped as Harris predicted – 600 acres were devastated 12,000 fires started and 45,000 people were made homeless. Regarding the factories, thirty-six had a 100% decrease in production and 350 had their production affected. Nine days after the raid Cologne was still cut off from communications by telephone or telegraph with the rest of Germany, and no mail was allowed to go out for two weeks and even then it had to be censored.

As it was, to their great credit Harris and Saunby achieved 1,047 aircraft and Bomber Command's operation to Cologne was a great success. For the first time a full-scale bomber operation was carried out and a real threat to Germany from the air had been achieved.

In this raid 250 factories were either destroyed or damaged and also a number of oil storage depots. In thirty-six factories not destroyed or damaged production ceased completely. One assumes that the workers were not keen to work owing to the bombing or that without the other factories being destroyed they could not function. The Germans in Cologne said it was the UK's revenge for the raids on Coventry. In the UK *The Times* reported 'Over 1,000 Bombers Raid Cologne "Biggest Air Attack of The War".' Churchill said 'This proof of the growing power of the British Bomber Force is also the herald of what Germany will receive city by city from now on.'

Leaflets were dropped to the German people with a message from Harris. He reminded them that for ten months the *Luftwaffe* had bombed the UK at such places as Coventry, Plymouth, Liverpool and London. The losses were high, 43,000 people being killed. He went on to inform them what they could expect in the future not only from Bomber Command but also the American Army Air Force.

The Cologne 1,000 bomber raid was followed by two further near 1,000 operations on Essen on 1/2 June attacking the Krupps armaments factory and other such factories in the area. On these occasions the magic 1,000 was not attained but 956 aircraft. Bremen was attacked on 3 June.

This without a doubt was the turning point in Bomber Command and the bomber offensive. The bomber offensive was now a reality and not just an idea. Over the next three years, the bomber offensive would be based on the 1,000 bomber raid to Cologne. But, a front-line force had to be built before this could come to fruition – the seed had been sown. The four-engine Halifax bomber was now in service and the Lancaster was on the horizon, both would play a major part in the bomber offensive over the next three years of the war. An important aspect would be the navigation, as locating the target accurately was vital. The birth of Gee to aid navigation was introduced in March 1942 on operations to the Ruhr and the 1,000 bomber raids to Cologne and Essen. The blind bombing aid Oboe was first used in December 1942, but had a limited range and was only suitable for targets in the Ruhr. The introduction of H2S enabled the range to be extended beyond the range of Oboe. In July 1943 the use of 'Window' packets of metal strips during the Battle of Hamburg totally confused the German radar system. On 31 July 1943 *Generaloberst* Weise sent a signal to Goering, and Milch, and to operational commands covering the telephonic arrangements he had made with Kammhuber. (Goering was the Commander in Chief of the *Luftwaffe* in Germany. *Generaloberst* Hubert Weise was in command of the *Luftwaffe* Centre and responsible for the Air Defence of the *Reich*.)

> The present enormous difficulties of defence against the heavy night attacks caused by the jamming of radar demand extraordinary measures everywhere. All crews must understand clearly that success can come only through the most self-sacrificing operations. I

therefore order the operations of *Geschwader* Herrmann, as previously laid down, over the target of attack. Moreover, insofar as no other favourable squadrons are to be put into operations over the flak area. Flak to be restricted to 4,500 metres when night fighters are over the target. The operation of the *Fuhlungshalter* aircraft against the approach and the return flights of the enemy are to be furthered by all means. For the information of other arms of defence. The JDs are to inform the *Luftgau* and flak commands immediately formations take off. Flak divisions and *Luftgaus* to inform JDs currently of the probable target, first bombs dropped, dropping of target-markers etc. The night fighters *Gruppen* are to be despatched at times calculated to enable them to arrive simultaneously with the enemy formations over the target. For this purpose, the searchlight organisation and flak navigational aids are to be at their disposal.

In August 1942, the Pathfinders had been formed under an Australian, Don Bennett, who as well as being a pilot was also a first-class navigator and had a ground engineer and wireless operator's licence. The role of the Pathfinders was to locate, illuminate, and mark the target for the main force bombers following behind.

In November 1943, came the Battle of Berlin, sixteen raids on the 'Big City' as the bomber crews knew it. The raids continued to March 1944. This battle had been preceded by the Battles of the Ruhr and Hamburg. Up to the end of 1943, the German night fighters worked over the target on the *Wilde Sau* principle, the radar equipment being in short supply for pursuit night fighting. The *Wilde Sau* (Wild Sow) worked by using close co-operation by night fighters and the flak guns over the target area and a dependable control of single-engined fighters over a wide area. They picked up the bombers by the use of their A1 sets, visually in the light of flares, or when the bombers became silhouetted against the fires from below. But, it was on occasion hit and miss and with 'spoof' raids to other targets by Bomber Command the fighters would sometimes not make contact at all with the main attacking bomber force. The method of attack was changed to one of route interceptions. A beacon was used around which fighters were assembled and then fed into the bomber stream with the aid of beams directed towards the route the bombers were taking. The experienced fighter pilots who made contact with the bomber stream would drop flares to attract other fighters to the area, rather like the fly in a spider's web.

Pathfinder crews all had great experience with main force operations prior to being selected. The Pathfinders flew forty-five operations in a tour and set the foundations for an all-out bomber offensive on Germany. The duty of the Pathfinder Force was to illuminate and/or mark the target. Each man considered must have flown at least twelve operations.

Following Gee came Oboe to assist navigation and bombing accuracy. The disadvantage was that it had only a range of 300 miles, which was ideal for the Ruhr but no further.

The big breakthrough was the introduction of the Halifax and Lancaster heavy bombers.

But to counter balance this the German fighter defences had increased with much of its fighter units being based in Western France.

On 10 January 1943 a memorandum was issued by the Air Staff that all available heavy and medium bombers should be used for the forthcoming air offensive. This would exert direct pressure on Germany and would take the flak guns and fighters away from the Russian Front making a third front for the Germans to cope with.

Up to this time Bomber Command had not been in a position to carry out its long-planned policy of true strategic bombing.

Bomber Command had to find enough suitable aircraft, aircrew and airfields; cope with the difficulty of hitting the target in the weather conditions that had to be faced; and counteract the growing strength and effectiveness of the enemy's defences.

On 21 January 1943, a directive made the bombing and disorganisation of the German war industry the first priority, followed by the U-Boat building yards, aircraft industries, transport and lastly oil targets in that order.

On 27 January came the first American day attack on German territory, an attack on Wilhelmshaven.

In 1941 a bomber force of 4,000 bombers were proposed but despite being 30% short of this number Bomber Command was now preparing to mount regular raids into Germany using between 500 and 800 aircraft for each operation.

In the Ruhr there were thirty-one key cities and suburbs that were involved in the German war machine, including Essen, Cologne, Dortmund etc. On 5 March 1943, the bomber offensive began in earnest with attacks on the Ruhr and in particular Essen and the Krupps armaments factory. This has become known as the Battle of the Ruhr. This factory employed 150,000 and was the size of Central Park in New York. The defences were 1,000 heavy guns, 2,000 light guns and 500 searchlights.

This would be the twenty-first attack on Essen since the war began. For this operation 442 aircraft were despatched, the Lancaster having the more powerful Mk 22 engine as opposed to the Mk 20. After the attack on 5/6 March it was found that fifty-three separate workshops had been hit and thirteen main buildings destroyed or severely damaged.

By April No. 4 Group with its Halifaxes alone had carried out 755 operations and had losses of night fighters of 6.22%. Overall, in March Bomber Command had lost fifty-one aircraft and had twenty-six damaged. This went up in April to sixty-seven and thirty-three respectively.

In June sixty-four factories were damaged in Dusseldorf; these factories made machine tools and heavy armaments, one factory alone employing 36,000.

The Battle of the Ruhr really ended on 25/26 June with again an attack on Essen. The target was meant to be Hamburg but there was still smoke over the city from previous attacks and so the raid was switched to Essen. But the final operation was actually to Remschied in July when 273 aircraft were despatched with the railway line and centre the primary target. This was the third attack on the town and the most destructive. Engineering works that made crankshafts for aircraft, aero engines were destroyed or damaged and the main railway stations and goods depot almost completely destroyed.

During the period March to July 1943 a number of non-Ruhr targets were attacked. At Nuremberg the main target was the MAN factory, which made diesel engines for submarines. Munich was attacked in March and damage made to the BMW factory, which made aero engines. Attacks were made on Stuttgart, St Nazaire and Frankfurt,

For this raid 705 aircraft were despatched, and twenty-three aircraft failed to return. The targets during this period also included Essen, Dortmund, Duisberg, Bochum, Wuppertal, Krefeld, Oberhausen, Mulhiem, Gelsenkirchen and Kiel. Two raids were made on the Italian naval base at La Spezia and the Skoda works at Pilsen. Workmen had been transferred to this area from Essen and the severely damaged Krupps factory.

There were also two special operations during the Ruhr period. They were against the Baltic seaports of Stettin and Rostock. It had been revealed that a large quantity of German fighter and bomber aircraft had been concentrated at Stettin in preparation for attacks against Russia in the Eastern Front campaign. At Rostock the Heinkel aircraft works were the target but the operation was unsuccessful owing to the factory being covered by a smoke screen generated by the attack on Stettin.

In May 1943, Hamburg was listed as a target by Bomber Command, again as with the Ruhr in history it is known as the Battle of Hamburg.

On 1 June the Zeppelin works in Friedrichshafen where Wurzburgs were spotted by the PRU (Photo Reconaissance Unit) unit at RAF Benson were targeted. (The Wurzburg was the primary ground-based gun laying radar.) However, it was a difficult target being only 500 yards long and 350 yards wide and was heavily defended. It had the code name 'Belicose'. In the attack three acres were devastated in the area of the factory.

On 13/14 June the Deutsche Phillips factory at Aachen was destroyed. The day before this in an operation on Turin W/C John Nettleton VC was thought to have been hit by a night fighter and shot down. Also in this period there were four attacks on Cologne.

At the end of the war the Admiralty claimed that for every mine dropped the RAF sank an average of 50 tons of shipping. During the period of the Ruhr battle (March to June 1943) 1,485 mining sorties were carried out and 4,191 mines dropped over an area covering 1,367,135 miles. The areas mined were La Pallice, Frisian Islands, the Brittany ports and River Gironde.

In July 1943 a memorandum stated that attacks on Hamburg were in the pipeline with its ship yards, engineering factories and liquid fuel depots being the main priorities.

This was the first time 'Window' was used to affect the German radar system, giving the impression by the dropping of silver tinfoil that the force was something in the order of 12,000 aircraft when in fact the number despatched was 791.

In the attacks four main ship-building yards, including U-Boat yards, were destroyed or severely damaged.

A review of the February 1943 to February 1944 attacks against large centres of population concluded that they had an overall effect on the output of the aircraft industry.

In Germany there were 45 towns that contained one or more factories identified as being associated directly with the aircraft industry either producing finished aircraft, aero engines, components or semi-finished parts. These 45 towns had a total population of 17,500,000 and contained 233 identified aircraft, aero engine or associated factories. Of these twenty-one towns had been attacked, of which contained 176 factories and a population of 13,250,500.

These raids included heavy attacks on Berlin and Leipzig, which were known to be successful. Between them they contained 45% of these 176 factories and they were the most important.

On 3 November 1943, Sir Arthur Harris sent a memorandum to Churchill saying that priority should be given to attacks on Berlin. He said that Berlin could be wrecked from end to end if the USA came in with us and that it would cost 400 to 500 aircraft.

This support was not forthcoming and there were heavy losses over Schweinfurt in October. However, the CAS approved in essence the proposal and would leave it to Harris when despite poor weather and tactical conditions he carried out attacks on Berlin.

The attacks started on 18 November when 440 Lancasters and four Mosquitoes took off to attack the 'Big City' as Berlin was known to the aircrew of Bomber Command. This was followed by a further eight raids on Berlin in 1943.

The attacks continued in 1944 when 421 Lancaster's took off on 1 January.

However, on 2 January the weather started to set in with thick snow. Despite this the crews who had gone to bed at 9 am were woken again at 3 pm, being told that another op to Berlin was on again that night. Everyone who could be used, including the stations commanders, was out clearing the snow and 383 aircraft took off.

It was two weeks, 20 January, before the next operation on Berlin was arranged.

This was to be the largest mounted so far with 769 aircraft taking off.

The end of what became known as the 'Battle of Berlin' came on 24/25 March 1944. There were sixteen raids in all. The cost was 497 aircraft, of which 381 were Lancasters. Aircrew losses were 2,938 killed. The city of Berlin had first been attacked in 1940 and was again attacked in 1945, making a total of 255 attacks and 870 aircraft lost.

Berlin was the location of a number of manufacturers such as Siemens, Rheintal, Henschel, Dornier, Heinkel, Focke Wolf and the Daimler Benz engine factories. Plus this was the location of an important railway system in Germany and also the centre of the German Government Administration. The Alkett Armaments factory was also hit and set on fire. This factory, the major producer of guns and tanks, was completely destroyed. In six attacks on Berlin forty-six factories were destroyed and 259 damaged.

In ninety-four attacks in this period on twenty-nine industrial cities, over 2,400,000 man working hours were lost in the industrial area owing to the air attacks.

In total 326 factories were destroyed or damaged, including Krupps. These attacks were felt throughout German war production and included electric engineering plants, which were vital for synthetic oil production.

This fact was corroborated by Dr Albert Speer when interrogated in 1945. The Americans did contribute to attacks on Berlin with six in March 1944 and right up until March 1945.

A seventeenth operation to Berlin was planned for 21 June 1944 with a force of 2,000 bombers of which 700 were to be from Bomber Command and the remainder the US. They would also provide a fighter escort as it was to be a daylight attack. This never took place as on the 21st it was cancelled because the US had decided to split their force of 1,800 to only 600 with the remainder going to other targets. In consequence only Mosquito aircraft made an attack that night.

If one takes on board Dr Speer's view, production all but stopped from these attacks. Also, although he was able to bring production up to the level achieved before the bombing of Berlin he was never able to catch up on the lost production. The provision for the Army, Navy and German Air Force was far below what was needed.

In conclusion one has to say that the 'Battle of Berlin' was costly but certainly not a failure.

On 5 January 1944, a telegram was received in London from Washington with instructions that it should be despatched to CAS and General Spaatz of the 8th USAF. It said that with *Overlord* coming up the German air combat strength in its factories, on the ground and in the air constituted the primary objectives. The dislocation of the German military, industrial, and economical systems and disruption of vital elements of enemy lines of communications remained the overall missions of the combined air force in the UK.

It was estimated that the total output of aircraft of all types from the German industry was about 1,000 a month, of which approximately 750 were first-line aircraft and included about 255 bombers capable of bombing England.

There were approximately 150 airframe and component factories (thirteen of which turned out complete bomber frames) and 120 engine and component factories and component factories (fifteen of which turned out complete bomber engines; eleven made undercarriages, thirteen made crankshafts, casings, cylinder heads etc; four were aero engine ball-bearing factories; twenty-three important factories made large sectional parts, forgings, castings, etc; and fourteen aluminium and magnesium plants of which only twelve were important).

Of these factories three were in the Ruhr within 40 miles of the French frontier, three within 200 miles of the French frontier, two near Leipzig and one at Lauta near Dresden.

On 20 January a telegram sent from the Air Ministry to Washington said that after consultation with the RAF and USAAF leaders in the UK they were convinced that the ultimate objective of the *Pointblank* plan should remain as stated in the Casablanca Directive and that first priory should continue to be given to the attack upon the German Air Force fighter forces and the industry that they depended.

On 21 January 1944, a further paper was submitted entitled 'Progress of the Combined Bomber Offensive Against German Aircraft Production and Towns'.

Of the thirty-three important German Air Force targets, nine were destroyed by Bomber Command, five by the USAAF.

Also on the 21st Harris submitted a paper on the progress of the Combined Bomber Offensive against German aircraft production and the towns associated with it. He said it could be seen that with the exception of Mannheim, which was a high priority *Crossbow* target and subject to the restrictions imposed on operations by short nights, and moonlight and weather conditions, which forced Bomber Command into areas where no *Pointblank* targets exit, all bomber command attacks since the adoption of the CBC plan had been directed against *Pointblank* objectives. Success he went on to say was far greater than was expected when the plan was drawn up.

He said that this paper would dispel the view by some of the Air Staff Directorates that Bomber Command had failed to perform its full share in the execution of the *Pointblank* programme.

On 27 January Harris received a letter from the Director of Intelligence, which outlined the appreciation of the work being done by Bomber Command.

It went on to say that from a most secret source another achievement could be accredited to Bomber Command. Two German fighter wings that were planning to re-equip over a ten-day period early in January had only just finished their re-equipping after twenty-eight days out of front-line combat. The factory that should have provided their new aircraft was Leipzig Mockau.

On 28 January a new directive reaffirmed that the two first priority targets were the fighter aircraft and ball-bearing industries. The objective was to ensure the best possible use of the short time remaining before *Overlord*. A maximum effort of strategic bomber forces was to be concentrated upon key installations in German fighter aircraft industry and ball-bearing industries and towns associated with these key industries.

In January 1944 there were in Germany 6,716 heavy guns, 8,484 medium/light guns, 6,320 searchlights and 1,968 balloons in a new reorganisation of the entire direction of the air policy and the control and directions of fighter units, as well as directing the strength of flak artillery.

On 27 March 1944, the Combined Chiefs of Staff issued orders giving control of all the Allied Air Forces in Europe to General Eisenhower the Supreme Allied Commander and his deputy Air Chief Marshal Tedder. This was passed on 1 April.

In early 1944 German officials in charge of aircraft production programmes stated that Allied bombing had destroyed or seriously damaged 75% of aircraft plants.

Bomb Tonnage Dropped on Aircraft Industry by British and United States Air Forces		
RAF	29,000 out of a total of 1,060 tons dropped	2.75%
US 8th AF	47,671 out of a total of 691,470	6.87%
USA 15th AF	14,000 out of a total of 545,000	2.55%
Total	90,671 out of 2,296,470	3.95%

On 17 April came a directive to the USSTAF and Bomber Command in support of *Overlord* during the preparatory stages.

The particular mission of the strategic air forces prior to the *Overlord* assault was:

(a) To deplete the German Air Forces and particularly the German fighter forces and to destroy and disorganise the facilities supporting them.
(b) To destroy and to disrupt the enemy's rail communications, particularly those affecting the enemy's movement towards the *Overlord* lodgement area.

The prime objective of the US was the German aircraft industry, and ball-bearing production.

At the end of the war Bomber Command had carried out 754,818 sorties and dropped 1,463,423 tons of bombs.

Chapter 5

The German Defences

———m———

In the late 1920s the Germans developed a number of new anti-aircraft weapons and in the early 1930s with the help of Swiss and Swedish companies they developed a 20-mm rapid gun for low altitude work, and a 37-mm gun for low and medium altitude altitudes.

In 1935 a section was set up to chart the objectives requiring protection against aerial attack. This section was known as the 'Air Protected Objective Charting Section'. The responsibility of its operation was given to the German Air Force. The German anti-aircraft authority was called *Flakarilueri*, or flak as it became known, which meant 'Defence Against Aviation'.

The famous 88-mm gun was used in all theatres by the Germans but it is best remembered in the air war in its original role as an anti-aircraft gun, although it was also used to great effect in the Western Desert. Its original design was the 75-mm model and this then became the 88 mm. It was first used in 1928 with the first models known as the Flak 18, which then became the 88/L56. It fired a 20.3-pound shell up to an effective range of 26,000 feet and a maximum of 32,000 feet. It was used in the Spanish Civil War as an anti-aircraft gun as well as an anti-tank gun.

The Germans also developed concrete blockhouses on which they placed anti-aircraft artillery.

In December 1939, a force of Wellington bombers attempted a daylight attack on Wilhelmshaven. In the approach flight its radio traffic was picked up by German interceptor units who, in contravention of their orders, immediately passed the results (location, height, course etc) direct to the fighter authority concerned. As a result German fighters were directed to a favourable point for interception and, as is known, obtained good results.

After this direct landline links to the operational units was strongly advocated, and although there was some opposition on security grounds the idea was taken up. Out of this came the reporting centres, which were responsible for the collation and evaluation of intercepted, and direction finder signals and their distribution in standard form to the interested parties.

The reporting centre set up on the Channel coast, Meldekopf Birk, was to supervise fighter operations, and Bomber-Meldekopf Zeist in Holland was set up for the special support of German night fighters.

The following were the main sources from which the Signals Intelligence drew their conclusions:

1. The traffic of every RAF bomber airfield was covered day and night.
2. The covering of radio transmissions on airfield frequencies disclosed such things as postponement of operations or very active take-off traffic.
3. From meteorological messages one could tell whether a particular airfield was fit for operations or not.
4. Direction finding tuning traffic.
5. Tuning traffic or Air Sea Rescue boats before RAF bombing operations.
6. H2S and H2X interception.
7. Engine trouble and SOS interceptions.
8. Wireless transmission from Group HQ to some or all of the units in the Group to break off operations.
9. Transmissions of the AEAF aircraft reporting centre in the vicinity of London call sign Q58, and known to the Germans as Freischuetz-Meldungen. Whenever this centre passed a long message in the late afternoon, which was transmitted by the Paris repeater, it meant that the RAF was going to mount a major raid or that RAF formations would pass over France.
10. Interception of 100 Group airborne jammers positioned over the North Sea or Belgium or Dutch territory that then flew with the bomber formation to Germany.
11. There was no certainty that because of jammers a raid was being mounted but if there was no sign it meant there was no raid that night.

But in May 1940 when the bombing offensive began in earnest the Germans were not prepared and thought that a ring of searchlights around the main cities would be sufficient. They only had a few radar detectors along the North Sea coast and only one fighter unit of fewer than fifty fighters to cover such a big span of area.

They soon learned that this was not going to work and General

Kammhuber was put in charge of night fighters in the *Luftwaffe*. He added more searchlights, but in a line that became known as the Kammhuber line that covered the approaches into Germany over Holland and Belgium he also increased the ground control radar along these routes into targets in Germany. The Freya radar detector would identify targets up to 100 miles away and then transmit to a Wurzburg unit with a range of 40 miles. A second Wurzburg would follow the dispatched night fighter, which created an accurate plot that enabled ground controllers to guide the pilot to make an interception.

The Germans knew that No. 5 Group of Bomber Command RAF had small pockets of specialist formations such as No. 617 Squadron who attacked the dams, helped No. 9 Squadron to sink the *Tirpitz*, and attacked bridges and port installations and so on. According to German reports this group caused German Air Force Signals Intelligence the maximum amount of worry. On one operation over Munich it was not until the formation was actually over the city that the first radar interceptions were made. Munich was caught completely by surprise and no air raid warning was given.

No. 3 Group Bomber Command RAF carried out a number of daylight operations and once again the aircraft were over the German frontiers before a warning was given. In many cases the radio transmissions of Fighter Command escorts gave the first indication of daylight attacks. The special duty squadrons from Tempsford were never intercepted before or during an operation, only on the return flight at best.

According to German intelligence the radio discipline of No. 8 Group, the Pathfinder Group of Bomber Command RAF, was above average, and often only detected from the Group HQ's meteorological transmissions. On the other hand the Mosquitoes, which regularly attacked Berlin at the end of the war, were always picked up in the area of the Frisians by means of H2S interceptions and direction finders.

In 1943, it was calculated that by the end of the year the German Air Defence for the Western Front would be 68% of the total single-engine and twin-engine fighters (1,650 aircraft). By the beginning of 1944, 75% of the aircraft would be required on the Western Front to oppose the Anglo-American bombing offensive. The remainder were spread out widely between Norway and the Loire Estuary.

On 1 January 1942, Germany had 1,360 fighters and was making them at a rate of 600 per month. This was remarkable as they had completely re-equipped the whole of the German single-engine fighter force with the latest marks of German fighter, the Bf 109 (G) and the Fw 190.

At the time it was obviously their aim and if it was allowed to continue the bomber offensive would be virtually made impossible. Only the bombers could prevent this occurring.

In February 1943 on the whole German Western Front the single-engine fighter force was between 400 and 450 aircraft, of which approximately 100 were in the Pas de Calais and Belgium areas operating between the district of the Seine and the Dutch coast. In June 1943, there were eighteen *Gruppen* of night fighters in the *Reich*, five more than at the end of 1942.

As the Allied bombers in the west became more active the activity of the *Meldekopf* became more important for both advance warnings and route tracking. The advance warning supplied by the *Meldekopf* was usually short term, for example hours or even minutes. The long-term forecasting of major Allied operations was provided by strategic evaluation (operative *Auswertung*). As the war progressed the evaluation gradually increased through knowledge of Allied traffics, so that they could often calculate enemy intentions from the most minute indications. The traffic of every RAF bomber airfield was covered day and night. On certain airfields definite indications of an impending operation such as tuning traffic or radio silence was observed. The coverage of radio transmission traffic on airfields with frequencies of over 5,000 kc/s or of 6,440 kc/s disclosed such things as postponement of operations or very active take-off traffic. From meteorological messages one could tell whether a particular airfield was fit for operations or not.

Direction finder section tuning traffic, tuning traffic of Air-Sea Rescue boats before bombing operations and H2S and H2X interceptions were all signs of an operation being 'on'. Wireless transmission orders from Group HQ to some or all of the units in the group to break off operations were passed in the Bomber Code but most were deciphered. Interception and direction finding of AI by the escorting fighters remaining close to the bomber stream would give away the position of the bomber stream.

The transmissions of the AEAF aircraft reporting centre in the vicinity of London, call sign Q58 (and known to the Germans as Freischuetz-Meldungen), worked on several frequencies, both HF and LF. It transmitted blind for the benefit of all interested parties such as the anti-aircraft defences and night fighters, to warn them of impending operations by single aircraft or formations. These messages were passed on in a three-letter code, which had been used for a considerable time, but was never broken. It was, however, inferred that the longer the message, the greater would be the size of the raiding force and the longer the route. The longest messages were passed before major RAF and US Eighth Air Force operations. In the Paris area there was a similar radio station, which repeated the messages when the track of the bombers lay over French territory. Whenever Q58 passed a long message in the later afternoon, which was re-transmitted by the Paris repeater, there would be a major RAF attack and the formation would fly over France. If the operation had to be cancelled on account of deteriorating meteorological conditions, a message was transmitted 'Cancel my message No.....' This was passed at once by the German Signals Intelligence service to the relevant quarters.

All the Germans required to know was the general track of the bomber force. Then by the use of long-range radar warning system and the Observer Corps the direction was determined. Once this was established a controller would assemble their fighters in a more or less central position and then progressively feed them into the bomber stream whatever its ultimate direction. Thus small angle deviations of the bomber route were not likely to upset the Germans to any great degree.

The fighters would be placed over a stationary electronic beacon where the pilots would orbit and wait for instructions from ground controllers and be directed to the RAF bomber stream. This was known as *Zahme Sau* (Tame Boar).

In July 1943 came the *Wilde Sau* (Wild Boar) raids in Germany to combat the 'Window' radar countermeasures of the RAF. The idea was to concentrate German fighters high above targets where they could spot the RAF bombers against the fires burning below. One allowed the attacking bombers to drop the initial bombs to start fires and then attacked them from above. The flak gunners were told to set the fuse on their guns so that they detonated below the night fighters' patrol altitude.

In 1943 the flak defences were in need of re-organising and large batteries were concentrated and mobile, including railway, flak were brought in. Also, flak ships were operated on the coast. The popular 88-mm gun could fire fifteen rounds per minute and fired 20-lb shells.

After the Dambuster raid in May 1943 a new system was developed to knock down low-flying aircraft with a single hit. This system became the 55-mm gun but it was still only in late development when the war ended. Each industrial town had about thirty searchlights and sixty heavy and light guns.

In March 1944 when Dr Albert Speer took over the aircraft industry fifty different types of fighters were being produced. On 1 March fighters were given the priority over tanks, U-Boats, flak guns and V-Weapons.

Between 1 January and 1 April 1944 there was no appreciable change in the distribution of the German Air Force fighter force, of which approximately 70% continued to be absorbed in the air defence of Germany against Allied day and night bombing from bases in the UK and Italy. Such was the priority accorded to the maintenance of the maximum possible fighter strength in Germany, notwithstanding the critical military situation that developed on the Russian Front during this period.

While in the first quarter of 1944 the strength of the German Air Force as a whole tended to decline from the peak figure reached on 1 January 1944, fighter strength remained almost unchanged at that level. Thus the effects of the day and night bombing on aircraft factories and German industry generally during the autumn and winter of 1943/4, together with heavy losses sustained in opposing escorted Allied day bomber formations attacking Germany, succeeded in arresting throughout the first quarter of 1944 the steady expansion, particularly with regard to fighters, which took place during the last three months of 1943. The successful daylight attacks in the latter part of February 1944, mainly against the German fighter factories, didn't by 1 April produce any noticeable effect on the actual strength of the German fighter force, although units equipped with Bf 109s showed some signs of decline in strength. This result was, however, only achieved by a return to a policy of conservation, which showed itself during March in an increased reluctance to engage escorted bomber formations attacking Germany except by single-engine fighters, and then only under advantageous conditions such as might fortuitously occur, e.g. during a temporary absence of fighter cover. The almost complete elimination of the twin-engine day fighter for interception purposes during March except in some circumstances was attributable to heavy losses, which reduced production, particularly of Me 110s, was unable to make up.

Although the weight of the bombing offensive increased during the first quarter of 1944 both by day and night, the total loss inflicted on Germany industry, as distinct from the particular effects on certain armaments industries, was probably less than in the last quarter of 1943, mainly owing to weather conditions. But despite this the offensive continued to keep German industrial production down to the level to which it had been reduced by the summer attacks.

For the first time there was during the winter of 1943/4 little if any recovery in German industrial production. This failure of German industry to make its normal winter recovery, combined with the general deterioration of domestic conditions mainly caused by the bombing offensive, appreciably reduced Germany's capacity to sustain a third major active land front.

The heavy raids on the single-engine fighter production in February meant a decline in the German Air Force as a whole. Also, the attacks on the German long range bomber (LRB) production contributed to the weakness of the LRB force available to oppose Operation *Overlord*.

These day and night attacks forced the German High Command to retain some 70% cent of the total fighter resources of the German Air Force in Germany and Austria, leaving important military targets in France and the Low Countries almost without fighter protection. This meant that the Allied bombing offensive against Germany during the first quarter of 1944 not only reduced the potential air opposition to *Overlord* but also resulted in targets in the operation being virtually unopposed.

With the exception of the raids on Me 110 production at Brunswick, on the Fw 100 factory at Oschersleben in January, and on the Dornier factory (Me 410) factory at Oberpfaffenhofen in March, precision attacks on the aircraft industry during the first quarter of 1944 were confined to a series of successful operations between 20 and 25 February. As a result of these raids heavy damage was made to the output of single-engine and twin-engine fighters and long-range bombers and transport aircraft.

Before these February attacks, a substantial recovery in production had taken place, and the rate of output of operational aircraft had probably reached about 1,450 a month by 19 February 1944, of which about 750 were single-engine fighters. In February this did not exceed 1,250, of which only slightly more than 600 were single-engine fighters. In March a further reduction to about 1,100 probably took place, of which about 500 were single-engine fighters.

The assembly factories most seriously affected were the following:

Messerschmitt, Regensburg (Bf 109)
Erla, Leipzig (Bf 109)
Gothaer, Gotha (Me 110)
MIAG (Me 110)

Production was thought to have been stopped at all of these plants for the remainder of February and March.

On 2/3 and 14/15 January 1944, when the bomber operations lay across the Germans' very popular Beacon 'M', the loss rate was well above average. Twenty-seven aircraft were lost on 2/3 January to Berlin, and thirty-eight on 14/15 January to Brunswick.

In 1944, intelligence reports indicated that a small proportion of the German night fighter force had been fitted with a fixed upward-firing gun. The Germans equipped with this type of armament would try to achieve surprise by positioning themselves below and slightly astern of the bomber, and without being seen by the rear gunner. This would call for the utmost vigilance on the part of the Fishpond operator in the bombers to pick up the approaching enemy fighter from below. (Fishpond was an extension of H2S airborne radar and designed to give early warning of German night fighters approaching from below up a range of 30 miles.) A German prisoner of war who had been a flight mechanic in the *Luftwaffe* with IV/NJG 3 at Sylt and had flown a number of times as a gunner said that the Me 110s were delivered to the *Gruppe* with a crew of three and a heavy armament, which included an upward-firing cannon. They were, however, delivered to the NJG 3 *Geschwader* HQ at Stade with a crew of two, a pilot and wireless operator. The radio was placed between the pilot and wireless operator. The after part of the aircraft had a large extra petrol tank. The modifications were made in the airfield workshops. Here the petrol tank was removed and a seat fitted for a gunner in its place. In the after part of the aircraft two fixed upward-firing 20-mm FF (Forward Firing) cannon were installed. The upward-firing cannon was fitted on two brackets, one on each side of the cable with the muzzle of the cannon protruding some 10 to 15 cm through the Plexiglas roof of the cabin. It was set at an angle of 45 degrees in a forward direction. The cannon was sighted and fired by the pilot who was provided with two Revi sights set one above the other in the forward part of the cabin slightly above the pilot's head – the lower Revi was set at 0 degrees and the upper one 45 degrees. The gunner as well as operating the machine-gun on the Me 110 was also responsible for making sure the cannon worked satisfactorily and for replacing the ammunition drum, which initially carried fifty rounds and later ninety.

The first indication of the use of this weapon was when returning damaged aircraft were examined and it was concluded that the enemy must be using an upward-firing gun. On 21/2 January 1944, a Lancaster bomber, LM 436 of 207 Squadron, was homeward bound from Magdeburg when fighter flares were spotted and a Ju 88 fighter seen below the rear gunner at a distance of 500 yards. It continued to follow the Lancaster for about 45 miles and then positioned itself in such a way that the rear gunner could not get his guns to bear. It opened fire several times and managed to damage the bomber but not enough to prevent it arriving back at base safely. When it was later examined the damage was found to have been caused by a 20-mm cannon and fired from directly below. Over the next few months there were many instances of aircraft returning with damage that was at first thought to have been caused by flak, but on examination was found to have been caused by a 20-mm cannon shell from a vertical or near vertical position below the bomber. The height at which the aircraft had been flying and the density of the shell strike on the aircraft made it certain that the shell had not come from the ground.

In January 1944, 3.2% aircraft were deemed to have been destroyed by the upward-firing gun. In February this increased to 11.4% and in April it reached its peak of 13.3%. From then on the percentage decreased until August 1944 when a 0% reading was found.

Since December 1942 the monthly reports on losses and interception of Bomber Command aircraft in night operations had drawn attention to the following:

- A high proportion of attacks were made on our bombers from below.
- There was a consistently high proportion of cases in which the attacking fighter was not sighted.
- A high proportion of damage resulted from such attacks.
- Members of bomber crews thought they had been hit by flak, but the subsequent inspection of the damage revealed that it had been caused by fighter attacks. The bomber was hit without warning by cannon shells. Neither fighter nor tracer was seen and the direction of attack was unknown. Tracer was seen striking the aircraft from somewhere below, often steeply below, but no fighter was seen. The bombers were hit by either by unseen fire or by tracer seen fired from some position below and the fighter was subsequently seen breaking away below. In a very few cases the fighter had been almost directly below the bomber just before it opened fire. Since the beginning of 1944, from the crews of missing aircraft who had evaded and returned, there were nineteen reported with some degree of probability to have been shot down by fighter enemy fighters equipped with upward-firing guns. The engines and fuel tanks of heavy bombers were much more vulnerable when attacked from below than from astern.

In December 1943, Paul Zorner was flying a Me 110 with SNZ equipment (night fighter radar). His aircraft was also equipped with the *Schrage Musik* upward-firing cannon, but he remembers that at that time as it still showed difficulties in adjustment. Major Schnaufer Kommodre of NJG 4 considered that in the later stages of the war (presumably 1944) 50% of the attacks on bombers were carried out with upward-firing guns. With the lesser experienced pilots in the *Luftwaffe* the upward-firing cannon was very popular. One reason for this was the difficulty the Ju 88 and the Me 110 had matching the speeds of the Lancaster and Halifax when approached from astern, and below, for an attack with normal firing guns. If the bomber corkscrewed it was most difficult for the fighter to gather speed quickly to follow in the downward dive of the bomber. Schnaufer had attacked twenty to thirty bombers with his upward-firing cannon at a range of about 80 yards, of this number only about 10% saw him at a range of approx 150 to 200 metres. The German pilots would aim to hit the bomber between the two nacelles on either side, or if the rear gunner became troublesome they would focus their attention on him.

The bomber crews thought they had been hit by flak, but the aircraft that got back showed evidence that they had been attacked by a fighter. The bomber was hit without warning by cannon shells. Tracer was seen striking the aircraft from below, often steeply below, but no fighter was seen.

The German pilots had the greatest respect for the mid upper gunners on the bombers at the commencement of the bomber's corkscrew. They said that as they approached from below and the bomber commenced to corkscrew with a dive in their direction it gave the mid-upper gunner a perfect view and a good chance to fire. This would normally be at fairly close range.

Schnaufer and other experienced pilots usually carried flares to drop when they found the bomber stream. These flares were of great assistance to the lesser-experienced pilots and enabled them to find the stream and its direction. All pilots considered the corkscrew a most effective evasive manoeuvre but were of the opinion that a corkscrewing Halifax was an easier target than the Lancaster, although the Lancaster caught fire more often when hit than the Halifax. Their view of the Halifax was that it was a robust but slower aircraft than the Lancaster, less manoeuvrable and with a poorer search. Schnaufer said the more violent the dive of the bomber in the corkscrew, the more successful, as the night fighter could not match its speed. He added that the manoeuvrability of the Lancaster amazed him. The banking search was considered most successful, as the pilots could not tell whether they had been seen or not and this certainly put them off attacking.

The maximum night fighter effort put up against any one of the Allied raids was 150 to 200 fighters.

There were 100 German fighters in the Pas de Calais and Belgium areas in February 1943. The flak strength was doubled by bringing in the mobile reserve, which included railway flak and consolidated large units of two to three single batteries at all important targets. The number of guns in each battery was increased to six and eventually eight. The number of 10.5 mm guns was increased and the first 12.8 mm static batteries came into operation in Western Germany. At the end of 1943, the strength of the air defences was 1,000 heavy flak batteries, 450 light flak and 300 searchlights. The *Heimatflak* or Home Guard Flak personnel had been utilised in considerable numbers. The total flak manpower amounted to 1,200,000. The heavy flak defences were sited according to calibre and performance. The inner gun ring was located within the bomb-release line. Two thirds of the inner ring guns were high performance 10.5 mm, 12.8 or 8.8 mm and were capable of firing across the object as well as out well beyond the bomb-release line. The outer ring was located near or before the bomb-release line and at an average distance of 6,000 metres. Two thirds of the outer ring guns were 8.8 mm calibre. The northern approach to the principal objective was provided with part of a third ring of guns. These positions were the northern defences of the Halle and the industrial area at Orgazitt. To the west defences were supplemented by the incomplete defences of Wintershall. To the east and south-east were a number of advanced batteries to tie-in the Halle-Leuna defence with those of Leipzig and Bohlen-Zeitz. The maximum distance between sites was 5,000 metres and the average distance was 2,500 to 3,000 metres.

The heavy flak sites were provided with light or medium flak protection. The defences were divided into three main sections. The northern section was *Flak Untergruppe* Halle, the central section *Flak Gruppe* Merseburg and the southern section *Flak Gruppe* Weissenfels. All three were under the command of the 21st Flak Brigade at Bad Lauchstadt.

The Germans used a 15-cm pyrotechnic rocket to simulate 'Pathfinder flares'. The projector comprised sixteen launching crates, in two rows of eight with various coloured rockets ready for firing. In January 1944, there were 6,716 heavy guns in Germany and 1,225 on the Western Front. There were 8,484 light and medium guns in Germany and 4,200 on the Western Front. Some 6,320 searchlights in Germany and 560 on the Western Front supplemented this. There were also over 2,000 barrage balloons.

The 88-mm Flak gun was the one that all aircrew knew about. It could be used horizontally as artillery and also as an anti-aircraft flak gun. It took some 8,500 rounds to down a single bomber. By the end of the war flak gunners would be responsible for bringing down 5,400 US aircraft.

The grenades or shells fired by this gun were 88 mm in diameter (hence the name). They weighed 9.27 kg each and could be fired up to a height of 14,690 metres. If they made a direct hit they immediately exploded or could explode at a pre-determined height. The gun had a crew of six and it could deliver eight grenades per minute.

Besides the Home Guard Flak there were German Air Force Auxiliaries (*Luftwaffenhelper* – schoolboys of the upper forms of high and medium schools. German Air Force Flak Militiamen (*Flakwehrmanner*) were men not normally liable for military service but who were conscripted for flak units. They carried on with their normal work but were called up for training and air attacks. As far back as 1942 the Hitler Youth was used in flak units to replace trained men needed in other theatres.

All male Germans born between 1883 and 1925, apart from doctors and pharmacists, were liable for service in the Home Guard Flak. The Ruhr area was the most heavily defended. In February 1944, 60% of the guns were 88 mm and 40% were of heavier calibre.

In night fighter areas flak units had the right to fire up to any height and also to fly balloons at a maximum height. In light flak areas the units could fire up to 1,000 metres or 3,200 feet.

On cloudy nights only a limited number of searchlights in a belt would operate. They would follow an aircraft along the base of the cloud in order to indicate to the fighters where the attacking bomber was. On clear dark nights they illuminated the target to permit a high degree of searching in a cone formation producing a wall of light ahead of the bomber, which may be visible to fighters attacking from the rear compelling the hostile bomber to run the gauntlet of light and to fly close to one of three beams or groups of beams. This meant the bomber became visible from the ground allowing other lights to engage. Other searchlight groups had two-metre master lights, which worked with the flak guns. These could be dipped to indicate to the fighters the direction of the bomber force. The lights were used in belts, a belt consisting of ten to fifteen, or twenty to thirty lights set 1,000 to 2,000 yards apart. In flak gun defended areas this distance was spread 3,000 to 4,000 yards apart. A radar-controlled flak gun fired with the help of searchlights and a six-gun battery, which could fire around a bomber at 20,000 feet. The blue appearance of some searchlights when laid close to the aircraft was caused by the high current density being passed through the arc.

The searchlight defences of objectives in the Halle-Leuna, Bohlen-Zeitz and Leipzig area were the responsibility of the 73rd Searchlight Regiment with its headquarters at 14 Flak Division at Leipzig-Schonau. The regiment consisted of five searchlight battalions.

They were sited in groups containing three to five normal lights and one master light. This was usually provided with a sound locator and a radar set.

The searchlight belt consisted of approximately 300 lights deployed to a depth of 15000–20,000 metres along the approaches to the defence areas. The searchlight crews were told not to cone a bomber with more than six searchlights when working with fighters. Larger groups of lights would blind the defending fighter pilot, as well as the bomber crew.

In the early part of the war the *Luftwaffe* used the 150 cm *Flakscheinwerfer* 37 searchlight operating on units of up to sixty-four lights,

which had listening sound locators. Later in the war a brighter 200-cm
Flakschwerfer 40 came into action, which was positioned close to the radar
system. Once the searchlight locked on to the bomber the brightness blinded
the bomb aimer and made it impossible for him to do his job of plotting the
target below.

Albert Speer said in 1945 that the defence against air attack as an overall
problem was regarded as being the natural responsibility of the *Luftwaffe*, at
least for two years of the war. Ground anti-aircraft defence was regarded as
being rather a minor portion of the defence scheme. Operationally it was
considered that the essential co-ordination of ground anti-aircraft defence
with the fighter aircraft defence could best be obtained by having the whole
system under one command – which obviously had to be the *Luftwaffe*.

As regards anti-aircraft weapon development, Speer said that in his view
the Army rather than the *Luftwaffe* was better suited to run it, as they were
more accustomed to handling guns than the *Luftwaffe*. The actual
development work on anti-aircraft ground weapons was carried out by the
appropriate *Entwicklungs Kommission* in the Speer industry.

The early warning procedure was conventional. In addition, in the
Halle-Leuna area three giant Wurzburgs of the 21st Flak Brigade provided
inland plotting for the Halle-Leuna defences. Warning was always adequate,
usually before the attacking force approached within 200 kilometres of the
defences.

In July 1940, there were the following defences in Germany:

	Heavy guns	Light/medium guns	Searchlights
January 1941	1,692	3,996	1,716
January 1941	2,300	5,832	1,824
January 1942	3,999	5,256	2,088
January 1943	4,491	6,456	3,330
January 1944	6,716	8,484	6,320
March 1945	5,614	3,984	4,880

In addition there were guns positioned in France, Holland and Belgium.
There were also flak ships along the French coast.

In 1943, 70% of these defences of 900,000 men and 75% of the heavy
guns, mainly 88-mm flak guns, were located on the Western Front of
Germany.

To counter the heavy raids by Bomber Command the old scheme of
'sector' defence was discarded and in its place **Grossbatterien** or large

batteries were introduced. The guns used were 105 mm and the new 12.8-mm guns. The 88-mm guns had a maximum horizontal range of 16,600 feet and a ceiling range of 34,770 feet. They could fire fifteen rounds per minute. The 105-mm gun had a range of 19,100 and 37,000 feet respectively and could also fire fifteen rounds per minute.

On 19/20 February 1944 the flak was slight but when encountered heavy. Searchlights were unable to penetrate the cloud but some illumination of the cloud layer was effected. Heavy predicted flak with searchlight co-operation was experienced at Texel. Defences were experienced at Stendal, Halle and Merseburg.

This cat and mouse game went on throughout the war – as soon as one side found a method of beating the defences the other side came up with a countermeasure. This was often made confusing for the enemy by sending one force to one target to mark it with flares and then bomb it while the main target was stacked, thus setting up two targets and splitting the night fighter forces. The Light Night Striking Force of 8 Group, equipped with fast Mosquitoes, were by the end of the war masters at this tactic.

On New Year's Day 1945 the *Luftwaffe* made a last desperate attack. They flew 800 sorties, most of them at low level, against Allied airfields destroying 127 aircraft and damaging 133. But their losses were heavy, with 200 aircraft lost to flak and fighters.

Chapter 6

The German Aircraft Industries

—∞—

In 1911 the firm DFW was established at Leipzig-Lindenthal to build French Farman-type aircraft.

In 1913 Hugo Junkers formed the Junkers Motor Works.

In 1914 the German aircraft industry had ten aero engine and fifty aircraft and parts companies. By 1914 and the start of WWI they had built 107 aircraft and by 1917 820.

In 1917 Junkers-Fokker was formed by merging two companies.

In 1919 DFW became ATG, formed to build transport equipment. In the five years since WWI the company now had twenty-six aero engine and thirty-six aircraft companies with a monthly production of 2,000 aircraft. Under the Treaty of Versailles in June 1919 the manufacture and import of aircraft, parts and equipment was severely restricted. This was monitored by the Inner-Allied Military Control Commission of which one section dealt with German military aviation and another with civilian. The treaty required the surrender of all military aircraft, some 15,000 aircraft, 28,000 aircraft engines and sixteen airships. As well as this all the hangars were destroyed.

To overcome this Germany continued military aviation experimentation in Russia. And firms such as Albatros, Blohm, Voss and Krupp were prepared to produce aircraft and submarines in Russia but supervised by Germany. Also in Russia, Junkers who were to feature heavily in WWII were to construct an aircraft and engine plant.

Gliding was not, however, banned and the Germans considered this a way of instilling air-mindedness in German youth. The single wingspan became a part of the German glider design. Gliders were of course used in the early part of WWII but after the disaster in Crete in May 1941 the whole concept of airborne troops by glider was disbanded on the order of Hitler.

But in 1921/22 restrictions were reduced and light aircraft industry began again.

However, the treaty unfortunately did not stop the manufacturing of commercial aircraft and companies making these were set up in neutral countries. For example, Junkers was set up in Russia, Sweden and Turkey, while Rohrback was set up in Denmark, Heinkel in Sweden and Dornier in Italy and Switzerland. Although civilian aircraft they were designed to be easily converted into military aircraft such as the Me 108 civilian aircraft, which became the Bf 109 military fighter. Flying clubs were set up throughout Germany flying engine and glider aircraft. Schools were set up for airline pilots but with the idea of them being bomber pilots.

In 1926 all restrictions were abolished and so names that were synonymous with German aircraft in WWII, such as Arado, Dornier, Focke-Wulf, Junkers and Heinkel, began production. Between 1927 and 1931 funds for the development of the German aircraft industry were 84 million Reichsmarks but in 1936 the figure had risen to 980 million Reichsmarks.

In 1926 Daimler-Benz was created with the merger of Benz with Daimler Motoren Gesellschaft but the company was forced to supplement its existing automobiles and truck production with entry into the aviation engine market. After WWI there was no real need for this but Daimler -Benz had realised that there was an opening in the market. In the early 1920s small aircraft were allowed to be built as long as the design could not in any way be thought to be of a military nature. By the late 1920s companies such as Heinkel, Dornier and Junkers were developed names that were to become household in WWII. They were developing single and multi-engine light transport aircraft but with limited range and carrying capacity.

With the accession of Hitler to power in Germany in 1933, and the appointment of Herman Goering as Air Minister, plans followed immediately to build up the German aircraft industry, despite the Treaty of Versailles, which forbid the building up of military aircraft in Germany. A number of plants in Germany – Arado, Erla, Fieseler, Focke-Wulf, Heinkel, Junkers, Klemm, Messerschmitt and Rohrbach – were the foundation upon which the German aircraft industry was rebuilt.

The Government paid the development costs, when required and necessary. A number of firms, the biggest including Weser, Henschel, Blohm and Voss, Gothaer, and Allgemeine Transportanlager GmbH, were brought into the industry before the war. Junkers and Arado were owned by the state.

In 1933 when Hitler came to power Dr Knauss, a former WWI flyer and now a general at the Air War Academy, sent a memo to Erhard Mulch the Managing Director of Lufthansa (and also a WWI flyer) in which he said that air power would be the decisive weapon in the future.

Knauss proposed the creation of a large heavy bomber force. A four-engine bomber to be built by Dornier had already been commissioned but its progress met opposition as it was not necessary and a twin-engine bomber would be far more effective.

In 1933 Hugo Junkers was not interested in rearmament but there some, including Messerschmitt Adolph Rohrbach and Heinkel, who were keen on it. However, later Junkers was very much involved in military aircraft developing for example the Ju 52, Germany's transport aircraft.

A 1,000 aircraft building programme was the start of the massive rearming in Germany but in 1933 only 197 were accepted. The others were rejected. By the end of 1933 no fewer than twenty-five models were under development and by January 1934 the number had risen to a monthly high of seventy-two aircraft manufactured compared with thirty-one in 1933.

In 1933 ATG was taken over by Koppenberg.

In January 1934 came the first program for the aircraft industry with the plans to produce 3,715 aeroplanes and nicknamed the Rhineland Program.

The principle of local dispersal was applied to the layout of new aircraft plants. As a precaution against bombing the German Air Ministry restricted the total ground areas covered by individual buildings, except in rare cases, to about 75,000 sq feet.

This meant that the usual plant consisted of several buildings distributed over an area of 30 or 40 acres. Even before the war some plants were equipped with an elaborate system of underground bomb shelters.

Converted textile and car barns were used and many of the new buildings built during the war had wooden roofs. Metal shelves and storage bins were not available, which increased the fire hazard. Brick walls and wooden posts were the most easily wrecked by bombing and could be easily destroyed with 500-lb HE (high explosive) bombs and incendiaries. Some of the pre-Hitler industry buildings were of this type. Steel structures could have a section of the roof blown off with 500-lb bombs but unless there was direct hit on a girder or column the building would remain standing and could be repaired within a matter of days.

The principal machinery was used for the fabrication of parts, hydraulic presses, stretchers, punch presses, power brakes, metal shapers, shears, routers and a varied assortment, but there was not a large number of machine tools for machining forgings and castings.

German practice corresponded rather closely with American practice but the German presses were far greater than that of America. But even the massive equipment could be destroyed by fire.

Assembly jigs and holding fixtures were necessary to ensure that many structural parts, ribs, longerons, stiffeners and skin were put together accurately in the desired aerodynamic form. German practice with such equipment was well advanced. The production of the principal German aircraft, especially the Fw 190 and the Bf 109, by several licensees would have been most difficult, and interchangeability of parts would not have been possible, if the assembly tooling problem had not been solved.

Two basic types of assembly tooling were used by aircraft manufacturers: the Dornier system, which minimised the use of assembly jigs, and the Aircraft Manufacturers' Association 'Standard' system. Each plant or licensee was provided with a set of production jigs (also a master jig) with which to keep the production jigs in adjustment.

German techniques were generally line production similar to the American technique, with the notable difference that operations were broken up among several buildings in the same location or dispersed over a wide area.

The use of mechanised assembly and mobile jigs was common but not universal in German plants. They were vulnerable to bombing, but since the usual practice was to have two or more installations in separate plants for each assembly or subassembly, another line could be operated double shift until the damage to the first could be repaired.

The result in 1935 was that for the new *Luftwaffe* nearly 2,500 aircraft had been delivered and 800 were ready for operations.

The choice of a fighter was easier and in 1933 a search for a new fighter started. In this year the Bf 108 was low-wing monoplane with a metal frame designed by Messerschmitt. This became the basis for Germany's new fighter, the Bf 109.

By the time the war broke out the industry was in a strong position, and with the exception of a big plant at Wiener/Neustadt, and a few small ones in occupied countries, the Germans made no attempt to broaden the bases of the industry throughout the war. In fact the German aircraft industry was the leading light in the aircraft industry.

In 1935 the *Luftwaffe* was officially formed with 1,000 aircraft and 20,000 men.

In 1936 the Germans got the chance to test their air force in the Spanish Civil War. The German force was known as the Condor Legion.

The Bf 109 was the star of this force. Not only aircraft but the flak batteries used later in WWII were put to use.

Because the Bf 109 was a short-range fighter a long-range escort fighter was also needed and so the Me 110 and Me 210 became main production aircraft.

In 1937, with the output steadily increasing, it was established that 500 airframes per month were being produced. General Erhard Milch, State Secretary for Aviation, stated that the output could be trebled if necessary on the outbreak of war by employing three shifts instead of one; moreover, it was known that even at this juncture the industry was working at far above normal peacetime pressure so that if the war broke out little difference would be experienced in putting the industry on a war footing.

In 1933 in Germany it was estimated that by 1938 the aircraft industry would be up and running. Among the plants was ATG of Leipizg-Mockau. They also had plants at Leipzig-Eutritysch and Grosstschocher.

It was estimated that by 1938 the *Luftwaffe* would have 11,732 aircraft, with 2,370 combat planes and 6,298 trainers. In 1938 four air fleets were formed consisting of bomber, fighter, and other units.

The aircraft engines for bomber aircraft were believed to have been made in eight factories, at Munich, Stettin and Eisenach. The monthly output at the end of 1937 was over 1,000 engines, but this was not the maximum as the industry was still expanding. The industry enjoyed many advantages in the pre-war years having the complete backing of the state, and its requirements were met whenever the necessary facilities existed and on a lavish scale. The pre-war factories were modern and well dispersed internally and sited outside the big industrial towns. They were embodied with up-to-date production methods. All schemes, design, patients and production techniques were under general rationalisation and techniques were pooled.

The aircraft industry was well housed as a result of the expansion of facilities between 1934 and 1941. Most of the buildings were of steel frame. Some were hangar type with wide clearances. Others were the monitor-roof type with overhead cranes and monorail systems. Saw-tooth roofs were also widely used but there were no blackout type buildings.

The steel buildings were less vulnerable to air attack. 500-lb bombs would blow off sections of the roof, dig craters in the ground but unless there was a direct hit the building would not collapse.

In Spain, the Germans were able to observe the behaviour of three main types, the Bf 109, He 111 and the Ju 87 or *Stuka* as it became known, which at the beginning of the war was more than adequate to support any air force then envisaged. The component industries were, however, not so lavishly stocked, as were the airframe and engine plants. There were instances of entire production being concentrated in one place such as Bosch at Stuttgart, producing all the aircraft magnetos up to September 1943 when the factory was dispersed. But, on the whole there was a multitude of different firms involved and it was unreasonable to expect Allied intelligence to detect the bottlenecks. In the UK, in contrast, the industry did not succeed in establishing a powerful industry by 1939, nor did it have the opportunity of testing out its own aircraft under wartime conditions.

But, once the war had begun the German industry made good progress and there was no complacency against the situation and what was required – a heavy bomber and heavily armed fighter. Between January and September 1939, the aircraft industry doubled its monthly output.

In Germany, the outbreak of war and the events between 1939 and 1941 made little impression on the German aircraft industry. The aircraft produced were thought to be adequate in numbers and quality to meet the demands required by the German High Command. The warning, however, that went out to the Germans after the Battle of Britain went unheeded as to the role air power was to play.

They felt that the war would be won on the ground and not in the air. Subsequently, no pressure was put on the German aircraft industry to increase its output or to produce better aircraft, particularly bomber aircraft between 1939 and 1943.

The aircraft industry built pre-war and in the first two years of the war worked on a single-shift basis. This had an important bearing on strategic bombing. In theory half the plant capacity could have been destroyed and the other half by working two shifts could have produced as many planes as before. In early 1939 the average production was 133 fighters and 217 bombers per month.

The rate of aircraft production in September 1939 was 800 machines a month, of which between 250 and 280 were fighters, including both single-engine and twin-engine types. A peak production of 2,000 a month was to be reached by the end of 1940. Two further programmes were drawn up in the course of 1940: this increased the peak output to 2,300 per month, a rate that had to be reached by the end of the year. None of these programmes was attained within the scheduled time. In Czechoslovakia the Skoda factory was in full production.

In 1940 Dr Tank of Focke-Wulf became critical of the German Air Ministry when after the Battle of Britain he tried to direct attention to the need for a high-altitude fighter. But he was told to forget the matter as the war was being won on the ground.

In Britain, however, it was quite the reverse and the outcome of the war lay, it was felt, in the air and so the aircraft industry was faced with expansion and development under direct air attacks that brought continual dispersal and blackout. The subsequent rate of expansion up to 1942 after it doubled in 1939 was as expected slower, as material, labour and factory space were short. Two or three shifts were being operated in the factories to try and quicken things up and raise production performance.

On 1 January 1942, Germany had 1,360 fighters and was making them at the rate of 485 per month. By December 1942, Germany had 1,660 fighters and was making them at a rate of 600 per month. By March 1943, this had risen to 1,820 fighters and advanced to 700 per month.

In Germany the RAF attacks on plants and factories had caused little damage or delayed production. The US daylight attacks in 1943 caused serious physical damage to some plants but did not affect their basic production potential and the German defences succeeded in inflicting a loss rate that caused a temporary suspension of their raids. The Focke-Wulf plants around Bremen moved to Marienburg, Posen, Cottbus and Sorau, plus other small plants were moved out of the range of the Allied bombers. The Bf 109 production was centred on three large assembly plants – Leipzig, Regensburg, and Wiener Neustadt. The idea was to build fully integrated complexes within an area of about 50 miles containing special factories with their own components-producing factories, fuselages, wings and other components. Each complex would be known as an *Ausschuss* and each would be under a Chief Engineer known as *Ausschussleiter* with an office at the assembly plant. One of the *Ausschleiter*s selected to head the pilot complex would lay down the production methods to be implemented by the others.

The various *Ausschusse* engaged in the production of one type of aircraft were collectively known as the *Sonderausschuss*, and the *Sonderaussleiter* was responsible for the production of that particular type of aircraft. He also had the power to divert components from one *Ausschuss* into another that had a temporary shortage.

Air raid precautions were taken by organising single shifts so that if one assembly plant or component were to be damaged by bombing then the personnel would be transferred as a body to one of the corresponding plants of another *Ausschuss* where by working a second shift production could be more or less maintained. In the German aero engine industry Junkers Motorenwerke had come to be regarded as the specialist in engines for bomber aircraft. The Dessau factory concentrated on research work and on the development of new engines. In the early part of 1942 the total war production in air armaments was 43% at a cost of 3 billion Reichsmarks; in the second half this dropped to 38%, but at an extra 3.4 billion Reichsmarks.

In June 1943, the Italian Air Attaché and his assistant were summoned to the General *Luftzeugmeister*'s department to attend a conference that had been called to explain the German production system, and to force the Italian Allies to adopt it in their own industry. General Milch addressed the heads of the German *Luftwaffe* production and planning sections, and also the heads of the industrial council, with the following words:

> We must not speak theoretically of victory. We must admit that the allies are much stronger in the air than we are. They are building more than three times the number of aircraft than Germany is, and if we cannot carry through our air production programme then Germany must lose the war.

The production of the Bf 109 aircraft was carried out on a conveyor belt system, each conveyor belt being designed for a monthly production of 300 aircraft. The target for the number of aircraft produced was 1,100 to 1,200 each month but by August 1943 this had not been reached. At Leipzig the number produced was 130, at Regensburg 200, and at Wiener/Neustadt 280 making a total of 610. Up to the end of August the precision bombing had been sufficiently serious enough to force the Germans to disperse factories but to continue on the mass production lines. It was felt that if they did revert to the old system of dispersing there would be a period of complete shambles and production would suffer. It was felt that a plan was in operation by the Allies to attack the aircraft industry sufficiently enough to make the Germans once again start to disperse the factories.

The plan for dispersal provided for the breaking up of production and the establishment of multiple sources for each part, subassembly and even final assembly. Karl-Otto Saur, Chief of the Fighter Staff, was in charge of the dispersal of the aircraft industry. The twenty-seven main aeroplane plants would be dispersed to 729 small plants.

The line production was as closely articulated as in the American aircraft plants, so any one unit or assortment of units could be destroyed by bombing without stopping the flow of production but its efficiency did suffer.

When Italy surrendered the German Air Ministry tried to integrate the Italian aircraft industry with the German aircraft industry. By 1943 all training aircraft and a large number of transport aircraft were being made in France, Holland, Hungary and Czechoslovakia. The Vichy Government of France refused to produce aircraft directly to be used for military purposes.

In January 1943, the Combined Chiefs of Staff approved a directive to the British and United States Bomber Command in the United Kingdom with the following order of priority of targets:

a. German submarine construction yards
b. The German aircraft industry
c. Transportation
d. Oil plants
e. Other targets in enemy war industry

The aim as far as the aircraft industry was concerned was the Fw 190 and Bf 109 plants with the idea of crippling the German defences not only in the Mediterranean, but also over Germany itself, which would open the way to a daylight offensive by the RAF and USAAF.

On 10 June 1943, the aircraft industry became the top priority and the order of targets was changed to:

a. German air industry
b. German submarine production and pens
c. German armament production
d. Axis oil production
e. Axis transport
f. The German will to resist

This was given the code name POINTBLANK.

Major General Eaker of the USAAF was asked for his opinion of the Combined Bomber Offensive paper. He replied with his comments on this paper on 15 April 1943. He was in full accordance with the policy recommended. He said that linking day bombing (by the USAAF 8th Air Force) and night bombing (by RAF Bomber Command) would unquestionably cause damage both to material and morale on a scale that the enemy would be unable to sustain.

The 8th USAAF was to attack the principal airframe and other aircraft factories while Bomber Command was to attack industrial towns in which there was the largest number of aircraft component factories – most of them were further east or south of the Ruhr.

After the raids on Hamburg in July 1943, Milch, Galland, and Speer pressed for priority to be given to the building of fighters, but it was light bombers that got the priority as in the opinion of the German High Command only by retaliatory attacks could the war be won. This theory in fact lasted until 1945 when four-engine bombers were still being built. The attacks in the last six months of 1943 resulted in 2,000 fewer German aircraft being built.

In August 1943, a Central Joint Committee known as the Jockey Committee was formed, which was separate from the Casablanca Policy of

January 1943. Its policy was the dislocation of the German military industry and economic system. It met each week to decide on the target to be attacked. In Germany the military officers and industrialists were amazed at the accuracy of the Allied intelligence on strategic targets.

In Germany Professor Messerschmitt expressed himself as highly critical of Goering and Milch for failing to provide the workers, materials and machine tools required for the expanding programme in August and October 1943. He also complained that the German Air Force suffered from deficient leadership. One of the principal complaints was that young pilots who had not distinguished themselves in combat had been placed in positions of great responsibly. He also criticised Goering and Mulch for failing to see the need to construct a fleet of long-range bombers to supplement submarine warfare in the Atlantic. This failure was part of the general failure to determine which of the thirty-five types of aircraft in production should be curtailed in order to make a place for four-engine bombers. It was Messerschmitt's poor opinion of the Air Ministry that caused him to suggest to Saur in 1943 that Speer take over the German aircraft industry.

At a conference in October 1943 in the UK, a decision was sought as to the immediate future with regard an all out effort by both bomber forces to complete the destruction of German fighter plants, or, an all out effort by both bomber forces in the area of German cities.

An informant in Germany stated that the first essential was to cripple fighter production, as this was then the branch of the industry that the Germans themselves considered to be vital. As the Bf 109 was the fighter produced in the largest numbers he recommended that the production of this type should be the first to receive attention. He suggested the offensive be started with raids on the three Bf 109 *Ausschuss* at Leipzig, Regensburg and Wiener/ Neustadt. The informant recommended that the attacks should take place with no more than three weeks between all three, thus, denying the Germans the possibility of switching their labour from bombed to unbombed factories. The same type of plant should be attacked in each *Ausschuss* and he suggested that the fuselage factories were the most vulnerable.

His reasoning was that in the German aircraft industry the work on fuselages was the most complicated and those factories making fuselages contained the largest number of jigs and machine tools. He also recommended attacking the aero engine production as well.

Hitler and his High Command feared the daylight precision attacks on individual factories, but the German people feared the night attacks more.

Hitler, however, openly boasted he could control the morale of the people by means of his party organisation.

In November 1943, a man who had been the Italian Assistant Air Attaché in Berlin was interrogated. He said that in June 1943, Milch said the following during a meeting, which included all the heads of the industrial council:

> We must not speak theoretically of victory. We must admit that the allies are much stronger in the air than we are. They are building more than three times the number of aircraft than Germany is, and if we cannot carry through our air production programme then Germany must lose the war.

He had said in October that 1,800 aircraft were produced in September, and in August 1,900, whereas in July it had been 3,000.

The Leipzig complex was even less advanced than Regensburg, but in August 1943 it was developed rapidly and the man being interrogated estimated that, all things being equal, it would reach the final figure of 300 aircraft per month within four to five months. The plant was 4 miles from Leipzig's city centre and made Bf 109 fighters.

The strength of the German Air Force on 1 December 1943 was estimated to be 5,150 aircraft. On the 2nd, the priority list of targets of the air forces in the UK was Erla Leipzig, which had Bf 109 components in Heiterblick and Leipzig Mockau where the Bf 109s were assembled, and Regensburg, where at Prufening and Obertraubling Bf 109s were assembled and components made.

ATG as well was in 1940 certainly focusing on building the fuselage and tails for the Ju 88. The final assembly and test flying was then carried out at Leipzig-Mockau and this continued until June 1944. The company also rebuilt many badly damaged aircraft that it had manufactured.

Also at Leipizg-Mockau the Ju 188 was built and first assembled in January 1944; some of the production was interrupted by US bombing attacks on 29 May and 20 July 1944. Despite this building continued until January 1945. As well as the Ju 188 they also were involved in the building of the Ju 388 fast bomber produced at Merseburg.

On 5 January 1944, a telegram was received in London from the US President. It read that he desired a consultation between the Chief of the Air Staff, and the Commanding General US Strategic Air Forces, Europe. The telegram included the following:

> The destruction of German air combat strength in its factories, on

the ground and in the air constitutes the primary objectives, the progressive dislocation of German military, industrial and economic systems and disruption of vital elements of enemy lines of communications remain the over-all missions of our combined bombing forces.

An outline plan was to be prepared and submitted by 20 January 1944, which included timing and a priority list of targets for a combined bomber offensive. A telegram reply was sent from the Air Ministry on the 7th, endorsing the view that the German fighter forces and the industry and its dependants were to be given first priority. After consultation with the Commanding General, the CinC Bomber Command, and the Air CinC Allied Expeditionary Air Force, the Chief of the Air Staff reviewed the progress of the combined bomber offensive, with particular regard to the short period remaining before Operation *Overlord*, and the invasion of Europe.

The German Air Force and its industry were, as previously agreed, given top priority.

On 13 January the Chief of the Air Staff sent a telegram to the Prime Minister.

He once again endorsed the task of the German Air Force and its industries as being a first priority. The order was:

Single-engine fighter airframe and component production
Twin-engine fighter airframe and component production
Ball-bearing industry

On 20 January a further telegram was sent to Washington from the Air Ministry. After consultation with the General US Strategic Air Forces, the CinC Bomber Command and the Air CinC Allied Expeditionary Air Force, the Chief of the Air Staff said:

We are convinced that the ultimate objective of the POINTBLANK plan should remain as stated in the Casablanca directive and the first priority should continue to be given to the attack upon the German Air Force fighters forces and its industry to which they depend. The reduction in the German fighter strength is in fact an essential prerequisite to progress towards the ultimate objective of the POINTBLANK plan and is a vital requirement in creating the conditions necessary for OVERLORD.

On 27 January 1944, the Air Ministry sent a letter to Air Chief Marshal Sir Arthur Harris CinC Bomber Command and the Director of Intelligence. It said that two German fighter wings, which were planned to re-equip over a ten-day period, early in January 1944 had only just been completed and had been out of the line for twenty-six days. The factory that should have provided their new aircraft was Leipzig-Mockau. It was suggested that the raid on this plant in December 1943 was responsible for this delay, although this was not completely certain, and that the factory had just been short of components. It was strongly felt that Bomber Command was responsible for this unwelcome delay.

The German aircraft production was until February 1944 under the control of the Air Ministry in Germany. This was under the control of Goering and the Director of Aircraft Production was Field Marshal Milch. He urged an increase in fighter production but Hitler, Goering and the General Staff were opposed from the outset so he set up several new plants in Austria and Czechoslovakia.

On 13 February 1944, a top-secret message was sent to Eisenhower in London from the Combined Chiefs of Staff. The message stated that the overall mission remained:

> The progressive destruction and dislocation of the German military, industrial and economic system, the disruption of vital elements of lines of communication and the material reduction of German air combat strength, by the successful prosecution of the combined bomber offensive from all convenient bases.

On 17 February 1944, an Air Ministry signal gave the following information:

> Revision of target priorities and approved by the Combined Chiefs of Staff.

> German Air Force
> Berlin
> And other industrial areas

The first priority was German single fighter airframes and airframe component production. Twin-engine airframe and airframe component production and installations supporting German Fighter Air Forces were next in priority.

The concept was the overall reduction of German air combat strength in its factories on the ground, and in the air mutually supported by attacks by both Strategic Air Forces.

Attacks on 20 February to 31 March resulted in a reduction of the completion of Bf 109s by 60%; 60% from April to June; and 25% from July to September. This represented a loss of about 2,000 to 2,500 aircraft.

It was estimated that by 1 April 1944, the strength of the German fighters would be 5,450 of which 2,400 would be on the Western Front. Of these it was estimated that 1,150 could be employed during the first day against the cross-Channel operations in April east of Cherbourg.

As the efficiency of Daimler-Benz increased in the design and production of high-performance engines, the most well known Mercedes-Benz engine was the DB601 due to the first application of direct fuel injection. This engine was used in most of the German fighter and bombers in the Spanish Civil War, the Battle of Britain and the remainder of WWII. The most successful of these, the Bf 109, was designed with the DB601 engine in mind. It also helped to power the Dornier D11 and Do 215 German bombers. The Heinkel He 112 and the Me 110 used to attack the B-17 and Avro Lancaster bomber forces during 1942/5 also used this engine. In 1939 this engine, used to power a Bf 109, created a new world speed record of 468.9 mph.

In a study by Air Ministry Intelligence it was estimated that between July 1943 and December 1944 the Germans were denied 18,000 aircraft of all types. This could have been more if they had not dispersed their plants but the losses were put down to airframe plants and direct losses caused by dispersal and the inefficiency attributed to these dispersals. The attacks on the aircraft industry had been a success.

The one thing that seems to be missed or overlooked is that although aircraft production increased in 1944 it was still far below the estimated production of months before had these attacks not taken place. Albert Speer said this in 1980 (he told the Author in a visit to him).

After the heavy attacks in February 1944 Milch approached Albert Speer, the Minister of Armaments, and told him that only 10% to 40% of the March production could be expected. He asked Speer to take charge of 'defensive' aircraft production. During these February attacks twenty-three airframe and three aircraft engine plants were hit.

As a result of this meeting the *Jaegerstab*, the committee for the production of fighter planes or fighter staff, was set up under the direct of Speer and Milch, with Saur as its executive head, on 1 March 1944. Many underground and other dispersal factories for the *Luftwaffe* had also been started.

'A survey in Germany said that more aircraft were lost out of production because of dispersal than because of direct bombing.'

Saur stated that by the end of February seven of the original buildings of the German aircraft industry had been destroyed or damaged. Attacks in January and February 1944 against factories producing the Me 110 were reported to have destroyed 465 machines in the final stages of construction, or standing on factory airfields.

Included in these attacks in February were the first raids on factories making Ju 188 and Ju 88 bombers, namely Junkers at Bernburg and ATG at Leipzig. The Bernburth attack was successful and production was put out of action until the end of March. The raid on ATG was so successful and yet production continued.

When Speer took over there had been fifty different types of fighter being produced. He said that he had blueprints every few months and that if a programme lasted three months it was a miracle. He was able to reduce this number but only by rebuilding and dispersing the shattered industry to reduce it to below thirty-eight.

Although the bombing offensive increased by day and night during the first quarter of 1944, the total loss inflicted on German industry (as distinct from the particular effects on certain armament industries) was probably less than in the last quarter of 1943 mainly due to weather conditions. Despite this the offensive continued to hold German industrial production down to the level to which it had been reduced by the German summer attacks.

The damage to aircraft plants was greater than to aircraft production. Up to 1 March 1944 75% of the factories producing airframes and engaged in main assembly work had been damaged. This was 75% buildings and 25% on machine and tool shops.

Although production increased new pilots was the main problem and a lack of fuel.

By the end of 1944 transport was so disorganised that material was not being delivered to the manufacturers and even if the material was finished it could not be taken away.

Also, although not open to direct attacks, engines etc could not be delivered to the factories. And by the time the war ended production was nil.

By October 1944, when most of Germany's best workers were called up for military service, their places were taken by older men, foreigners, prisoners of war and part-time workers.

a. German men and women	52%
b. POWs and Jews	12%
c. Foreigners	36%
d. Women	23%

Not all of these foreign workers were 'slave' workers. A large number came voluntarily to Germany to take a part in Hitler's New Order. Of the 'slave' workers the Dutch were the least cooperative.

Bombing of three aircraft factories began on 13 August 1940 and continued to 8 April 1945. In all, thirty-seven raids were made and included Leipzig-Mockau and Leipzig Taucha.

In 1945 at the end of the war all the aircraft plants including ATG at Leipzig were stripped of their presses.

Chapter 7

Leipzig

—∽∽—

L eipzig was first documented in 1015 and in 1165 received its town charter and rights as a market town. Due to its strategic placement along the market routes to Prague, Berlin and Frankfurt, Leipzig quickly experienced a flurry of commercial activity, which continues today. It is situated 134 miles from Berlin.

The Electorate of Saxony was created in 1423; Leipzig was an important commercial centre in the area of Europe and was full of European scholars and traders.

In 1481 the first book was published in Leipzig and the city has continued to be a centre of publishing and printing. In 1497 the right to hold fairs was granted to the growing city of 10,000 inhabitants.

In 1409 the University of Leipzig was founded, which makes it one of the oldest in Europe.

In 1813 Napoleon was defeated to the south of Leipzig when he took on an army of 370,000 with an army of 198,000. He lost 73,000 men in battle and his opponents lost 54,000.

Johann Sebastian Bach moved to Leipzig in 1723 and he remained here for the rest of his life. During his time as the cantor of Thomaskirche (Thomas Church) the choir was fifty strong; today this has risen to 100. He died in 1750. Another famous composer, Felix Mendelsson, lived in Leipzig.

Richard Wagner was born in Leipzig in 1813. It was here that his great compositions were created.

Martin Luther (1483 to 1546) the religious reformer was active in Leipzig.

In 1839 came the first long distance rail service from Leipzig to Dresden. This connected Leipzig with Dresden and was soon after called the 'Dresdner Bahnh of the Magdeburger'.

The first German labour party, the GGWA, was founded in Leipzig in May 1863.

The industrial expansion was based on a railway line from Leipzig to Dresden. From this single track came the economic development and the vital factor in the unification of Germany in 1871.

At the beginning of the twentieth century with a united Germany, the Saxon industry continued to develop and contributed powerfully to Germany's industrial strength.

Leipzig was one of Germany's major cities and the largest in Saxony. It also had the largest railway station, Leipzig Central Station, in Europe. It had twenty-six platforms and a huge transport hall.

The people of Leipzig were very proud of their station with its four good yards and small marshalling yards formed a block in the centre of the city. It had been built with the idea of impressing visitors to the Leipzig trade fairs. It had been erected in the years 1902 to 1915 after the German states Prussia and Saxony agreed a new station had to be built. All the facilities were doubled: one set for the Saxony, and the other Prussia.

The marshalling yards were at Wandren and Engelsdorf west and east of the city, the former with a maximum daily wagon capacity of 4,500, the latter 3,700. A smaller marshalling yard was at Mockau north of the main station.

Wahren lay on the electrified line to Halle and was connected to all the main lines from Leipzig by lines that passed around the city. One line from Wahren passed through Mockau, where it crossed by the electric line from the main station to Bitterfield and Magdeburg, connected with the lines from the main station and the south to Cottbus, crossing near Engelsdorf. Another line from Wahren connected with Grosskorbothat-Mockau Main station and forked at Leipzig-Plaswitz station, one line proceeding via Gera to Plauen, the other via Gashwitx to Plauen.

The main importance of Leipzig lay in its own industry, and that of the Saxon towns nearby. The immense value of local industrial traffic and the importance of the great trade fair was evident by the number and size of its goods yards, the impressive size of its post office sorting sidings and the grandeur of its main station. There was much through traffic from the Ruhr to the east.

There were two main municipal power plants in the city, both of 50-100,000 kW capacity, and a subsidiary station at Gennewitz. The city gas works were to the south of the city. Both the gas and electric plants were close together.

In the centre of the city were engineering works Hugo Schneider AG making machine tools, light arms and ammunition, Kollman Werks AG producing torpedo components, and the textile factory Leipziger Wollkazmerel.

In the western outskirts of Leipzig were located engineering firms and textile works, including a subsidiary of E Bedker AG producing light metal castings for the aircraft factory and Deutache Kugellager fabrik Gm producing ball-bearings.

Outlying targets during WWII included the aerodrome on which there were three assembly works belonging to Eral ATG and Junkers. Also Erla had a fuselage plant at Heiterblick and the Mitteldeutaene Motorrenwerke had a large aero engine factory at Taucha. At Rackowitz 6 miles north of Leipzig there was the Leipziger Leichtmetall-Werk, which produced magnesium alloys.

In 1913 a monument was erected, the Volkerschlachtdenkmal, to celebrate the 100th anniversary of the Battle of the Nations.

The first German long distance railway line across the eastern Ore Mountains was opened in 1873 between Leipzig and Dresden.

In 1933 the population of Leipzig was 714,000, and in 1941 it was 707,000. Its chief industries were aircraft construction, forty-five factories making aircraft and aero engines, light engineering, metal workings, rayon, paper and printing. Of lesser importance were the textiles, electrical apparatus, and musical instruments industries. It was a great commercial centre of special importance with its fairs, book and fur trade. As a cultural centre it was the seat of the supreme law courts and university.

On a map in 1934, its total area represented 110 square miles and its administrative area covered an area of 50 square miles or 33,000 acres. This was made up of a built-up area of 7,600 acres, which took in homes, gardens, factories and yards. An area of 4,100 acres was made up of streets, squares, railways, open spaces of parks and cemeteries. Most of the city of Leipzig was situated on the eastern side; the western side was smaller and housed the important urban area with its outlying suburbs. Boulevards, public buildings, railway station and yards encircled the old town. The circular railway bound the south-east section of the city and east of the Bavarian station to the south and exhibition buildings, seventeen in all, totalling an aggregate floor space of 170,000 square feet, which during the war was reported as being used for factory floor space.

The industrial area was clustered in four principal districts:

> The Central, around the central railway yards.
> The Northern lay on the north side of the central railway yards
>   and followed the railway due north as far as the aerodrome.

> The Western, lay west of the river plain and was a large fully built-up area in the heart of the urban area of Lindenau; factories extended into open land along the railway to the north and south.
> The Southern, a smaller district than the others, lay by the railway running south from the Bavarian station including the gas and electricity works.

The railway encircled the outskirts of the city. There were six blocks of railway yards, which terminated in the central station penetrating right to the heart of the city. It ranked with Hamburg and Berlin as the most densely populated city in Germany, and was 540 miles from the Wash.

The factories engaged on aircraft production were:

> Erla works employed in aircraft assembly.
> Allgemeine Transport employed in aircraft assembly and aero engines
> Mitteldeutsche Motorenwerk making aero engines

Other factories making war material were:

> Bussing making tanks and armoured fighting vehicles
> Meir and Veukelt making tools
> Hugo Schneider making light arms, small arms and ammunition

The city lay on flat land at the confluence of two small rivers – the Weisse Elster and the Pleisse. The factories were clustered in four principal districts. The main built-up area was west of the Pleisse Plain and had an area of 7 square miles.

The central railway yards, congested old town, modern public buildings on and adjacent to the boulevards and inner tenement areas all formed one compact fully built-up target area of 3 to 4 miles. The old town was vulnerable to fire, but the wide boulevards would act as a firebreak. On the boulevards were modern buildings, which would stand up best to bombing.

Leipzig was predominately a city of tenements, and ranks with Hamburg and Berlin as one of the most densely peopled cities in Germany. They were very vulnerable to bombing.

On 9 November 1938, the Nazis in Leipzig destroyed Jewish synagogues as they had done all over Germany.

On the 10 August 1939 a report in Leipzig said that the people were resigned to the fact that war was about to commence.

Leipzig was taken by American troops of the 69th Infantry Division known as the 'Fighting 69th' on 20 April 1945, Hitler's 56th birthday. In

July 1945 the Americans gave up control of the city to the Russians and it remained part of East Germany until 1989 when Germany was reunified. During the battle for Leipzig a sub camp of Buchenwald Concentration Camp, Leipzig-Thekla, was discovered. At its height, having been built in 1943, it had 1,400 prisoners. When the battle was going on tremendous atrocities to the prisoners took place. The Allied Military Government ordered the local establishment in Leipzig to provide caskets for the dead prisoners of which some 300 had been shot. And on 27 April a full funeral was organised with a guard of honour from the surviving inmates carrying flags from many nations in Europe that had been incarcerated there. In 1993 the 69th were recognised as the liberating unit at the US Holocaust Memorial Museum. In taking Leipzig the 69th suffered 1,506 casualties, of which 384 died in battle. In 1950 Leipzig started to recover from its wartime damage.

The movement to pull down the Berlin Wall, which was built in 1961, started in Leipzig. But it was not until 1989 that the wall was pulled down and Germany was again united.

It is now a centre of culture, printing, music and trade in Germany. It is often called 'Paris in Miniature' because of the beautiful art, music and films produced there. It has a sister city Houston.

Today it has a population of 480,000 and its religion is 44% Protestant and 37% Roman Catholic. Its main industries are publishing, printing, manufacturing and chemicals. Its exports are chemicals, agriculture, machinery and paper. And it imports oil and natural gas. They have a President and a Head of Government. It has sixteen states that are responsible for schools and other local matters. It also has a mayor.

During WWII there were said to have been eighteen air attacks on the city. They included:

1. 22/23 May 1940 – an attack on Merseburg near Leipzig
2. 26/27 August 1940 – an attack on Leipzig
3. 20/21 October 1943 – an attack on Leipzig
4. 3/4 December 1943 – an attack on Leipzig
5. 19/20 February 1944 – an attack on Leipzig
6. 6/7 December 1944 – an attack on Merseburg
7. 16/17 January 1945 – an attack on Zeitz oil plant
8. 13/14 February 1945 – an attack on Bohlen near Leipzig
9. 10 April 1945 – Leipzig Engeldorf and Mockau marshalling yards.

Situated 30 miles from Leipzig was one of the most notorious Allied prisoner of war camps, Oflag IVC, a *Sonderlager* or Special Camp in the village of Colditz.

The Tower, or Great Castle of Augustus the Strong of Saxony, stood above the village of Colditz and on the banks of the River Mulde in Upper Saxony. Since 1800 it had been a prison and then from 1828 up to 1939 an asylum. It was in November 1940 that it became a Special Camp or *Aper Mit Besonderer*.

The prisoners kept in the castle were prisoners of war who had escaped many times from other camps and it was thought that putting all the 'bad apples in one basket' would eradicate the problem. But of course if you put men with such skills together then you are asking for trouble, and they certainly got it.

The castle had been built in 1158 after Emperor Frederick Barbossa appointed Thimo 'Lord Colditz'. When it was sold in the fifteenth century it ended 250 years of rule by the Lords of Colditz. In 1504 it was set on fire by accident but it was rebuilt in 1506. In 1933 under the Nazis it became a political prison for communists, homosexuals, Jews and other 'undesirables'. In 1945 at the end of WWII the Russians turned the castle into a prison camp for local burghers and non-communists. Then post war it was again a hospital and psychiatric clinic.

Two flak divisions were formed in Leipzig on 2 in July 1938 and 17 April 1942 but both were later moved to the Russian Front and Italy.

Today the castle is a museum and a popular venue for WWII enthusiasts. In 2006 it was the venue of the 2006 World Cup Draw. In 2012 the city bid for the Olympic Games but did not make the final selection, which of course was won by London.

After the wall came down in 1989 the railway station was reconstructed and in addition to its role as a station it has become an excellent shopping centre. Its promenades are one of Germany's most modern shopping and service centres. It covers about 30,000 square metres on three levels with about 140 shops and purpose-built parking decks.

In 2006 about 40 miles from Leipzig in an area around Koethen, which was heavily bombed in July and August 1944, more than 2,100 undetonated explosives were discovered over a period of seven days.

Chapter 8

Target Leipzig

—ɷ—

The first heavy bomber attack on the city of Leipzig in WWII was on 20/21 October 1943. For this operation 358 aircraft were despatched, of which 287 attacked the target and fifteen were missing, eighteen were damaged by flak and eight by enemy aircraft. This was an all Lancaster force.

It had been attacked on a number of occasions in 1940/41. The first occasion was on 22/23 May 1940, when Merseburg near Leipzig was attacked and it was attacked again on 26/27 August 1940, when the Mockau works and the power station were attacked by twenty-eight aircraft and 42 tons of bombs were dropped. On 22/23 May the Hampden forces were recalled because of bad weather over the UK airfields, but one Hampden did not get the recall and bombed Merseburg.

In those early days of the war known as Code H 131 (the code name for bombing operations at that time of the war) Pilot Officer Bancer attacked the local gas or power station and Pilot Officer Reed bombed north-west of Hanover, having failed to locate the primary target at Merseburg.

The plan of attack in October was route marking with thirteen blind markers and ten backers up dropping red spot flares in the area of Bremen and yellow TIs (Target Indicators) near Stendal both on the outward and inward routes.

On the homeward route, and in the area of Hanover, red TIs were to be dropped. The target marking was carried out by blind marking (Y-Type) aircraft detailed to drop yellow TIs over the aiming point. If the cloud was less than 7/10 each aircraft was also to drop a string of flares; the first bundle twenty-four seconds before the TIs, the second eighteen seconds before and the third at the same time as the TIs and the remainder at six-second intervals thereafter. Visual markers were to mark the exact aiming point with red TIs. If this was not possible they were to aim green TIs at the centre of the yellow TIs with a three-second overshoot. Backers up were to maintain marking with green TIs in order of preference: reds, centre of yellows or centre of greens overshooting in either of the two last-named eventualities by three seconds. Supporters were to identify visually, otherwise aiming at the centre of the yellows. The main force was to aim at the reds, or the centre of the greens. All Y-crews (H2S) were to carry red flares plus green stars for use in unfavourable cloud conditions. Zero hour was set at 2100 and the duration of the attack was from 2056 to 2111.

The Pathfinder force consisting of forty-six Lancasters was to drop 'Window' at a rate of one bundle every two minutes for part of the trip and then one bundle every half minute for the latter part of the trip and into Leipzig. This was to be carried out on the return trip also.

The weather forecast was 10/10 to 6/10 cloud en route with good visibility and no moon in the target area with winds of 40 to 45 mph.

Throughout Yorkshire, and Lincolnshire the air was full of throbbing engines of Bomber Command aircraft. On a bomber station there were over 2,000 men and women whose sole task was to get twenty aircraft and 140 aircrew off each night and deep into enemy territory.

They were to become the pioneers of victory in Europe and the ending of the war.

A bomber station was like a small self-contained town with a great number of buildings and a network of roads connecting it all. The aircrew are like guests at a hotel, coming and going all the time, some having finished a tour of operations, usually thirty, or others making that one-way trip and becoming a prisoner of war or a casualty of war.

To every aircraft were ten ground crew, each having a special task, such as riggers, instrument repairers known as ' bashers', armourers, electricians, and so on but all vital to the maintenance of the aircraft and the safety of the crew. Every time the aircraft went out and came back, and that's if it did, a thorough check was made for damage or engine problems.

On 20 October 1943, 358 Lancasters were despatched, of which 271 (75.7%) attacked the city. Fifty Lancasters (14%) attacked other targets and twenty-two (6.1%) aborted with technical problems, manipulation errors or crew failure. Fifteen (4.2%) failed to return and thirty-three returned damaged. One German night fighter was reported to have been shot down. Of the missing aircraft five were thought to have been lost on the outward journey and a sixth on the homeward route, all in the area of Texel. Five aircraft were observed to fall victim to flak, one in the target area. One aircraft from 5 Group ditched in the sea 60 miles off Grimsby with engine failure; five of its crew were rescued.

Ten Mosquitoes carried out diversionary attacks on Berlin and succeeded in diverting many of the German night fighters from the route of the main force to Leipzig.

Four Mosquitoes bombed Emden on Oboe and five attacked the power station at Braunweiler. Four attacked the power station at Knapsack and four attacked Cologne instead because of the failure of their precision devices. Twelve Stirlings laid sixty-three mines off the Frisians and twenty Whitleys and Wellingtons dropped leaflets over towns in Northern and Central France.

Of the twenty-three blind markers despatched, seventeen reached Leipzig but only seven dropped their TIs or flares, which were immediately obscured by cloud. Of the total main force aircraft despatched, 239 claimed to have attacked Leipzig; of these eighty-three aimed their bombs at suspected TIs or flares and eighty-nine bombed blindly at the estimated time of arrival but no concentration was achieved.

Photographs taken nine days later revealed a number of points of damage in the city and on the outskirts of Leipzig. This included a group of factories, which was engaged in making building machinery, accumulators and chemical goods. Five warehouses at the goods junction at Neustadt were gutted and part of a workmen's barracks belonging to the Allgemeine Transport Anlagen GmbH was demolished and scattered damage had been caused to business and residential property.

In the target area only slight flak was found although in the later stages of the attack this became moderate. But although the searchlights illuminated the cloud they were unable to penetrate it. However, at Texel accurate predicted flak was found in co-operation with searchlights and eighteen aircraft were hit. Three running fighter commentators were heard coming from Stade, Deelan and Berlin. At Deelan they soon handed over to Berlin, but Stade continued alone. They were somewhat confused as to the actual target thinking it was Bremen, Hanover or Berlin.

The fighters did arrive eventually at Leipzig but not until 2124 hours and very few combats took place. What fighters were found on the outward route were identified as Ju 88s. The one German fighter lost was reported as being shot down by a Lancaster of No. 1 Group.

The weather conditions found were not that predicted in the briefing. In the weather forecast given to the crews they had been warned of some thick cloud en route but this proved to be an understatement, certainly as far as Steve Bethell (an air gunner with 467 Squadron from RAF Bottesford) was concerned. His pilot Flt Lt McCelland soon encountered cloud and deteriorating weather conditions. The aircraft was being buffeted in all directions and ice became the major hazard with thick layers forming on the leading edges of the wings. This occasionally broke away and crashed along the side of the aircraft. There was a constant flash of lightning and thunder all around the aircraft. Steve at first thought it was flak but it was the stormy conditions that were worrying rather than enemy gunfire.

The winds forecast were 50 mph over the North Sea, 65 mph over the Dutch coast, and 45 to 55 mph over Leipzig.

When McCelland was about an hour from the target one of the starboard engines went u/s (unserviceable) due it was thought to icing and the aircraft began to lose height. The pilot ordered the bomb aimer to jettison the 4,000-lb bomb being carried in order to stabilise the aircraft and to maintain height. When they arrived over Leipzig they were surprised to find a few gaps in the cloud. However, they found no sign of Pathfinder flares or markers, just some scattered bunches of incendiaries. There appeared to be no other aircraft in the target area so they proceeded to bomb and then headed homeward.

Steve described their return on three engines as a nightmare, with the aircraft tossing about violently and the leading edges of the wings and the windscreen covered in ice. The ASI (airspeed indicator) was useless and Steve's intercom froze up.

They landed back at base more than an hour late and with very little fuel in the tanks.

The operation had been a complete waste of effort and time and everyone knew it would mean another visit in the future.

As well as the fifteen aircraft missing thirty-three were damaged:

a. Eighteen by flak
b. Eight by fighters
c. Two collided with other British bombers
d. One by incendiaries
e. Four to other causes

Fighters on the outward route, two south of Groningen, two between Texel and Leeuwarden, and one south-west of Oldenburg, shot down five of the fifteen missing aircraft. A sixth was destroyed on the homeward run in the Texel area. Five were seen to be shot down by flak, one over the target, two possibly at Emden, which was well off track, and two more between Texel and Leeuwarden. The remaining four losses could not be accounted for.

A Lancaster of No. 408 Squadron was rammed by another aircraft while on the perimeter of its airfield and was badly damaged. At Linton-on-Ouse Lancaster DS726 taxied into Lancaster DS771, which had stopped short of DS774.

W/O Claude White of 100 Squadron had flown on a number of operations when he took off in Lancaster DV189-B-2. En route the intercom went u/s and then a mechanical fault put the port engine out and then caught fire. They were still able to carry on and bomb the target but it meant they were seventeen minutes behind the main force of bombers. On landing the flames flared up and threatened to engulf the whole of the Lancaster but after getting all the crew out he stayed behind to turn off the petrol cocks and switches. For this operation he was awarded the CGM. The next night he was on the battle order to Kassel, his twenty-ninth mission.

F/Sgt Frederick Stuart of 426 (Thunderbird) Squadron RCAF was also on the operation to Leipzig and took off in Lancaster DS686-D. He was attacked by a fighter on several occasions before reaching the target. The Lancaster was hit by an Bf 109 on the tailplane, fuselage and wings, knocking out the mid upper gun turret and wounding the mid upper gunner. The windscreen had been shattered and the Gee apparatus made u/s. Nevertheless, they went on to bomb the target and had a safe return. Despite the damage Stuart made a superb landing. He had completed twenty operations and was also awarded the CGM.

Sadly, only two months later he failed to return from an operation to Frankfurt and is today buried in the Rheinburg War Cemetery.

For the crews that returned to base the wireless operator would call the watchtower and would normally receive a reply from a WAAF. Each station had its own call sign. For example, on one station it was Parsnip. The pilot would be told where to land on the runway or told to circle, particularly if an aircraft was coming in damaged or with wounded aboard. The end of one operation but with many more to come.

Chapter 9

The Second Attack

—⚡—

The second major attack was on 3/4 December 1943, at the time the Battle of Berlin was being mounted by Bomber Command. For this attack 527 Lancasters and Halifax aircraft were despatched, of which 451 attacked and twenty-three were missing. (The remainder turned back with engine problems or did not take off.) As a feint to confuse the German fighters eleven Mosquitoes of 139 and 627 Squadrons were despatched to Berlin, dropping green and yellow TIs as well as high explosives. The first four were to make a dummy run from the route marker TI north of Hanover and aim yellow TIs at the northern edge of the fires, still burning from the previous night's attack on Berlin. The rest of the force was to aim green TIs at the centre of all visible TIs. 'Window' was to be dropped at the rate of four bundles per minute en route to Berlin. The feint was successful and took the defending fighters away from the main objective, at the time the attack on Leipzig was being carried out. Zero hour was set at 0400 hours and the duration of the attack was from 0358 to 0414 hours.

The Lancaster force came from 1,3,5,6 and 8 Groups and the Halifax force from 4 and 6 Groups. En route to Leipzig all primary blind markers were to drop yellow TIs north of Hanover and red TIs 9 miles west of Brandenburg (either on H2S or visually), green TIs 6 miles south-east of Frankfurt and 10 miles south-east of Coblenz on the return route. They were to attack the aiming point with red TIs and release one bundle each of Wanganui flares using H2S. (The Wanganui, named after a town in Australia, was a sky marker flare that lit up the area for about two minutes.) Secondary blind markers were to keep the aiming point marked with green and Wanganui flares using H2S.

Early backers up were to aim greens at the centre of the reds; if the cloud obscured the TI they were to bomb the flares.

Late backers up were to aim at the centre of the greens and supporters were to bomb blindly. The importance of accurate timing was especially emphasised to those aircraft. The main force aircraft were to bomb the centre of the green TIs if visible, otherwise they were to bomb the flares in the same way as the supporters. 'Window' was to be dropped at the rate of one bundle every two minutes within 30 miles from the target in both directions and one bundle per minute for the rest of the way home.

'Window' was the code name for quantities of a conductor of electricity paper-backed metal foil cut in the form of strips and released in the air in order to produce echoes in radar equipment resembling those produced by aircraft. The number and length of the strips in the bundles used by Bomber Command were chosen so that the echo sent back to the enemy's flak or fighter control, or to his airborne radar, by each bundle when dispersed in a 'cloud' was equal to that reflected by a heavy bomber.

Over Leipzig the cloud was forecast as 10/10-layer cloud with tops at 5,000 to 6,000 feet with no moon and the winds were forecast as up to 35 mph.

A request came from Canada that a bomb be dropped on Germany in a token of one million dollars in war savings stamps contributed by the citizens of Ontario and this was carried by an aircraft of 432 (Leaside) Squadron RCAF based at East Moor, Yorkshire. Twelve ABC-carrying aircraft to help disrupt the German fighters were mingled in the bomber force. (ABC aircraft carried special operators who spoke and understood German. They would listen in to German radio and jam instructions being given to German night fighter pilots.)

Of the 527 aircraft that were despatched 428 attacked the primary target Leipzig (81.1%), nine attacked alternative targets and sixty-seven aborted with technical trouble, manipulation problems, icing up or crew error, and twenty aircraft failed to return (4.4%).

Nick Knilans, an American pilot serving with 619 Squadron at Woodhall Spa, was in one of seven aircraft despatched from 619. The weather forecast given in the briefing at Woodhall Spa was heavy cloud and icy conditions on the way to the target, and on the return, foggy conditions were forecast to have set in. Nick nearly crashed on take-off. It was pitch black and his eyes were glued to his instrument panel. Just as the aircraft lifted off the artificial horizon showed his port wing dropping so he applied starboard rudder and aileron but nothing happened. The instrument showed him diving to port and as he looked up he saw the nearby base of Bardney. The little aeroplane inside the artificial horizon was tumbling all the way over to port. He righted the Lancaster and used the lights at Bardney as a horizon. He had a decision to make: go on to Leipzig or abort and return to base. On the squadron aborting was known as a 'Boomerang'. He decided the risk was too great and climbed to 5,000 feet over the North Sea and jettisoned his bomb load and made a safe landing at base. As he was driven back to the Petwood Hotel, the 619 Officers' Mess, he found himself whistling and felt it was a way of letting off steam after the tenseness of the last hour.

The Pathfinders used two Lancasters to drop sky markers over the cloud, and with the aid of Mk III H2S they were able to find aiming points in Leipzig. The attack started at 4 am and the main force crews found a good concentration of flares to aim at. The concentration of bombing was reported as one of the best ever seen and was maintained throughout the attack, which lasted less than thirty minutes. The glow of the ground markers in the same area could also be seen through the thin cloud. The smoke rose to a height of 12,000 feet, and some crews reported having seen a built-up area blazing furiously. One aircraft that bombed at 4.25 am reported large fires in an area 2 miles square.

German fighters were seen en route but few over the target until the latter part of the attack when large numbers were seen over Leipzig and Berlin. The searchlights were ineffective against the cloud and flak was slight to modest. Over Dessau to the west of the target there was considerable flak.

The eleven Mosquitoes from 139 and 627 Squadrons made a divisionary raid on Berlin and dropped yellow and Green TIs in addition to high explosive bombs.

Photographs taken ten hours after the raid showed the whole of the centre part of Leipzig obscured by smoke and fires still burning. The German fire service in Leipzig became completely unorganised due in part to five units having been sent to Berlin to put out the fires from the night before. According to Dr Goebbels Leipzig was unprepared and the fire service inadequate. The smoke was billowing up to 20,000 feet. German radio broadcast that a formation of bombers had attacked Leipzig and dropped a number of bombs. The terror attack, it went on to say, destroyed several districts of the city and a number of public buildings. Among them some of cultural importance were severely damaged. Photographs taken two weeks later revealed the extent of the devastation. Nearly 30% of Leipzig lay in ruins by this single attack. The greatest damage was around the central station affecting the railway station itself and neighbouring goods sheds, and the town gas works. Of the seventeen large exhibition buildings used for the world trade fairs in Leipzig, and now used for the building of Junkers aircraft, not one remained intact. Some, including the largest hall, which boasted an unsupported roof span of 321 feet, were completely shattered. Nearly fifty other factories and seventy-seven small industrial premises were affected. The wool-combing plant of the Leipziger-Wollkammered, the third largest of its kind in Germany, was more than one-third destroyed. Nearly half of the branch factory of the Erla Maschinenbaiu, which produced aircraft components, was wrecked. Most of the goods sheds and rolling stock in the main station were gutted but the railway station, the largest in Europe and a junction on the supply route to the Russian front itself, suffered only damage to its roof and lights.

The Bhuthner facility, formerly a piano-making factory but now an ammunition boxes assembly plant, was in the heart of Leipzig and close to aircraft factories and a 'buzz' bomb plant. It was completely destroyed by fire after being bombed. They had been forced to stop making pianos by the Nazi Government but in 1990 following German reunification they again went back to becoming a private company making pianos.

The district office of the Nazi Labour Party was destroyed and also the headquarters of the 35th SA Brigade. In all, 564 acres in the fully built-up area of the city was devastated. Over 150,000 and possibly up to 200,000 were made homeless in Leipzig and 1,182 were killed.

The bombing photographs taken by 432 Squadron were sent to Royal Canadian HQ in London.

The production losses caused were later traced to fifty-one fuselages and two weeks' production capacity.

The defences over Leipzig were a loose barrage of moderate intensity up to 20,000 feet but the searchlights could not penetrate the cloud. En route, accurate heavy flak was encountered from Egmond. The fighter commentators plotted the bombers accurately along the route as far as the turning point and numerous encounters occurred in this area.

Of the twenty-three missing Allied aircraft five were seen to go down on the outward route between Egmond and the east coast of the Zuider Zee. Three of these were lost to flak – two at Egmond and one in the Zwolle/Meppel area. Fighters shot down the other two. Fighters shot down five other aircraft between Quackenbruch and the turning point. In the target area one was shot down by flak and two by fighters. The only evidence of a loss on the homeward route was to flak at Jerva. Of those that returned twenty-nine were damaged of which four were written off and scrapped.

One aircraft of 50 Squadron flown by Flying Officer Mike Beetham (later Chief of the Air Staff and Marshal of the Royal Air Force) was attacked by a fighter and had its No. 2 port tank holed and port flap holed and the main plane on the port side exhaust stub hit. There were also bullet holes through the port inner propeller and the port aileron was damaged.

During the action the guns froze up. He had taken off at 12.30 am and landed at 8.10 am.

Another aircraft from 50 Squadron was flown by F/Lt James Lees RCAF who when some miles from the target was shot by an enemy fighter.

The rear turret was rendered unserviceable and the main hydraulic gear was damaged. The windscreen near the pilot was shattered causing intense cold in the cabin. Nevertherless, the resolute pilot flew on to the target, executing his attack, and afterwards flew the aircraft back to base where he effected a masterly landing despite having two tyres burst and without the use of flaps. He had already successfully completed five operations to Berlin during the Battle of Berlin. He was awarded the DFC for this operation. On one operation he was reported missing on an operation to Milan until word came that he had crash-landed in North Africa and he later returned to the UK on a transport aircraft. Sadly, he was killed flying in a Dakota on 15 September 1946 aged thirty-two and is buried in Chilliwack Cemetery, Little Mountain, British Columbia, Canada. His name is recorded on the Abbotsford War Memorial in Canada.

This attack on Leipzig was described as the most precise bombing attack ever carried out on a target covered in cloud – all thanks to H2S. One of several photographs taken from the cathode-ray tube of the Mk III H2S showed an image of Leipzig at a range of 8 miles. It was so clear that copies were sent to the men who had invented it and made H2S work.

Two Lancasters collided over enemy territory but no serious injury or damage was incurred. Five aircraft were damaged from bombs dropped from above.

War Correspondent Colin Bednall flew with Flight Lieutenant Utz, an Australian flying in Lancaster JA683-E-Edward of 460 RAAF Squadron. Before taking off, Group Captain Hughie Edwards VC DSO DFC, the station commander at RAF Binbrook, presented Colin with his own good luck charms, which he had carried in his own many bombing operations – a 5 lucky dice and a St Christopher medallion. Colin at first said he would rather not take them as he might lose them but Edwards simply smiled and pushed them into his pocket. Taking off on a long haul in the darkness was anything but glamorous and one's mind became full of grudges. 'Damn the night.' 'Damn the cold.' 'Damn the Hun.' 'Damn everything including the job of war correspondent.' In a short time they began to roll down the runway and past the runway lights. In the dark he could hardly make out the features of the crew and until he returned he only knew them by their Christian names and their voices over the intercom. Because George, the

Anti-aircraft guns protecting the towns and cities in Germany. (*IWM*)

Pre-war Leipzig Railway Station. (*Alan Cooper*)

Leipzig Railway Station looking North-east of the city. (*Alan Cooper*)

Last minute instructions for Lancaster W4964 of 9 Sqn.

103 Squadron - Norman Storey on top with his crew. (*Norman Storey*)

Lancaster W 4380-S flown by P/O Lasham of 9 Sqn.

To the aircraft. (*M. Emery*)

Those last few minutes. (*Alan Cooper*)

The pre-operation supper. (*Alan Cooper*)

A 4,000lb 'Cookie' bomb being loaded into a Lancaster of 460 Sqn. (*W/C Cairns*)

A crew briefing at 460 Sqn. (*W/C Cairns*)

Debriefing after an operation. (*W/C Cairns*)

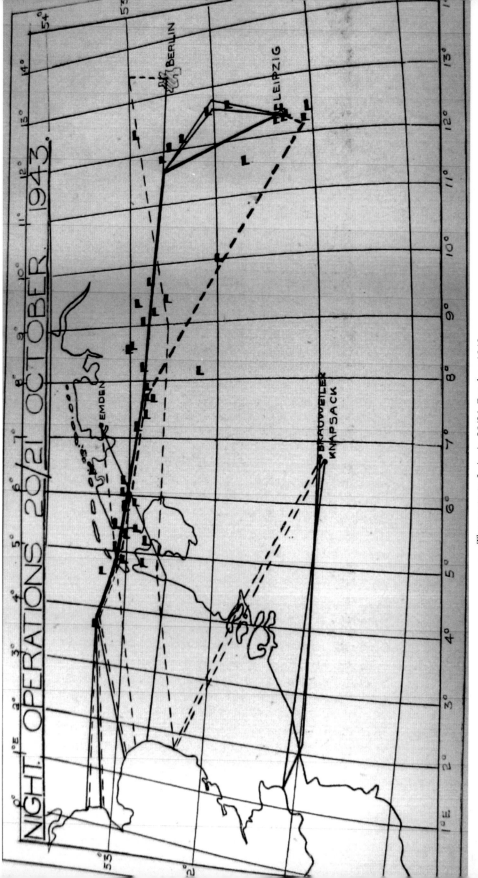

The route to Leipzig 20/21 October 1943.

Aircraft Factory (*Mockau*) Leipzig.

Aircraft Factories (*Mockau*) Leipzig.

Aircraft factory (*Mockau*) Leipzig.

Major Paul Zorner.
(*Paul Zorner*)

Me 110 night fighter interior layout.

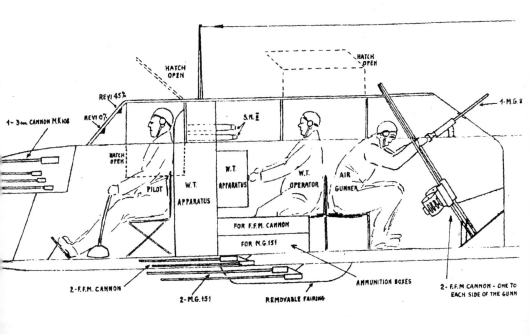

MODIFIED Me 110 NIGHT FIGHTER

SECRET

YEAR 1944		AIRCRAFT		PILOT, OR 1ST PILOT	2ND PILOT, PUPIL OR PASSENGER	DUTY (INCLUDING RESULTS AND REMARKS)
MONTH	DATE	Type	No.			
						TOTALS BROUGHT FORWARD
FEB	15	D.H.82	DE354	SELF	—	19 22
"	15	"	"	"	AC Rowe	5 9 12 13 14
"	16	"	"	"	—	22
"	16	"	"	"	Sgt Goodbody	20
"	19	HALIFAX III	LK762	P/O DOWNS	SELF CREW	OPS. LEIPZIG. (79 A/C LOST)
"	23	DH82	7787	SELF	—	20
"	23	"	"	"	—	22
"	23	"	7787	"	AC ROYSTON	12 13
"	23	"	"	"	ROYSTON	12 13
"	23	"	"	"	ROBINSON	9 12 13 14
"	23	"	"	"	ROBINSON	12 13
"	24	"	6950	"	—	25
"	24	"	"	"	AC ROYSTON	5 12 13
"	24	"	"	"	AC BEER	10 11 12 13 17
"	24	"	"	"	AC SMITH	9 12 13 14
"	24	"	"	"	—	19 20 22
"	24	"	"	"	—	25
"	24	LINK		SELF	—	3/4
"	24	DH82	DE471	"	Sgt SOMERFIELD	26
"	24	DH82	892	"	Sgt ROBERTSON	26
"	25	"	5136	"	—	27
"	25	"	5136	"	AC ROSE	5 9 12 13 14
"	25	"	5156	"	AC KILLICK	9 12 13 14
"	26	"	5136	"	P/O GREGORY	Ferry-9

GRAND TOTAL [Cols. (1) to (10)]
1149 Hrs. 510 Mins.

TOTALS CARRIED FORWARD

P/O Downs log entries. (*P/O Downs*)

Route to Leipzig 19/20 February 1944.

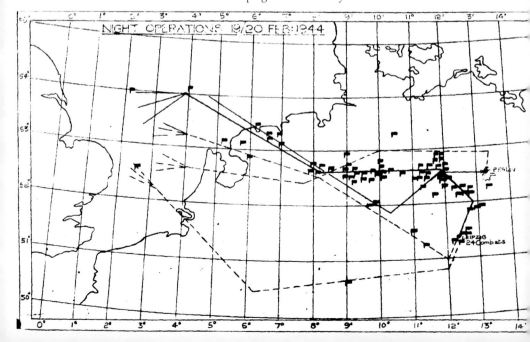

Roy Child, top right, and crew. (*Roy Child*)

Ken Davies and crew. (*Roy Child*)

Roy Child on his return from a PoW camp. (*Roy Child*)

Roy Child. (*Roy Child*)
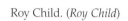

Ken Davies. (*Roy Child*)

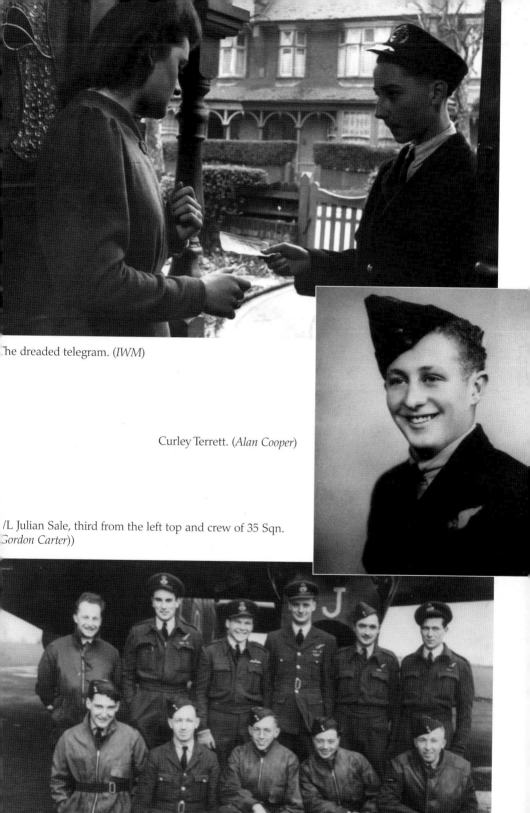

The dreaded telegram. (*IWM*)

Curley Terrett. (*Alan Cooper*)

/L Julian Sale, third from the left top and crew of 35 Sqn.
Gordon Carter))

The Berlin War Cemetery. (*WGC*)

F/Sgt K Williams and his crew of 158 Sqn who failed to return.

I.S. 9.(W.E.A) 2514/1343

WARNING AGAINST GIVING INFORMATION ABOUT YOUR ESCAPE
OR HOW YOU EVADED CAPTURE

This applies to Members of all Services and continues even after discharge therefrom.

1. It is the **duty** of all persons to safeguard information which might, either directly or ~ectly, be useful to the enemy.

2. The Defence Regulations make it an **offence**, punishable with imprisonment, to ~lish or to **communicate** to any unauthorised person any information or anything which ~orts to be information on any matter which would or might be directly or indirectly useful ~e enemy.

~. This document is brought to your personal notice so that you may clearly understand ~mation about your escape or how you evaded capture is information **which would be** ~l to the enemy, and that therefore to communicate any information about your escape ~w you evaded capture **is an offence under the Defence Regulations.**

~. You must not disclose the **names** of those who helped you, the **method or methods** ~ich you escaped, the **route** you followed or how you reached this country, nor must you give information of such a general nature as the **names of the countries** through which ~ravelled. All such information may be of assistance to the enemy and a danger to your ~ls. **Be specially on your guard with persons who may be newspaper repre- ~tives.**

~. **Publishing or communicating** information includes :—

  (a) publication of accounts of your experiences in books, **newspapers** or periodicals (including Regimental Journals), **wireless** broadcasts or lectures :

  (b) giving information to friends and acquaintances either male or female, in private letters, in casual conversations or discussions, even if these friends or acquaintances are in H.M.'s or Allied Forces and however "safe" you may consider them to be.

F.O. (557-44)
A.C.I. (1896-43) } prohibit lecturing by escapers or evaders to any unit without
A.M.C.O. A89-44 } prior permission of the Admiralty, War Office, Air Ministry.

~E COMPLETED IN THE PERSON'S OWN HANDWRITING.

~have read this document and understand that if I disclose information about my escape, ~n of capture I am liable to disciplinary action.

~ _William Robertson_   Date _1979_

~ame (Block letters) _WILLIAM ANTHONY ROBERTSON_

and Number _F/o 244850_

158 Sqdn.

Witnessed by _Wmss_

Warning against giving information about escape.

The areas of Leipzig attacked.

USAAF attack on Leipzig 3 July 1944.

Another shot of the
USAAF attack on
Leipzig 3 July 1944.

The attack on Leipzig
railway station.

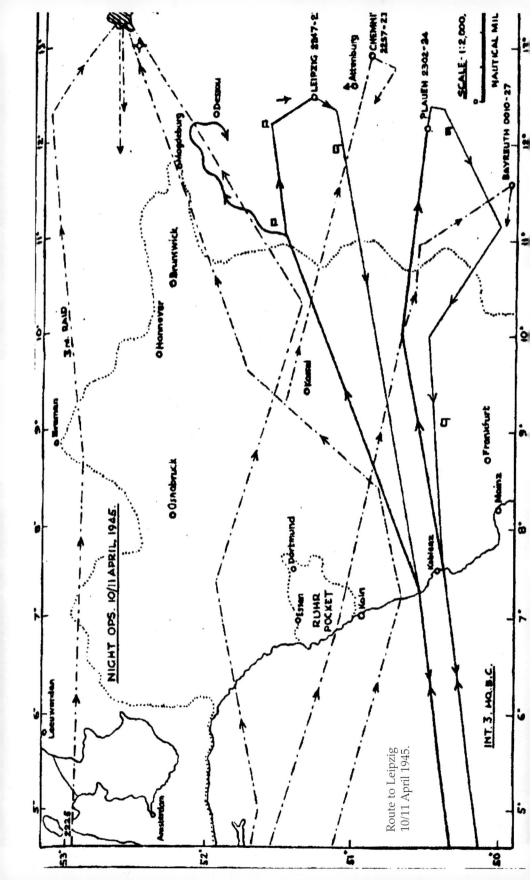

NIGHT OPS. 10/11 APRIL, 1945.

Route to Leipzig
10/11 April 1945.

SCALE · 1:2,000,

NAUTICAL MIL

INT. 3. H.Q. B.C.

f 109 German night-fighter. (*IWM*)

O Tom Smith and his crew's burial site.

German radar.

The Bach statue in Leipzig. (*Alan Cooper*)

automatic pilot became useless, Flight Lieutenant Utz was resigned to having to handle the controls throughout the flight. Colin could see he had severe cramp during the flight and that he was bouncing up and down to try and ease the stiffness in his legs. At the briefing after landing a flight lieutenant said it was the best concentrated attack he had ever seen. A warrant officer said he had seen fires 200 miles away from the target on the homeward journey. They had taken off at 2352 hours and landed at 0726 hours. His first task was to thank Group Captain Edwards and return his lucky charms.

Colin had received a very interesting letter just before he reported to 460 Squadron at Binbrook:

> Dear Air Correspondent – After the last war manufacturers of machinery in this country were put out of business by products of Leipzig dumped on the world's markets at cut-throat prices. The whole of this city's great manufacturing resources must have been turned over to war production. Is Leipzig going to be allowed to get away with it again? This is a vital matter. Can't you do something about it?

In Leipzig Heidi Herrman was celebrating her twelfth birthday the next day when she heard the bombs crashing down and saw the light of the fires through the cellar window.

When the all clear came all the windows were smashed. In one house that was destroyed a young girl that had gone back to pick up a doll was killed.

Chapter 10

The Third Attack

—〜〜—

On 1 February 1944, a newly formed Mosquito squadron, 692 Squadron, joined 35 Pathfinder Squadron at RAF Graveley. On the 10th, the King and Queen visited the station and spent over an hour in the Control Tower, which of course was the hub of any station. Although the airfield has long since gone back to being farming land the Control Tower still remains but is now a house with a sloping roof.

At this time 70,000 men at Anzio in Italy had made their landings and the monastery at Monte Cassino had been bombed and reduced to ruins. In Berlin, at the height of the Battle of Berlin, 140 factories had been bombed and destroyed or damaged. The wall of the prison at Amiens in France had been breached and a number of French resistance fighters had escaped from the Germans hands and certain death. The man who led this force was Group Captain Percy Pickard. Sadly he died in the attack.

On 13 February, Ju 52 aircraft were seen at AG Assembly and Ju 88 aircraft at Mockau, both in Leipzig. On 14 February, fifteen navigators were selected from each group in Bomber Command. With the aid of API, Gee and H2S, it was their role to determine the wind direction and strength en route to a raid on Leipzig coming up in the next few days. Their findings would be sent back to Group HQ. They would then be sent to the meteorological staff at HQ Bomber Command. On 17 February, a memo was sent to the CinC Bomber Command, Sir Arthur Harris, and to the Commanding General of the US Strategic Air Force.

Your overall mission remains the progressive destruction and dislocation of German Military, Industrial and Economic Systems, the disruption of vital elements of lines of communication and material reduction of German Air Combat strength by successful prosecution of Combined Bomber Offensive from all convenient bases.

The primary objective was depletion of the German Air Force with a primary importance upon German fighter forces by all means available, including attacks against flowing precision targets, industrial areas and facilities supporting them. The equal first priority was German single-engine fighter airframe and airframe components production, and the twin-engine airframe component production and axis controlled ball-bearing manufacture. The second priority was installations supporting the German Air Force; the overall plan was to deprive the German Air Force of 43% of its fighter aircraft and 65% of its bomber aircraft.

On 18 February, the crews at RAF Breighton, the home of 78 Squadron, were celebrating and relaxing on a stand down from operations. Tom Smith and Bernard Downs, both pilots, decided to spend a few hours in Leeds. They cycled to Wressle Street Station and caught a local train to the Yorkshire city. A meal and a few drinks at the Yorkshire Hussar, Robin Hood and the Griffon followed. Then on to the local Mecca dance hall. The last train left at 10.30 pm, by which time all the pubs had closed and the blackout was in force. The streets were deserted. Somehow Bernard got separated from the rest and missed the last train back to camp. This meant waiting on a cold and uninviting station for the early morning train.

The morning of 19 February 1944 was a bleak winter's morning, dry but with a chill wind and typical Yorkshire smog. Bernard arrived at the Officer's Mess dishevelled, unshaven, and bleary eyed. When he arrived in the dining room Tom Smith was already eating his breakfast. When he saw Bernard he smiled as if to say where have you been? A hurried slice of toast followed then a rush to get cleaned up. He checked that his crew were all there and at 8.45 am reported to his flight commander. It could be 'No operations', 'Operations on' or possibly a late decision. As it was a little late the flight commander came back to say 'Okay chaps, ops are on tonight.'

The third and final major attack on Leipzig was on 19/20 February 1944. The pre-briefing for pilots and navigators was called for 11 am, which meant a late afternoon take-off and a possible chance of a snooze for Bernard. He and Tom went to the briefing together. It was to be their fifteenth operation so they had got to half way to completing a tour of operations. They thought with the Battle of Berlin the target would again be Berlin or the 'Big City' as they called it. Better the one you know than the unknown was their sentiments. No trip to Leeds this night.

The briefing room was blacked out and a guard posted on the door. The navigators were deep in maps, charts, and navigation logs. At one end of the room was a large sheet, which covered a wall map and the target for that night. However, just as the briefing was to begin the telephone went and the call taken by the commanding officer. It was a brief call and he turned to face the crews awaiting his briefing and said 'Sorry chaps, the time over the target has been put back, the pre-briefing for pilots and navigators will now be at 5 pm.' The take-off time was now midnight. On leaving the briefing room Tom told Bernard to get his head down and that he would keep him informed if need be. Tom had recently become engaged and planned to marry in Easter 1944, the time he would finish his tour of operations.

At 78 Squadron they had recently been equipped with the Mk III Halifax but as they say in Yorkshire 'You get nowt for nowt'. The improvement in speed and altitude over the Mk II was paid for with an increase in fuel consumption, which meant a lesser bomb load.

In Leipzig the important areas were the largest railway station in Europe; Allgemeine Transport involved in aircraft assembly and aircraft engines; Mitteldeutsche Molorenwerke making aircraft engines; Bussing making tanks and armed fighting vehicles; Meir & Weukelt making tools; and Hugo Schneider making light arms, small arms and ammunition. In addition there were the seventeen large former exhibition buildings, totalling an aggregate floor space of 170,000 square feet.

At 1 pm a weather forecast was supplied to the air staff of Bomber Command; this had been acquired by a Pampa flight of 1409 Flight based at RAF Wyton. A Mosquito ML906 flown by Flight Lieutenant G.W. Roberts forecast 10/19 cloud at Leipzig itself for the operation and predicted that all the clouds would be freezing and ice forming. A further forecast at 1615 hours showed little change on this occasion. Again in Mosquito ML906, flown by Flying Officer R.D. Mattock, 1409 Flight forecast cloudless skies on Berlin but 10/10 cloud over Leipzig and a wind of 100 mph!

Some 823 aircraft were detailed for Leipzig. Forty-nine aircraft were detailed for 'Forget Me Not' mining operations at Kiel Harbour, consisting of forty-five Stirlings from 3 Group and four Halifaxes from 35 Pathfinder Squadron at Graveley.

Twelve Mosquitoes were detailed for an offensive sweep to Berlin and sixteen Oboe-carrying Mosquitoes attacked German night fighter airfields at Venlo, Leewarde, Twente, Gilze Rigen, Deelen, and Volkel. Finally, two Mosquitoes were detailed to attack military constructions at Sottovast and Herbouville. Twelve Mosquitoes of 100 Group were to make a Serrate sweep over enemy territory with a view to detecting and confusing the enemy radar systems. (Serrate was a radar detection and homing device used by Allied aircraft to track German night fighters.) From 100 Special Duty Group one Halifax was detailed to patrol the North Sea to Heligoland and one Wellington flew off the Dutch coast between Ijmuiden and Terschelling.

Finally 5 pm came and Tom Smith and Bernard Downs settled down

THE THIRD ATTACK 101

behind closed doors for the briefing. The sheet was removed revealing a large map with a red tape running across to the target. The black board contained a series of tracks and times. At the head of the board in large capitals was written LEIPZIG 19/2/44. All the aircraft would carry a similar bomb loading consisting of one 2,000-lb high explosive and 4,000 lb in canisters of incendiaries.

The main briefing was at 2130 hours. The route, the Pathfinders' role and weather were fully discussed. Tom was to fly in an earlier wave than Bernard and would be over the target between 4.10 am and 4.14 am. Finally, the Commanding Officer said 'Have a good trip and good luck.'

The plan of attack was that the Pathfinders using primary blind markers with mixed Parramatta (red TIs) and Wanganui (green and red stars) would mark the target.

If H2S became useless they were to hold their markers and act as supporters. Thirty primary blind markers and twenty-five blind backers up were detailed, all from No. 8 Group of the Pathfinder Force. Plus, thirty Lancasters of No. 1 Group were to act as supporters aiming at any TI that was visible or bombing on H2S. The main force aircraft were to aim at the centre of all greens or at the centre of release-point flares if the Pathfinders found the cloud too thick. The time of marking by the primary blind markers was 3.58 am and the duration of the attack twenty-one minutes.

'Window' was to be dropped on the inward and outward journeys at the rate of two bundles per minute within 50 miles of the target in both directions, and one bundle per minute for the rest of the journey. The route took the bombers eastward across the North Sea then a feint diversion was carried out south-eastwards towards Berlin with a final run in towards the target for about 50 miles. The outward route was on a heading south-west for about 30 miles before turning north-west and home to base.

Some 170 Lancasters were detailed from No. 1 Group; 140 Halifaxes from No. 4 Group; 209 Lancasters from No. 5 Group; thirty-one Lancasters and ninety-eight Halifaxes from No. 6 Group; and eighty-nine Lancasters, seventeen Halifaxes and seven Mosquitoes from No. 8 Group.

It was time for the crews to get dressed. On went the woollen 'Long John', extra roll neck sweaters and fur-lined flying boots. The flying helmets, gloves, parachutes and Mae Wests were checked. The gunners had additional outer clothing with electrically heated gloves and insoles for their boots, something they would certainly need on this operation.

Tom had been allocated his usual aircraft LW367-Q-Queenie but Bernard was allocated LK762-Z as his aircraft was unserviceable. They would normally travel together to the aircraft, which were normally parked side by side. But because of the change of aircraft they travelled in separate transport. Before they got into the transport Tom said 'Have a good trip, see you for breakfast.'

The ground crew were waiting for the crews and the pilot to sign the Form 700, which meant he accepted the aircraft as being serviceable. At 11.30 pm the crews started to board the aircraft and the start-up procedure began. At 11.45 pm the aircraft started to roll forward from their hard standings and on to the taxi track. An airfield at night was a forest of lights – white, red, amber, green, and blue some bright and some dim. At 11.55 pm at the runway holding point, there would be a pre-take-off check. Checks were made of the fuel, flaps and fine-pitch – there were twenty-seven items in all to check. There was a short green flash from the controller's caravan then a turn on to the runway. At 11.59 pm there was a long green flash, then it was throttles open and Z-Zebra started to move forward slowly at first but building up momentum. The tail lifted off the runway at 100 mph to 115 mph and 33 tons of aircraft with its bomb load took to the air.

Flying Officer Charles Parker was a pilot instructor and attached to No. 78 Squadron for one week. A week before a colleague attached to No. 78 Squadron had flown on operations with Flight Lieutenant Denman in 'B' Flight. He suggested that Charles attach himself to Denman when he arrived at No. 78 Squadron. However, a flight sergeant was assigned to Denman and Charles Parker was detailed to fly as second pilot with Bernard Downs in 'C' Flight.

Soon the air all over Lincoln and Yorkshire was full of the sound of aircraft engines, Lancasters and Halifaxes taking off for a long flight to Leipzig in Eastern Germany.

From No. 1 Group there were 170 Lancasters of which 155 attacked the target and seventeen failed to return. From No. 3 Group there were sixty-two Lancasters of which forty-nine attacked the target and four failed to return. From No. 4 Group there were 140 Halifaxes of which 120 attacked the target and seventeen failed to return. From No. 5 Group there were 209 Lancasters of which 192 attacked the target and twelve failed to return. And from No. 6 Group there were thirty-one Lancasters of which twenty-eight attacked the target and five failed to return, plus 98 Lancasters of which eighty-two attacked the target and eighteen failed to return. No. 8 Group sent out eighty-nine Lancasters of which eighty-three attacked and six were missing, also seven Mosquitoes all which were successful and all returned.

Of the main force that went out sixty-nine failed to return (9.7%) and of the 113 Pathfinders sent out ten failed to return (8.9%). A total of 25,552 tons of bombs were dropped by 730 aircraft that attacked the target, including two 8,000-lb bombs, 469 4,000-lb bombs, 201 250-lb bombs, 1,202.5 high explosive bombs and 1,352.7 incendiaries plus 184 flares.

Chapter 11

To the Target

—⧈—

A total of 823 aircraft were despatched to the Germany city for the third assault. The Pathfinder force consisted of 138 aircraft, the main force of 430 Lancasters and 262 Halifax aircraft.

Along with this eighteen Lancasters carrying ABC operators were spread throughout the attack. 'Window' was to be dropped at two bundles per minute within 50 miles of the target (in both directions) and one bundle per minute for the rest of the journey. All the Mosquitoes despatched were to drop 'Window' at maximum rate.

The first crew to take off for Leipzig on 19 February was Flying Officer Taylor of 166 Squadron from RAF Kirmington. He took off at 11 pm in Lancaster ME638. He was closely followed by Flight Lieutenant Hart of 103 Squadron and Flight Lieutenant Newton of 9 Squadron at 11.04 pm and 11.05 pm. At Tholthorpe, aircraft of 425 Squadron had problems taking off because an aircraft of 420 Squadron became bogged down prior to take-off and blocked the runway. At Skipton-on-Swale Halifax HX316 ran into LW433. Both were 424 Squadron aircraft. The pilot of LW433, Canadian Flying Officer Krampe, had stopped for cockpit drill prior to take-off when suddenly he saw another Halifax coming towards him. It was HX316 piloted by 1st Lt Compton. Krampe opened his throttles and tried to turn to starboard to avoid a collision but as he did so he was struck by the other aircraft and the rear gunner, Sergeant Bottrell, also a Canadian, was severely injured and later died. The reason for the collision given by Compton was that he was blinded by the glare from outside his aircraft. Sergeant Bottrell was later buried in Harrogate Cemetery, the resting place for many wartime Canadian airmen.

Gordon Ritchie took off smoothly and headed out towards the North Sea and apart from his trepidation it could have been another training flight. Squadron Leader Peletier was completely undeterred and the Fishpond device used by the wireless operator to detect other aircraft in the dark remained in working order.

At 11.30 pm Bernard Downs and his crew climbed aboard. 'Hold on to your hats, here we go,' said Bernard. This was break or make time for a heavily loaded bomber. At 11.59 pm the green light from the Control Tower came, the signal that the runway was clear and they could take off. The throttles were opened by Downs with the assistance of the flight engineer and slowly Z–Zebra rolled down the runway building up speed as the flare path lights flashed by ever more quickly.

It was now Sunday 20 February 1944. As they gained height the lights of the airfield below became dimmer, but the lights of Holne, Melbourne, Pocklington and Elvington and other airfields could still be seen brightly shining in the dark. The sky was now full of red, green, and white aircraft navigation lights; whichever direction you looked they were there. A slow climbing orbit brought them back over the base at a height of 6,000 feet and then on an eastward course at a speed of 155 mph. Ten minutes later they crossed the coast at Hornsea. Here the navigation lights were turned off, an all blackout security check as a small chink of light could be seen for miles in the air at night. It was now pitch black and to all intents and purposes they were on their own. The only thing that broke the murk was a red glow and short flame from the starboard engine. The exhaust stubs seemed to be very bright in the darkness; not too bright they hoped, as the German fighters would be around as soon as the force was picked up on the radar.

In 35 Squadron, Bill McTurk found his aircraft heavy on take-off from Graveley. The bomb aimer had failed to lock the throttles open so for a while things were a little dicey. Len Young of 103 Squadron ran into trouble before taking off. During the engine run up the port inner engine D–Dog JB555 started to overheat. This was not very unusual to a point, but when the temperature went up to 100 degrees and white vapour appeared on the slipstream they felt that something was amiss. The ground crew sergeant tried to convince him all was well and not to worry and abandon the aircraft. But, he was the pilot and had responsibility for his crew and decided to take the reserve aircraft. In a similar experience a Warrant Officer Townsend had taken the spare aircraft and had not returned. He had usually used D–Dog on ops and so there was an omen about changing from this aircraft and taking the reserve. Len went for the spare A–Able ND363 and it was later discovered that D–Dog had a coolant leak and would have failed on take-off. If this had happened there would have been another casualty report to write. Squadron Leader Douglas Haigh DFC of 576 Squadron flying LL748-A2 had his starboard inner engine lose power but without seeming to have a fault so they continued on course.

Squadron Leader W. Walker, an Australian, was flying HX340-N of 158

Squadron and was making his way to the perimeter track when he saw another aircraft crash on take-off, which lit up the sky. Pilot Officer Jennings in HX351-S had taken off at 12.08 am. Within eight minutes he had crashed at Catfoss and he and all his crew were killed. It put Walker off and he went off the track and into the mud, but by quick thinking he opened all four engines into full boost and was able to keep moving and back on to the perimeter track. He took off in murky rain, and the airspeed indicator started to rise to a respectable speed and then suddenly went backwards, staying at 50. Despite this he was able to get the aircraft up to 10,000 feet and then levelled out.

Pilot Officer Bradburn flying in ND517-U of 44 Squadron took off at 11.53 pm but at 12.28 am he realised that he had no rear gunner. His normal rear gunner was Flight Sergeant Lloyd but for some reason he was not there for the take-off. The bombs were jettisoned at 2,000 feet and they returned to base landing at 1.04 am.

At Waddington Lancaster LL792 of 467 Squadron Flight Lieutenant D.S. Symonds, an Australian, taxied out for his twenty-ninth operation and collided with the starboard engine of Lancaster LM440. The accident was blamed on snow building up on his windscreen and obstructing his vision. Flying Officer D.C. Harvey, also an Australian, had stopped in LL653 to allow LL792 to pass when his starboard engine struck the port wing of LL792.

Flight Sergeant Kingham of 514 Squadron was taxiing when his port wing tip struck the front turret of LL620 and Flying Officer J.R. Laing also of 514 Squadron struck an engine stand or trestle, which should not have been there. These were some of the problems aircraft and crews had before they had even taken off.

The raids on the Dutch airfields and the mining operation at Kiel prior to the main raid to Leipzig caused the earliest night fighter reactions ever recorded (ninety-five minutes) timed at 12.09 am and gave the fighters plenty of time to concentrate at their respective beacons. Hostiles were first plotted by the Germans 130 miles north of Texel and later reported at 120 miles north of Leeuwarden, 28 miles east of Zwolle, and the Rotterdam and Denhelder areas. This also gave rise to some confusion in plotting during the first stages of the attack. The bombers were due to cross the enemy coast at 1.43 am, one hour and thirty-five minutes after the night fighters of NJG 1 and 2 were airborne. At 12.09 am they were ordered to make for an area around the island of Wangerooge, having been told that many enemy aircraft were more than halfway on their journey from Norfolk to the Dutch coast. At 12.16 am they were diverted to intercept a few bombers that were already over Holland. This must have been Mosquitoes, as at this stage they were said to be flying at first north and then east of the Zyder Zee over Rotterdam and a few north of Amsterdam, all on a southerly course. At 12.38 am units of NJG 1 and 2 were ordered back to beacon L and then five minutes later to Vechta. At 12.48 am the fighters were sent to beacon Q, and ten minutes later further messages suggested that other aircraft of NJG 3 were brought down from Schleswig and others brought up from Stade to join them there. From 1.05 am to 1.59 am night fighters from beacon Q were being ordered up to Heligoland and being told there was no flak there at all. *Feldwebel* (Sergeant) Rudolf Frank of NJ 3 claimed he had shot down a Lancaster at 1.53 am in the area north-west of Delmenhorst, which was probably the first aircraft lost that night. *Feldwebel* Frank was later killed in action on 26 April, 1944. The fighters of NJG 5 were airborne at 12.59 am and sent to Vechta and fighters of NJ 6 to beacon M near Stendal at 1.27 am where later a very large number of interceptions were made. Here they were in an excellent position to make contact with the bomber stream. It meant the area of beacon M was the track of the fighters and bombers.

Early on the Germans thought the target was Berlin and Leipzig was not announced as a target until the attack was about to begin. At this time a number of bombers were seen in the vicinity. In the nose of Bernard Downs' aircraft bomb aimer Tony Sherwin had little to do but keep a look out for fighters; his main job would come later over the target. He would be the man the rest of the crew would be relying on to do the job that they had made the trip for. The navigator Bill Hendry was calculating and recalculating the route. Bill Garget the wireless operator was manning a listening watch on his wireless; later he would be responsible for despatching 'Window'. Flight Engineer George Jupp was checking the engine performance and fuel gauges, and when he was not doing this he was keeping a watch from the astro dome. The two gunners Bob Dawson and Pat Joiner were in their turrets, cold and possibly bored, but still having to keep awake and alert.

It was now 1 am and they were out over the North Sea when the first problem occurred. The automatic pilot would not engage, which meant Bernard would have to fly the aircraft there and back manually. They were at 14,000 feet and climbing steadily. The engine power had dropped off in the thinner air and it was time to engage the higher supercharger gear. The engine gave a slight cough and then surged with renewed power and the rate of climb increased. At 1.40 am, now at 20,000 feet, they came to the first turning point, 120 degrees to the right. The speed increased to 160 mph, indicating a true speed of 230 mph.

At 1.50 am came those now immortal words from the navigator 'Enemy coast ten minutes'. This was confirmed by a burst of flak ahead and a few searchlights, a welcome they had become used too, and it was now time for eyes to be peeled by all members of the crew. It was now time to start dropping 'Window'. There was an occasional judder as they passed through the slipstream of another aircraft, and once or twice there was a warning from the gunners of another aircraft, but they proved to be friendly aircraft. Gordon Ritchie suddenly saw a fighter flare, which lit up the area like daylight. Then below there was an exchange of tracer and down went a Lancaster with flames pouring from the port inner engine.

This was war and the time to sit up, give one's eyes a rub, and look into the murky black for fighters. The gunners would make a search from top to bottom and back around again – one slack moment and they could be joining the Lancaster that went down with an engine on fire.

Ernest Windeat's aircraft met five layers of freezing cloud – the temperature outside was recorded at 22 below freezing and it was still falling. Severe icing of the wings, tail plane, prop spinners and air intakes could be seen in the dark reflections from stray shell bursts. Chunks of ice that had built up were breaking free to slither off with a rendering sound, and as it did the Lancaster would buck. The engine temperatures were at all times low; as a consequence the oil pressure was very high. Ernest reported his guns freezing up and was obliged to fire intermittent bursts to keep them free of ice and working.

When over the North Sea Len Young's bomb aimer discovered that some of the bombs were rolling about on the closed bomb doors so he opened the doors and disposed of them quickly. In Lancaster R5486 of 622 Squadron the wireless operator picked up a voice with an American accent, stating that he thought the bombers were heading for Berlin and promptly transmitted the engine noise on the same wavelength.

Sergeant Robert (Bob) Trett was a navigator with 102 Squadron at Pocklington. He and his crew were due to start ten days' leave at one minute past midnight on Sunday 20 February 1944. He attended the navigation section briefing, as he was the navigation leader at that time, but he was not on the list for the operation to Leipzig. He returned to his billet after collecting his pay, ration allowance, food coupons and a warrant to get him home. He locked away his flying kit and laid out his best blue all ready for a quick get-away. But, when he called back to the navigation section he found his name on the bottom of the operation list. The reason his crew were not on it and going on leave was that their own aircraft was due to be scrapped. Somehow the powers that be had got them another aircraft, Halifax

HY125-B for Boomerang. He went to his billet and unpacked his flying kit and then went to draw up a parachute.

He took off at 11.42 pm with Flying Officer Dean at the controls. Bob soon found the winds were to say the least crazy – up to 130 mph. They were therefore seventeen minutes early at the turning point so reduced speed and went south. They crossed the coast near Langeoog Island eleven minutes early and reduced speed even further to lose time. Near Essen they were seven minutes early and arrived at the last turning point at Stendal four minutes early. A course was worked out by Bob to fly two-minute doglegs to lose the four minutes but the pilot decided to fly an orbit with all the crew looking for fighters.

F/O William Blake of 428 Squadron was attacked by a fighter on the outward flight but before it could be beaten off the Halifax was badly damaged. Later it was hit by ground defences and the intercom cut and the supply of oxygen to the rear of the aircraft was lost. Despite this he attacked the target and dropped his bombs successfully and managed to fly the damaged bomber to an airfield in the UK.

Blake was awarded the DFC in March 1944. Sadly Blake, from Hamilton in Canada, was killed in action on 23/4 March 1944 and his name is on the Runneymede Memorial. His DFC was presented to his mother on 28 February 1946.

The damage to the Erla complex caused by this attack resulted in severe damage to almost all stages of production up to the final wing and fuselage erection at Heiterblick, and in moderate damage to the assembly shops at Mockau. The Erla complex was left more or less intact, with final capacity that could be restored by simple repairs within a month. Most of the press and machine capacity, however, and much of the capacity for preliminary work on fuselages and for sub-assembly and erection of control surfaces was destroyed.

Chapter 12

Combat with the Enemy

—⚬—

In Northern Holland a few sightings of German fighters were made and combats reported but the principal concentration of enemy aircraft was encountered in an area south of Bremen. From this point and right up to the target there was a constant succession of sightings and combats with enemy aircraft of all types. The principal German aircraft was the Ju 88 but Me 110s and a number of other unidentified twin and single-engine aircraft were present also. Of the fifty combats reported during this period over forty were with twin-engine aircraft.

In the target area a further thirty combats occurred, Ju 88s once again being predominant. It was estimated that 250 twin-engine and seventy-five single-engine German fighters were brought into action.

The three areas for combat covered the area from Texel to Leeuwarden. From the turning point at Stendal to the target area over half the enemy aircraft identified were Ju 88s and were the majority both along the route and near the target. In the Texal area an HS 129 enemy aircraft was seen. A Lancaster of No. 1 Group claimed to have destroyed a Me 110.

The first combat recorded was at 12.54 am. Flight Sergeant Soper of 15 Squadron flying in Lancaster ED310-M suddenly received a message from the wireless operator who was on watch in the astrodome that a Fw 190 was coming into attack at a range of 500 yards. The rear gunner got a sighting and opened fire with hits being seen on the fighter. Its nose came up and it stalled and appeared to fall out of the sky with flames coming from the engine cowling. The rear gunner sergeant was credited with having destroyed it.

At 2.10 am Flying Officer Healey flying Lancaster JB619-D of 419 Squadron was hit by a twin-engine fighter, thought to be a Ju 88. It collided with the Lancaster and damage was sustained to the mid upper turret and main plane. The rear gunner Sergeant Parkinson saw pieces break off the fighter and it broke into flames and fall to the ground. Healey having lost height in a spiral dive after the collision was able to regain control, jettison his bomb load and make it back to base where he landed at 3.39 am. Although he had only flown on twelve operations he was awarded the DFC for his superb airmanship on this occasion.

Flying Officer Williams also claimed a Me 110 at 2.27 am. He was flying Lancaster JB455-F of 75 New Zealand Squadron when he was attacked from 400 yards. His rear gunner returned fire and an explosion was seen in its cockpit. The mid upper gunner then fired and the fighter was seen to blow up and hit the ground. The fighter was claimed as destroyed.

At 2.41 am Flight Lieutenant Crawford of 550 Squadron came under attack from a Bf 109. Both his gunners, Sergeants Moss and Robertson, opened fire and the fighter was seen with smoke and flames coming from the engine. Flight Sergeant Lunn of 622 Squadron claimed a Me 320 destroyed. Flying Officer Toovey DFC and Bar of 50 Squadron was on the last trip of his first tour. At 2.57 am he heard strikes on his aircraft and dived to port but the fighter was not seen again.

By this time Pilot Officer Dowds had reached the briefing height of 22,000 feet and arrived at the next turning point and turned due east. If they stayed on this course it would take them to the Big City – Berlin. As they continued on this course, Berlin at the time was being attacked by the Mosquitoes with the aim of taking the German fighters away from Leipzig. So far this plan appeared to be working, certainly as far as Dowds was concerned. The hundreds of searchlights could be seen over Berlin but now it was time to start on a heading for Leipzig.

From 2.52 am to 3.14 am the Germans were reporting enemy aircraft as flying towards Berlin, and at 3.17 am they were reported to be over Berlin. This would have been the Mosquitoes. The German flying control in the Leeuwarden area was heard at 2.59 am to ask the fighters 'Have you made a *Sieg Heil?*' (victory). It was obvious the Germans thought the target to be Berlin. The Battle of Berlin was at its height at the time, so it would be the likely target. Fighters of NJG 5 received definite instructions to proceed to Berlin. At 3.36 am aircraft of NJG 6 turned north to join the bomber stream in the Bremen area. Aircraft of NJG 1, 2, 3, 5 and 6 were all identified as operating against the bomber stream. They had attempted to intercept the aircraft on mining operations but were then called to collect at Beacon L south of Osnabruck and then directed into the bomber stream.

An hour before arriving at the target area Flying Officer William Blake of 428 Squadron was attacked by a fighter and the aircraft was badly damaged. Shortly afterwards he was attacked three times by fighters but successfully evaded them and without incurring further damage. About forty-five minutes before reaching the target area he received a direct hit from flak, which destroyed the starboard rudder and cut off the entire intercom and the oxygen in the rear of the aircraft. The rear gunner Warrant Officer James Houston who had been instrumental in giving Blake the correct instructions to avoid the three fighter attacks was hit by a piece of flak in the shoulder and was without oxygen and the use of his intercom. The front of the aircraft was lit up like daylight; it was like a fly trying to break out of a spider's web. Despite the attacks Blake continued and bombed the target at 4.08 am.

Squadron Leader Douglas Haigh of 576 Squadron was on his second tour of operations. While climbing after take-off he had a loss of power on his starboard inner engine but decided to press on and attack the target. About 100 miles from Leipzig his rear gunner Sergeant Arthur Wright informed him that a single-engine fighter was coming in to attack. Wright opened fire and the fighter turned and was not seen again. Fifteen minutes later they were again attacked by a Me 110; both Wright and the enemy aircraft opened fire at the same time. As the fighter turned away it went into a slow spiral and was last seen going down with clouds of black smoke coming from it. Squadron Leader Haigh continued to the target and bombed it successfully.

Pilot Officer Reddish was on his twenty-fifth operation.

> I saw the inside of the cockpit of the fighter it was that close. I was just glancing through the nose when it flashed across in front and just underneath us, it was a Me 210. It happened just before we reached Leipzig and I thought he would hit our port wing. He was obviously not after us but on his way to Berlin. He could have hit us if he had not at the last moment seen us and banked steeply to avoid us.

Flying Officer Byford of 419 Squadron received a call from his rear gunner Sergeant Fraser that a Ju 88 was at a range of 1,000 feet and was ordered to corkscrew. Both Fraser and the mid upper gunner Sergeant Dugay opened fire at a range of 500 feet but after seventy-five rounds had been fired Fraser's guns stopped and then a cannon shell hit the turret rendering the hydraulics useless, which meant he could not turn it.

Byford's Halifax JP204-E was badly damaged in the fuselage and port wing and Dugay suffered a minor cut during the corkscrew after hitting his head on the ammunition tracks.

Flight Sergeant Horley of 434 Squadron spent his twenty-first birthday over Leipzig and because of the wind found himself over Bremen and all the flak the Germans could muster. This was added to by two fighters but as soon as they appeared off went the searchlights. Whether they were dazzling the fighter pilots or not matters little but for Horley it meant he escaped in the darkness and lived to have his twenty-second birthday. They were down to two engines on the return journey and at a height of 2,000 feet but were able to get one of the engines restarted and Lancaster L703 and its crew were able to make it back to base at Croft in Yorkshire. The aircraft was battered and damaged but the thing that the flight engineer Sergeant Stahler remembers is Horley shouting out to his navigator Flight Sergeant Wilson for a course out of the area of Bremen. The navigator replied to him 'Where to' and six voices in unison said 'Switzerland'. When all seemed lost a voice of the mid upper gunner Sergeant Forsyth, a Canadian, shouted out 'Keep it up lads we'll beat the dirty bastards yet.'

Gordon Ritchie had filled in for a gunner who had gone sick with eye trouble. It appeared his eyes had frozen up on a previous operation when he was looking below for fighters. To get a better view, he had kicked in the blister and his eyes had become exposed to the slipstream while he looked out for fighters.

For Sergeant John Carter of 115 Squadron, on his first operation, it came as a great shock to see so much fighter activity and aircraft being shot down. They had seen an aircraft ahead and at first thought it was a Mosquito but when it fell back and began to climb they became suspicious, suspicion that was justified as the aircraft turned out to be a Me 210. John yelled 'Port-Go' to the pilot Flight Sergeant Hemmings and he turned into a violent corkscrew. John did not want to open fire as it could attract a fighter that had in fact not seen them. After a couple of minutes they lost the fighter and went on to bomb Leipzig.

At this time Paul Zorner was at Lueneburg and for some months had flown a Me 110 with SN2 equipment (night fighter radar). In December 1943 the aircraft was subsequently equipped with the *Schrage Musik* upward firing machine-gun installation, which still showed difficulties in adjustment.

> If I'm right this operation was a few days after a new moon and the weather was clear over the continent. An old high-pressure system gave good visibility above 13,123 feet or 4,000 metres.
>
> At about midnight we received a pre-warning and we were informed that after midnight we had to expect the arrival of a strong enemy bomber force. At 0030 hours a message concerning the formation of strong enemy forces over Southern England came in. Around 1.00 am on 20 February 1944, we received the stand-by order and at 1.11 am I received permission to start.

Paul Zorner took off at 1.13 am and was ordered to fly to a pending position between Munster and Oldenburg. After flying for about an hour he was told that a strong bomber force had crossed the Dutch coast between Rotterdam and the Zuider Zee with a course east. At that stage nothing was heard about the possible target. New information received said that the enemy bomber force was on an easterly course in the north of the Ruhr. Somewhat north of their position they saw the first enemy bombers going down.

He had been flying for about two hours and only had one hour's fuel left when at 3.00 am his wireless operator, who was handling the radar equipment, detected a flying target with SN2 but he was unable to hold the target for an attack. However, at 3.02 am there was suddenly a Lancaster bomber ahead. He flew nearer and opened fire from a distance of 328 feet and an altitude of 19,000 feet; the burst hit the left wing and the bomber went into a diving spin and crashed at 3.04 am in the area of northern Hanover.

Minutes later there was another target. At 3.14 am he made another attack at a distance of 262 feet and moved with the left wing through his fire cone. As he could not see any fire Paul thought of making another attack and throttled back the engines. Suddenly, after twenty seconds the bomber exploded, a large fragment passing near to Paul's aircraft. The bomber had burst into several pieces and went down at 3.17 am; it crashed and scattered in the Wesendorf area.

He then saw a bomber climbing very close on his starboard side. At once he attacked the bomber with a burst into his port wing, which was instantly on fire. The bomber went into a rolling motion, as it did the fire expanded. Three minutes later it went into a dive and crashed at 3.26 am around the Gardelegen area.

The three bombers went down within twenty-six minutes in an area of about 62 miles. The next bomber went down at 3.41 am south of Brandenberg with a very large explosion and it was thought to still have its bomb load aboard. He had now been in the air for about two and a half hours and only had twenty minutes' flying time left. In twenty-six minutes he had shot down four bombers. When equipped with *Schrage Musik* Paul would always attack from behind and below. He would aim into the wings of the bomber or ahead so that the bomber would fly through his machine-gun salvo with one of its two wings. He had claimed two thirds of his victories with only one burst of fire; on one occasion he needed only six rounds of ammunition. The usual firing distance was six between 100 and 200 metres. Of his forty-four victories fifteen were with the use of *Schrage Musik*.

The German night fighter interception policy after the use of 'Window' was to concentrate long-range freelance fighters over the target where they attempted interception of the bombers either by the use of instruments or visually in the light of flares or when the bombers became silhouetted against the fires.

At 3.20 am Pilot Officer James Catlin of 166 Squadron was attacked by two Me 110s. His rear gunner Sergeant William Birch opened fire. Despite this the bomber was raked from rear to the front by cannon fire and the wireless operator Sergeant Thomas Hall and mid upper gunner Sergeant Tom Powers were both wounded. In the attack Birch's turret was put out of action. The navigator Pilot Officer Tony Pragnell was also wounded in the attack but it was the flight engineer Sergeant Barry Wright on his twenty-fifth operation that was badly wounded in the groin. His instrument panel was completely shot away and one petrol tank holed and empty. Despite his wounds he kept at his work and managed to keep all the engines running at maximum power. All the navigational aids were destroyed and all the lights on the aircraft were put out because of a short circuit. Also, all aileron controls had been lost, which made any evasive action impossible. A cannon shell had burst in the rear turret area scattering ammunition from the bulkhead to the turret. It also blew a hole in the port side of the aircraft of about 3½ feet square. The Perspex in the mid upper turret had been blown out and mid upper gunner Sergeant Powers had been knocked out. The bombs were jettisoned over the Stendal area when a second attack came from the port side.

Bill Birch gave Jim Catlin a good running commentary of the fighter's movements but because of the damage to the aircraft there was little he could do in the way of evasion tactics. By operating his turret manually Birch was able to get a good shot in and hit the fighter from whom black smoke was seen. It then burst into flames and dived to the ground. The first fighter to attack was also confirmed by the wireless operator as being hit. The crew was told by Catlin to put on their chutes and the bomb aimer Fred Sim, now redundant, jettisoned the front escape hatch. Thoughts of baling out had to be abandoned because of the badly wounded Barry Wright and the unconscious Powers. Tommy Hall was able to repair the intercom and the navigation lights, which they would need to land. The course for home was set by Tony Pragnell and passed to Catlin by Sim. As Tom Powers was a big man they were unable to release him from his seat and so he was left there. Because the hydraulics had been shot away the bomb doors were still open and the trim controls locked up as for a full bomb load. Jim was having great difficulty in controlling Lancaster LM383-C. To stop the aircraft climbing he had to apply a forward pressure to the control column. Near the enemy coast at Zwolle they received a welcome of flak, which came so near they could smell the cordite from the exploding shells coming in from the open front escape hatch. They crossed the Dutch coast south of Ijmuiden with Barry Wright still coaxing the utmost power from the engines, during which time he fainted no fewer than three times through lack of blood. On arrival back at their base they found it closed down because of bad weather and were diverted to Manston in Kent. The crew was ordered into the crash position.

The undercarriage was lowered manually. Both tyres were observed to have been punctured and may well have buckled on landing. However, they did not and they landed safely at 6 am. Tony Powers was cut out of his turret with an axe. When his flying suit was cut open pieces of shrapnel dropped on to the floor of the aircraft. He had by now started to come round and to take notice of those around him. He and Barry Wright were taken to hospital and Tom Hall and Tony Pragnell were given treatment and returned to their unit the next day. The aircraft was scrapped and broken up, where it lay on the field at Manston. The average age of the crew was twenty-two. Jim Catlin on his twenty-seventh operation was awarded an immediate DFC. Tom Hall on his twenty-fifth operation was awarded an immediate DFM and Barry Wright the highest award to an other rank other than the Victoria Cross, the Conspicuous Gallantry Medal. The other members of the crew Tony Pragnell and Fred Sim had already been recommended for the DFC too, and Tom Powers the DFM two days before the operation to Leipzig. This crew survived the war.

Warrant Officer Stanners was flying Lancaster JA673 of 156 Squadron when it was hit by a shell, which exploded under the aircraft sending sent it up 700 feet into the air. Over Holland a fire started on the port side and the decision was made to bale out but as they made for open ground to do so the tail of the aircraft snapped off and the aircraft went upside down and crashed north of Baarn. German soldiers arrived and recovered five bodies. One of the crew F/O Kingston, who baled out, landed in a haystack and was taken prisoner. F/O Kryskow RCAF died of his wounds. Sergeant Hughes in the crew had lost his brother F/O Richard Hughes on an operation to Hannover with 576 Squadron on 24 December 1943.

F/O Williams Blake, a Canadian, was hit by predicted flak while flying Halifax LW285-Z of 428 Squadron. The aircraft suffered severe damage to the starboard rudder and oxygen supply. The intercom was rendered u/s and one wheel had a burst tyre. He was then attacked by a Fw 190 fighter and again the aircraft was holed and damaged. This was not the last attack as some twenty minutes later they were again attacked by a fighter. Despite all this they went on to attack the target at Leipzig and Blake was able to fly the aircraft back to base in the UK.

He and his rear gunner were recommended for an award and Blake was awarded the DFC, announced in the *London Gazette* 10 March 1944. Sadly, he was killed on another operation on 23/4 March 1944, flying the same Halifax as the operation to Leipzig, and has no known grave. His award was presented to his mother on 26 February 1946.

At 3.56 am a message was heard from the Vecta area German fighter control: 'I have made four *Sieg Heils.*'

The enemy claims were 'Enemy aircraft penetrated over *Reich* territory and dropped bombs on some localities. The air defences brought down 16 four-engine bombers and 2 fighters. [Later the figure of sixteen aircraft was corrected to twenty-six].'

Nothing was heard from the aircraft reported shot down by the enemy intelligence.

For many others it was on to the target deep in Eastern Germany.

Chapter 13

Over the Target

—∿∿—

It soon became obvious to the bomber crews that the wind forecast was far from correct. Sergeant Richardson of 9 Squadron was one of the navigators selected to be a wind finder and took off from Bardney at 11.15 pm.

In 1944 winds were determined by selected aircrews and transmitted back to Group Headquarters. The winds found were telephoned to Command Headquarters and to the CFO (Central Forecast Office) at Dunstable. Here they were examined and plotted by Upper Air Forecasters at Command and CFO who discussed the results by telephone in the light of their upper air charts. In this way more accurate forecast values of wind for the aircraft on later stages of the route were obtained and were broadcast by wireless transmission from Command Headquarters to the aircraft at pre-arranged intervals.

The winds found by these selected crews were transmitted back to Group HQ. Richardson remembers the winds being forecast as up to 40 mph in the briefing but over Borkum he recorded a wind speed of 95 mph and over Kiel 108 mph. Being a tail wind it would mean the crews arriving at Leipzig far too early and having to stay in the target area far longer than they should. Ideally you arrived at the target, dropped your bombs and then got out.

Sergeant Cowman remembers the Bomber Command 'Health and Safety at Work Act 1944'. This laid down that to obtain protection you must arrive at certain points at certain times, give or take ten seconds, and that inbetween times you kept dead on track. With the winds being much stronger than forecast crews had to try and lose time somehow. But how? Squadron Leader Pelletier decided to make a dog-leg, which would lengthen the distance they had to travel to the enemy coast. The problem with a dog-leg course is that other crews would be trying the same tactics as soon as it was realised the winds were incorrect and the net result would be aircraft crossing each other's paths and possible collisions. For the next ten to fifteen minutes Sergeant Cowman sat glued watching the 'Fishpond' screen pinpointing aircraft on the screen and which appeared to be converging on them. He gave the approximate position over the intercom to the pilot and received the reply 'I see it.' Time after time he took evasive action, which undoubtedly saved them. In Cowman's opinion he must have had incredible night vision. How many mid-air collisions took place off the enemy coast we shall probably never know but it did reach a peak when Squadron Leader Pelletier said 'God they are putting their navigation lights on.' They eventually reached the enemy coast and Sergeant Cowman continued to feed aircraft positions to the pilot and the gunners.

There had been no provision on this operation for altering the zero hour and so it meant 800 aircraft all trying in their own way to lose time. Bob Trett crossed the enemy coast near Langeoog Island at 23,000 feet, an outstanding height for a Halifax, and eleven minutes early. The temperature outside was 40 below. They reduced speed but when they reached the next turning point near Essen and altered course for Stendal they were still seven minutes ahead of time. Now they were on an easterly course with a tail wind that had been relayed from Bomber Command HQ as 273 knots or 129 mph. At first they could not believe the figures they had received. Neither could Bomber Command HQ, hence the delay in relaying it to the crews.

Ernest Windeatt experienced wind problems and also icing. His wireless operator was busy sending out coded messages of course and wind correction in an effort to hold the main stream together. On a number of occasions they changed altitude to avoid icing conditions.

Roy Child of 7 Squadron was flying with Squadron Leader Davies and having found the winds to be incorrect he began to zig zag across the bomber stream. This of course soon led to near miss collisions – so close on one occasion that Roy heard the engines of the other aircraft. He pointed out to his pilot the danger they were in if they continued this zig zagging and he accepted the point and returned to a straight and level course. Some time had been lost and by flying at a slower speed than normal they should lose even more. Soon after take-off they had found the automatic pilot George was not working but decided to press on.

Leslie Bartlett found the winds had changed and they were getting to Leipzig too early. He had to do orbits outside Leipzig waiting for zero hour.

At 3.55 am Bernard Downs' navigator, Bill Hendry, came on the intercom. He said to Bernard 'Turn to 207 degrees, seventeen minutes to the target.' They had no sooner got on to this new course when the first of the Pathfinders' white target incendiaries cascaded from the sky. Bill came on the air again 'Five minutes to go, it's all yours.' The bomb aimer Tony Sherwin now came in to his own and would take over the proceedings. He came on to the intercom with the standard procedure we have now come to expect from bomb aimers or to give them their official title Air Bombers. 'Left, Left, steady hold it, doing nicely Skipper, three or four minutes to go.' All around aircraft were going in the same direction; searchlights were coning one or two. In front of them was a Lancaster with smoke coming from it. Suddenly, it rolled over on to its back and plunged into the ground. One of our aircraft was missing. The rear gunner called to say another Halifax was under attack from a fighter. Once again Tony came on the intercom 'Hold it Skip, right a bit okay bomb doors open, left, left, steady, steady, bombs gone.' The aircraft lifted in Bernard Downs' hands – having lost its heavy load it now felt free. Now the bombs had gone they would get about 10 to 15 miles more per hour. Below, the fires were raging but partially obscured by rising smoke. The barrage of anti-aircraft fire was still intense. It was now 4.30 am and time for a change of course to the north-west and the homeward run. Suddenly over the intercom came an Australian drawl. It was Pat Joiner. 'Jeeze that was a hot bastard.'

The lack of searchlights around usually meant fighters in the area. Gordon Ritchie remembers it being like a giant fireworks display and as light as day with bombs exploding, photo flashes going off and the flak from the anti-aircraft guns. One Pathfinder aircraft got a direct hit and there was nothing left but multi-colours of dust and fire where moments before there had been a four-engine aircraft and seven men. Their names in the future would feature on a war memorial as having no known graves.

As all this was going on the Master of Ceremonies, or Master Bomber as he was known, was instructing the main force bombers on the best target indicators to bomb on. This was the real thing, and certainly not a training flight.

Patrick Turner remembers how long it took on the bomb run into the target and then, having bombed, how long it took to get clear of the target area. Wing Commander Adams who came from Sussex said 'The whole area was lit up like daylight by searchlights shining on the clouds. I am told we nearly collided with a fighter but I never saw it.' Pilot Officer Reddish on his twenty-fifth operation did however.

I saw the inside of the fighter's cockpit it was so close. I was just glancing through the nose when it flashed across in front and just underneath us. It was a Me 210. It happened just before we reached the target and I thought it would hit our port wing. He was not obviously after us but on his way to Berlin. He would have hit us if he had not seen us at the last moment and banked steeply to avoid a collision.

Pilot Officer 'Pop' Marshall of 158 Squadron was detailed to stay over the target, having bombed in the leading wave, and to observe the effectiveness of the operation. It was his twenty-sixth operation and he had four to go before finishing his tour.

Sergeant Alan Morgan was twenty-one on 20 February and spent it over Leipzig. On approaching the target he saw a deep red explosion far bigger than he had ever seen before and about 10 miles from Leipzig. Sergeant Griffiths of 207 Squadron remembers still seeing Leipzig on fire 35 miles after they had left the target area. Flight Lieutenant Raymond, a navigator with 158 Squadron, said that a marked target is one of the most beautiful sights he had ever seen. The colour, and the lurid spectacular made it an awesome sight with the splash and mushrooming explosions of the 4,000 lb 'Cookies' a sight he will never forget even fifty years later. An American pilot Warrant Officer 'Tex' Mimms of 625 Squadron was flying Lancaster LM317-W. He remembers considerable fighter activity and the memory of the fighter flares has always stuck in his mind. He later joined the USAF.

Vic Southwell's aircraft bombed at exactly 4.08 am – the briefing time for bombing was between 4 am and 4.08 am so they were probably the last or one of the last to bomb.

In the crew of Squadron Leader Weller of 158 Squadron the bomb aimer asked for the bomb doors open, which meant sacrificing height and also 20 knots in airspeed. They were at 11,000 feet and had engine trouble. After dropping the bombs the lever used to close the bomb doors was activated but the warning light indicator refused to go out. The hydraulics had failed and the doors were still hanging open. The only means of closing them was manually – a long laborious task for the flight engineer, or whoever was available to do it. Whatever, it had to be done, as they could not make it back to base on three engines with the bomb doors open. A hand pump was used for the task and it seemed to take for ever. It was like trying to screw a very long screw into wood. Suddenly, the light went out and the doors were closed; it was then that they started to pick up speed.

The attack opened early with the first primary blind markers going down six minutes before zero hour. Thirteen primary blind markers managed to make it to Leipzig and bombed before zero hour. The blind backers up, of which twelve made it to Leipzig, dropped Wanganui flares at zero hour. The individual timing of the primary blind markers, with one exception, was good but the supporters' timing was very bad and the markers were spread 2 minus 5 and 2 plus 9, 3.53 am to 3.57 am. One supporter bombed as early as 2.15 am, one at 3.43 am and another at 3.49 am. The marking tailed off at 2 plus 8, 3.56 am and then there was a gap until 3.59 am when no release flares were burning over the target. Reports indicated that for the most part the main force bombed on Wanganui flares and was enthusiastic about the concentration of Wanganui flares in the early part of the attack.

Squadron Leader McLeish of 428 Squadron RCAF arrived sixteen minutes early and made a circuit and a second run on the target, both on H2S. Flying Officer William Blake was another to bomb late at 4.08 am despite at the time being attacked by a fighter and being hit by flak. Pilot Officer Ewens of 49 Squadron was engaged by a Ju 88 fighter on his bombing run but managed to elude him. Flt Lt Caunt of 166 Squadron saw a fighter over Leipzig attacking a Halifax on his port side.

One man who will never forget the operation to Leipzig was Ken Watkins. He was flying with Pilot Officer Bodgers of 576 Squadron when he got out of his seat to check the lead of the battery because the intercom had failed. However, his parachute harness accidentally knocked the main switch on the panel of his instruments, which put out all the lights. Later the switch was modified to prevent it happening again.

Pilot Officer Samuel Atcheson of 57 Squadron was on his nineteenth operation. His airspeed indicator became unserviceable shortly after take-off due to icing. However, he carried on and delivered an accurate attack on time at Leipzig. He was on his nineteenth operation, including twelve attacks on Berlin.

On 5 March he was recommended for an immediate DFC. This was approved and gazetted on 24 March 1944.

Chapter 14

The Home Run

—〜〜—

For some the journey home would be as eventful as the outward one. Sixty aircraft had to return without attacking the target: engine trouble, icing up, crew sickness and damage from fighter attacks were the main reasons for aborting the operation.

John Carter's aircraft after its brush with a fighter went on to bomb Leipzig and return home unharmed and to a welcome leave for the crew. After being over those bitter skies of Germany with battles going on all around, within twenty-four hours they were on leave in their own homes.

The crews of Bomber Command went right into the lion's den and some if they were lucky came back to the UK. Lady Luck would play a great part in this operation to Leipzig. For seventy-nine crews their luck had run out and there was no return to the UK.

Sergeant Wadsworth of 619 Squadron was on his homeward run but still in the target area when his rear gunner Sergeant Jay saw a Bf 109. At the same time wireless operator Sergeant Brady got a contact on the visual Monica, which closed to 700 yards. (Monica was a radar invention that warned Allied aircraft when they were being scanned by German ground or aircraft radar.) Jay gave the order to Wadsworth to corkscrew to port and then opened fire at a range of 500 yards. The fighter turned on its back and fell away in a vertical dive through cloud. Jay claimed it as damaged. In the action he had fired 200 rounds of ammunition. Attacks were being carried out by Ju 88s and Fw 190s all around the area of Leipzig and crews were having a running battle to get out of the target area on their homeward run.

Flight Lieutenant Fitch of 61 Squadron was attacked by a Do 327, which made a circuit of the Lancaster and then flew alongside for 400 yards. Fitch was asked to hold the aircraft steady by his mid-upper gunner Sergeant Whitehead who opened fire with a burst of 200 yards. Hits were seen on the German aircraft but there was no confirmation of its being destroyed.

The return trip for Gordon Ritchie was as bad as the outward. His aircraft was coned by searchlights and the rear gunner gave the order to corkscrew, upon which the pilot put the aircraft into a steep dive and Gordon was thrown all over the aircraft. He was not at the time in his mid upper turret and so had no belt to hold him still.

As they crossed the coast of the UK the dawn was breaking and by the time they landed the sun was coming out. His eyes were swollen and sore from the constant peering out into the dark but were soon back to normal. When you are young the body is very resilient and recovery is quick. Gordon's own pilot was also on his first operation as a second pilot or second 'dickie' as it was called. He said on return to Gordon 'That is two of us in the crew which have been on ops.' When they arrived back in their billet the rest of the crew, who yet had to face their first ops were full of questions. 'What was it like?' Gordon's reply was 'Firstly, who has a cigarette for an operational type?' For Gordon's pilot on this occasion his luck was to run out when his aircraft ditched on the infamous operation to Nuremberg on 30/31 March 1944. He was the only one not to get out into the dinghy and survive before the aircraft sank.

Gordon's pilot was himself to die later after being hit by flak on an operation to Normandy. Gordon went on to complete thirty-four operations, be awarded the Distinguished Flying Medal and become an officer.

After leaving the target area Pilot Officer Bernard Downs found he had lost 2,000 feet. Because in the briefing he had been told to return at a height of 24,000 feet he set about making up the lost height. Then he saw a bright parachute flare, and another to port and then another to starboard. Before long he was flying down an immense flare path laid by high-flying aircraft on either side of the bomber streams. This was a new tactic by the German fighters, lighting up the aircraft near the flare. The first reaction was to stick the nose of the aircraft down to get out and away from it, but at 24,000 feet at least they were out of the way of other aircraft and moving to the right or left would mean becoming vulnerable to the radar defences. The only available action was to try and climb even higher.

This Bernard did and got to 26,000 feet, and by then the flares were below and getting further away. The aircraft controls became more ragged the higher they got. The crew was becoming anxious, and the effects of lack of sleep were beginning to be felt with the previous night out to Leeds taking its toll. The temperature outside was now down to 40 below and even with the heaters going full blast they were just, able, to keep the temperature inside from falling below freezing point.

An added problem for flight engineer George Jupp was fuel. His calculations showed him that if they continued to climb at full speed they would not have enough fuel to make it back to base and would have to land in Norfolk 50 miles nearer than their own base.

The flares continued on both sides of the aircraft but after fifty minutes or so they suddenly stopped just as though someone had turned out the light.

They were now at the aircraft limit of 27,000 feet, and it was time to reduce speed and descend – much to the relief of Jupp. At 5.30 am and now down to 20,000 feet they crossed the Dutch coast north of Texel and could go even lower and increase speed to get home to base. The problem of staying awake was the predominant factor.

At 6.30 am and now down to 4,000 feet they crossed the coast just south of Hornsea when, over the radio, they heard the first aircraft landing at Breighton their base. It was somebody asking for landing instructions. At 6.45 am they reached Breighton. Dawn was now coming up on the horizon.

At 7.10 am the wheels once again hit the runway. They had made it. Despite fighters, flares, lack of fuel and sleep, they were home to fight another day. In Bomber Command there was always another day. At dispersal the faithful ground crew were waiting, always pleased to see their charge come home again. The crew jumped out and looked at their warhorse, which considering what they had gone through seemed unscathed.

At 7.45 am they were now in the briefing room at Breighton, where they were interrogated. How were the fighters? How did they attack? Were new tactics being used? This was all grist to the mill for the intelligence officer who would pass on the information to Bomber Command Headquarters. The returning crews were given hot coffee laced with rum.

The returning crews were being recorded on the operation board, but not as yet Q-Queenie. By 8.30 am the debriefing was over and they were free to do as they pleased. In the case of Bernard and his crew it was definitely sleep. At 9 am Bernard finally collapsed on his bed but still with the sounds of droning engines in his head. It was also on his mind that five aircraft, including his, had returned but not Q-Queenie. In his room there were a number of empty beds that emphasised that fact.

The crews still returning were still having confrontations with fighters. Despite being hit by flak Flying Officer Blake had reached Leipzig and on the return trip was attacked by fighters on no fewer than seven occasions but somehow reached his base. The rear gunner Warrant Officer James Houston had been hit in the shoulder and had his oxygen mask and intercom rendered useless.

On 21 February 1944, Blake was recommended for an immediate DFC. It was only his fourth operation and he had done remarkably well. His recommendation mentioned that he had been hit three times by flak on the outward journey, the first as he crossed the enemy coast and the second time at Grenorgen and thirdly at Celle.

On 29 February Houston was recommended for the DFM.

Flying Officer Lennard of 158 Squadron, having dropped his bombs on the target, found he could not close the bomb doors owing to the hydraulics being faulty. With them open he felt there was no way he could make it back and an attempt to close them with a hand pump had to be made. For the pilot, Squadron Leader Weller, this seemed to take for ever until eventually the warning light went out, which meant the doors were closed. He could then obtain more speed as the doors were causing considerable drag. He was, however, still flying on three engines. On coming down and out of cloud he saw a marvellous sight ahead – land, the UK. They had made it and landed at 7.49 am. They had been in the air for seven hours and forty minutes and when they landed had only ten minutes' fuel left.

Pilot Officer 'Pop' Marshall had a mixed crew of a New Zealander, a Yorkshireman, a Welshman and a Londoner. His wireless operator Sergeant Jones was hit by a piece of flak over the eye and on landing was taken to hospital. When the aircraft was later inspected, a hole was found in the port side near Sergeant Jones's wireless Perspex window.

Squadron Leader Haigh of 576 Squadron was also recommended for an immediate bar to his DFC, which had been awarded three years before in 1941. Despite engine trouble and being attacked by a fighter, he pressed home his attack and landed at 7.25 am. His rear gunner Sergeant Arthur Wright was recommended for the DFM. Despite having completed only seven operations he coped very well with no fewer than seven fighter attacks on his aircraft and was credited with having damaged one of the attacking fighters, which was last seen going down trailing smoke.

Flight Sergeant Gumbrell of 103 Squadron, flying Lancaster JB 530, crashed at his home base Elsham Wolds having made three attempts to land. Sergeant Osborne in his crew was killed but the remainder of the crew were unhurt, all having had a very lucky escape.

Warrant Officer Warner in Lancaster ND334 also crashed. Five of his crew were killed and two uninjured, including Warner. The two aircraft JB530 and ND334 collided in mid air. Warner, having opened up to go around again, did not see Gumbrell who had not been given permission to land whereas Warner had.

Warrant Officer Rollins of 576 Squadron found his brake pressure low on landing and could not pull up in time at dispersal. He struck an engine stand, which was sitting on the grass.

Flight Sergeant Farrant of 97 Squadron, landing in an extreme cross wind, swung to port. In so doing his port tyre burst, but the crew was okay.

Flying Officer Taylor of 166 Squadron, the first man off, made it back and landed at 7.10 am. The second man, Flight Lieutenant Hart of 103 Squadron, landed at 6.53 am and the third Flight Lieutenant Newton of 9 Squadron at 7.31 am. The last two crews to land were piloted by Flying Officer Rance of 425 Squadron in Halifax LW 375-P and Pilot Officer Merrill, also of 425 Squadron, who landed at 8.15 am.

When Merrill landed all that would return had, but there were many that did not return and touch down safely at base. There were many empty beds that morning and many empty places on the dispersals all over the UK. In fact, there were 555 empty beds in messes and billets in thirty-five stations throughout the UK, including six flight commanders. On returning to base Squadron Leader James Frazer Barron, a flight commander with 7 Squadron, a Pathfinder Squadron, said:

> It was one of the toughest I have been on, German fighters appeared to be waiting for us. Everywhere they laid an aerial of flare paths for a distance of 100 miles to the target. It was just like day and we saw kite after kite in combat and watched several going down in flames. We were highly relieved when we reached the target, bombed it and got out without trouble.

Squadron Leader Barron DSO DFC DFM was born in New Zealand and only twenty-three years old at the time of the raid on Leipzig. Sadly, he was later killed on a raid to Le Mans in May 1944, an operation to make the Normandy landings a success.

During the cold winter of 1943/4 the rear gunner in Bomber Command had three enemies – the three 'Fs'. They were Flak, Fighters and Frostbite. It was the latter that affected Norman Storey flying in the rear turret of a Lancaster of 103 Squadron from Elsham Wolds in Lincoln. The condensation in his oxygen tube froze and he was literally being starved of oxygen. He remembers feeling drunk. He remembers thrashing about in his turret, during which struggle the turret light somehow came on. The mid-upper gunner having seen this, and it not being something one did during an operational flight, reported it to the pilot. He in turn called up Norman on the intercom and from the response or lack of response he sensed something was amiss. He sent the wireless operator who was using a portable oxygen bottle back with a replacement helmet complete with oxygen mask. He removed the one Norman had on and replaced it with the one he had brought with him. However, during this time his head and ears particularly were exposed to the elements he suffered frostbite. On landing he was taken to the sick quarters where his ears were treated and then covered in bandages. He remained here for three days. On release he was allowed to wear a ladies' silk stocking acquired from the wireless operator's wife to wrap around his head and ears. This he wore when outside and while flying on operations for the remainder of the winter months.

He had a 'chit' from the medical officer to allow him to wear this stocking over his head much to the discomfort of the Station Warrant Officer.

Even on demob from the RAF he still wore a scarf over his head and ears during the cold weather. Over the years since the war the suffering and pain from this has diminished but even now on a very cold day he suffers a pain down the back of each ear – a constant reminder of 20 February 1944 and Leipzig.

Crews could still see the fires at Leipzig some thirty-four minutes after leaving the target area.

Chapter 15

Casualties

—⚊⚊—

Suddenly, as Bob Trett and his crew looked out for fighters they were attacked and hit by a Ju 88 from below. The wings of the aircraft were hit and set on fire. The words no airmen wants to hear, 'Abandon aircraft', came over the intercom and the radio sets and documents were destroyed. Below, huge fires were blazing. When Bob baled out he found himself heading for Brandenburg. He hit the ground softly in a snow drift and his chute got caught in the trees. The aircraft crashed near Leipzig. They had been shot down by Oblt Becker over Brandenburg.

The losses were devastating. Seventy-nine aircraft failed to return to base. These were the heaviest losses since 21/2 January 1944, when fifty-eight aircraft failed to return from a trip to Magdeburg. Of the 823 aircraft that were despatched 645 attacked the primary target Leipzig. The losses affected some squadrons more than others. One squadron lost four aircraft and a further six squadrons lost three aircraft.

Men such as Squadron Leader Julian Sale DSO DFC, a thirty-year-old Canadian and flight commander with 35 Squadron failed to return. This was one of four aircraft that failed to return to Graveley and 35 Squadron on this operation. His navigator Squadron Leader Gordon Carter DFC and bar recorded the trip to Leipzig in his flying logbook. They had become airborne from Graveley at 1 am on 20 February in conditions of hail, sleet and ice. They flew all the way against heavy defences when a Ju 88 fighter flown by *Feldwebel* Frank shot them down at Celle. The aircraft crashed at Berenbostel. It was Sale's fiftieth operation. The overload tank on the aircraft was hit and exploded in fire. Gordon baled out and landed in a forest unseen and unhurt. Julian Sale had stayed with the aircraft because his rear gunner could not bale out and also Julian thought he could crash-land the aircraft. He had on another occasion crash-landed on the base at Graveley and got away with it. On this occasion, although he survived the crash he was badly injured suffering a broken pelvis and serious internal injuries. On 20

March 1944, not being able to come to terms with his injuries and fearing that even if he lived he would be a cripple after having been a very fit man, he managed to get out of bed and to the window at the hospital in Hannover. He jumped out and was killed – a sad way for a man of such courage and standing to die. Today this brave man is buried in Choloy War Cemetery. He had already been shot down in May 1943 and managed to evade and get back to the UK. After his death he was awarded the DFC. Initially a further DSO to add to the two DSOs he had already been awarded was recommended but this was later changed to the DFC. In the recommendation for his immediate DSO the operation in which he was shot down and evaded was fully recorded. He had taken three months and travelled 1,250 miles through Germany, Holland, Belgium and France before getting back to the UK.

Gordon Carter, also Canadian, managed to cover 100 kilometres before being caught by the Germans in Nien-Am-Weser. It was also the second time he had been shot down and he had also returned to the UK via a boat from Brittany the first time. This time he was not so lucky and spent the rest of the war in a POW camp, landing back in the UK on 9 May 1945. His later life in a camp had not been easy. He and others were marched across Germany until liberated by the Cheshire Regiment 7 miles from Lubeck. The Germans had evacuated Sagan because of the approaching Russians from the East. After marching over 100 miles in very near freezing conditions they were out on cattle trucks and taken to a naval prison camp at Marlag Nord. Here they stayed as SHAEF (Supreme Headquarters Allied Expedionary Force) had given orders not to try and escape.

Warrant Officer Cross had been on his fifty-first operation of which twenty had been with Squadron Leader Sale.

His was one of four aircraft missing from the seventeen despatched by 35 Squadron.

Bernard Downs' friend Tom Smith did not return. He crashed at Kallenkote and he and his crew were buried in a churchyard at Steenwyke on Swolle, in Holland. It was mid afternoon when Bernard awoke but his hopes of Tom returning were dashed when Squadron Commander Guy Lawrence said 'Sorry, Old Chap, there's no news of Tommy Smith.' When he arrived back at his billet he was shattered to find that the RAF Police had been in and taken Tom's personal effects. This was the routine drill when men went missing, but nevertheless it was shattering.

On the morning of the 21st the morning papers conveyed front page reports of the raid on Leipzig with the shocking news that seventy-nine aircraft were missing. These were the heaviest losses suffered by Bomber Command to that date and the second heaviest throughout the bomber offensive. In addition to the losses many aircraft were badly damaged and crashed on return to base. Despite the losses life had to go on, the war still had to be won. However, the conversation was full of the raid and the losses. Bernard again enquired if there was any news of Tom Smith but as before he was told 'Sorry, there is nothing further, if we hear anything we will let you know immediately.' Tom and his crew were posted 'Missing, Presumed Killed.' After the war Bernard met Tom's fiancée Joan. She said she had hung on for news for a long time but no trace of Tom, his crew or his aircraft had come to light. Bernard still has a vivid memory of Tom as a rugged, cheerful, and dedicated young man, which will always remain with him. There have been friendships of much greater duration – but none so secure. Now many years on, 'Tom Smith, I salute you' were the sentiments expressed by Bernard.

Flying Officer Charles Parker was down to fly with Bernard Downs in LK762-Z Z-Zebra on the Leipzig raid. His colleague who had arrived on 78 Squadron earlier was flying with Flight Lieutenant Denman in LU816-N. He was also one of the missing. He had been shot down by Oblt Becker of NJG6. Denman was killed along with four other members of his crew and two were taken prisoner including a flight sergeant who had followed Charles into the Adjutant's office on arriving at 78 Squadron.

Flight Sergeant Leslie Burton was flying with 101 Squadron. His pilot officer was John Laurens DFM, from South Africa, who had joined the Grenadier Guards in 1935 after being wounded at Dunkirk and transferred to the RAF. They found the winds much stronger than forecast and Laurens, in attempting to lose time, began to dog-leg when suddenly in the area of Oldenburg the wireless operator Pilot Officer Cas Waight reported that a fighter was showing up on his equipment. Suddenly, a petrol tank between the port inner and outer engines caught fire and the flames quickly got worse. The bombs were jettisoned and they headed for home. But at 17,000 feet the crew was given the dreaded order to 'bale out'. The mid upper gunner Sergeant Bill Bolt baled out, but his chute failed to open. His body was found the next day by Mr A. van der Donk near a hedge, next to his house. He had suffered a fractured skull. When the port wing fell off Leslie was blown out of the aircraft; his last sight of the aircraft was the helpless Cas Waight from British Honduras caught in the burning aircraft without a chute on. The flight engineer Sergeant Alex Kibble from London got out safely and met Leslie on the ground. It was 2.35 am and the ground was frozen. Leslie had pain in his right leg and there was blood running down his nose.

The Buiter family in Tolbert, Holland, picked them up and gave help. Sergeant Bert Royston the rear gunner had been given up to the Germans by a collaborator, and the poor helpless Cas Waight had been thrown out of the aircraft without his chute and had hit telephone wires. He never did wear his chute in the aircraft as it impeded him working the radio; this sadly cost him his life. The pilot was found in the wreck of the aircraft. They were given help by various members of the Dutch underground but were later betrayed in Belgium after having been handed over to the Belgium White Brigade and were interned in a civilian prison before being taken to *Dulag Luft* at Frankfurt. From there it was a POW camp. They ended up at Fallingbostel in April 1945 where they were liberated by the 6th Airborne Division on 2 May 1945. The Russians liberated Flight Sergeant Ron Aitkin; the bomb aimer had also managed to evade capture for some while until he was also betrayed. He ended up in Stalag Luft III at Luckenwalde. Sergeant Jim Davies the special operator on the aircraft also managed to stay out of German hands for about six months when he was also betrayed along with Jim Aitken and ended up in Luckenwalde.

For many years after the war Leslie Burton who ended the war a warrant officer was the secretary of 101 Squadron Association. Sadly, he died on 17 April 1982 after two major operations from which he never recovered. His pilot John (Jack) Laurens and the mid upper gunner Don Bolt are buried in the village cemetery of Tolberdt a few miles south-west of Groningen and the wireless operator Cas Waight is buried in a cemetery at Noordwyjk. Of the seventy-nine aircraft that were missing, this was the only one from 101 Squadron that failed to return.

Ernest (Eric) Windeatt flew as a flight engineer with 106 Squadron. He and his crew were due to go on leave and had their passes all signed up and ready to go when the commanding officer Wing Commander Ronnie Baxter asked them to postpone their leave by twenty-four hours to enable 106 Squadron to make an all out effort in the number of crews despatched. En route they met severe icing and chunks of ice were falling off the aircraft with a rendering sound. The guns were freezing up and they were obliged to fire intermittent bursts to keep them working and free of ice. On the last leg and the turn-off point German fighters jumped them from above and also two other Lancasters that were three minutes ahead of time and on a true course. Eric described them as coming down like a hail storm. One fighter was hit and on fire, a Lancaster burst into flames, and they themselves were hit in one engine and to the fuselage, which made it impossible to open the rear hatch and all the crew except the rear gunner had to move forward to bale out. This it was later reported was the reason that the pilot Flying Officer Leggett lost his life – the fire took off the wing before he could bale out. Eric received frost bite to his hands and face having removed his helmet and gloves in preparing to put on the pilot's chute and also his own. He landed having baled out close to Berlin and was taken prisoner as were the rest of the crew. John Harrison was in the same crew. He remembers that the fighter came up from below and as John was about to fire he saw the fighter just below and to port. He gave the pilot the usual evasive drill but soon realised the aircraft was in trouble and not operating as it should be. The pilot then told the bomb aimer to jettison the bombs. By now the pilot Dicky Leggett was doing his best to fly the aircraft. As John made his way forward in the escape hatch his left boot became jammed fast and it was Dicky who got hold of it and pulled it off and out John went. He landed right on top of a German Air Force Camp and was captured right away. John was taken to Berlin and from there to *Dulag Luft* at Frankfurt and then *Stalag Luft* VI at Heydekruge.

Squadron Leader Kenneth Davis is today along with another member of his crew, Flying Officer Kenneth Marriott DFM, buried in the Berlin War Cemetery. He was flying in Lancaster JB468-U of 7 Pathfinder Squadron. Despite 'George' the automatic pilot not working on the aircraft they had decided to press on to the target. On reflection the surviving members of the crew thought they should have turned back to fight another day, having had a series of bad luck in previous trips. They had, like other crews, tried to lose time by zig-zagging across the bomber stream but this led to near collisions. One aircraft passed over so close that Sergeant Roy Child could hear the engines, so they abandoned this and carried on a straight course. The target Leipzig was now beginning to light up as the markers went down followed by bombs. Suddenly, there was an explosion under the aircraft and the aircraft started to burn. It would now appear they had been attacked by a *Schrage Musik* fighter. There was an explosion and then more flames in the fuselage. It was thought that in this attack Flying Officer Ken Marriott DFM was killed. The order to bale out soon came and Roy Child left his mid upper turret and went to the rear to get his chute and fix it to his harness. The flight engineer was having a problem getting the front escape hatch open.

Roy remembers:

I sat on the edge of the aircraft and fell into space. Coming down was an unbelievable sensation. I pulled the ripcord and the chute opened; I could still hear my aircraft quite clearly as I started to descend. I also heard the fighter go by below. They were the only sounds. It appears the rest of the bomber force had kept to their position and not tried to lose any time to ensure they arrived at the target at the correct time.

When he eventually landed on the ground it was into deep snow, and it was in this that he hid his chute; his escape compass he used to get some idea of direction but he later dropped it in the snow and it was lost. Having taken refuge in a church he was soon picked up when daylight arrived and he was taken to the local village where he came upon three other members of his crew. It was then that he heard that Ken Marriott had been killed and that the rear gunner and the pilot were missing. The local detachment of the *Luftwaffe* turned up and took them to the local air base. In the lorry they were taken in they saw something covered up in the lorry. They were told it was the H2S set from their crashed aircraft. They also learned that Squadron Leader Davis had been killed when he tried to crash-land the aircraft. At the air base a very proud *Luftwaffe* pilot came to see them; he claimed to have shot them down and had previously been on the Eastern Front. He said the raid on Leipzig had not been too successful; bombers were spread all over the target area trying to locate the target in the bad weather. His attack he said had been simple and the bomber had been doomed and of course it was.

The rear gunner Flight Sergeant Albert Grange had been badly injured as he had not been able to open his chute until it was too late and he died the next day. His grave to this day has never been found, but he is remembered on the Runneymede Memorial. He was thirty-two and came from Ripon, Yorkshire. He was recommended for the DFM the day he took off for the operation to Leipzig having flown forty-two operations. A great deal of his service had been in North Africa with a number of sorties on Tobruk and El Alamein in 1942.

Flying Officer Ken Marriott was twenty-four and had been awarded the DFM in 1942 after twenty-eight operations with 115 Squadron. In the last letter to his parents, dated 18 February 1944, his first thought was for his grandmother who had suffered an accident. In the letter he described one of his last flights when a Ju 88, which was finally shot down, and another beaten off attacked them. 'That meant we had Berlin to ourselves.' They then added their contribution to a 'Berlin which seemed all ablaze' and then started off for home, only to have another fighter attack them. After that his oxygen failed and after making an effort to get a fresh supply he dropped unconscious and was hauled to safety by the navigator with only forty-five seconds to spare.

Warrant Officer Derek Measures was flying a Halifax of 77 Squadron; he was hit en route to the target but was able to bomb Leipzig. But on the return trip the crew ran out of petrol and baled out south-east of Calais. After some time evading the enemy with the help of various people he eventually arrived in Antwerp but he was handed over to the *Gestapo* here and from September 1944 to April 1945 he was a prisoner at *Stalag Luft* VII and then *Stalag* III A.

At 78 Squadron Wing Commander Lawrence, the commanding officer, had twenty-one letters to write to the next of kin of the three crews missing from 78 Squadron after the operation on Leipzig. One was to Mrs Hemmings the mother of Sergeant Harold Hemmings who was in Tom Smith's crew. He and the rest of the crew of Halifax LW367-Q were all killed when it crashed. They were buried together in one grave, but later reburied separately by the War Graves after the war.

The losses suffered by aircraft on the Leipzig on this night were not only greater than on any other previous single bomber operation but proportionately they were larger than on any operation of comparable size. There were three possible reasons for this. First, there were unexpected variations in the winds, which caused many aircraft to be early at various points on their course and to have to use up time by orbiting, thus increasing the collision risks. Second, the resulting inevitable loss of concentration probably increased the flak losses on the route, which passed several heavily defended areas. Third, the enemy fighters in what appears to be an unfortunate accident rather than deliberate design, were steered into the bomber stream at an early stage and were able to follow RAF aircraft all the way to the target.

As the bombers approached the enemy coast on the outward journey, a number of aircraft with navigation lights on were seen travelling in the opposite direction. It would appear that some aircraft were early and forced to orbit in order not to cross the Dutch coast too soon. Two collisions were reported, one 50 miles off the coast and another in the area south of Emden. Losses occurred at Emden (two), Bremen (two), Hannover (one) and Antwerp (one). Along the route aircraft were lost to flak at Ameland, Groningen, Vechta, Celle, Stendal, and Overflakkee, and in the target area five were shot down.

German night fighters were assembled in the Hamburg area in response to the minelaying aircraft moving towards the Danish coast. The attacks on airfields in Holland engaged the attention of the fighter controllers and possibly prevented a whole-hearted attempt at interception of the minelayers.

It so happened then that the fighters were present in the Hamburg/Heligoland area when the main bomber force crossed the north Dutch coast and, being sent southwards from there, made contact with the bomber stream. From the area south of Bremen to the target, twenty aircraft were seen shot down by fighters and some twenty-five in all can be attributed to this cause.

Early on the Germans assumed that the target was Berlin, and Leipzig was not announced as the target until the attack on Leipzig was beginning. The bombers' route lay over the very popular Beacon 'M' where many of the bombers were intercepted and from 'M' to the route marker near Stendal a very large number of interceptions took place. Instructions were heard sending fighters to Beacon 'M' and from there they were in an excellent position to make contact with the stream.

In his diary Leslie Bartlett recorded:

Took off at 6 pm and it was a 'twitch' trip right from the beginning. Bad cloud to get through and bags of icing, but were lucky and found a break. From the moment we crossed the coast it was a battle, kites were going down left and right. To make matters worse the winds changed and we got there far too early and had to orbit outside Leipzig waiting for zero hour. The trip back was just the same, next day we heard the score 68 lost. What a price!

He ended with a tribute to Squadron Leader Ken Davies and his crew.

The difficulty is not so much to find a friend to die for as to find a friend worth dying for.

Our Lad

Every year there comes another
anniversary of the day we lost our lad.
Time dulls the agony.
But always on this sacred date he seems
to hover near as if he know we stood in
need of comfort and of cheer.
We look upon his photograph.
That face so young and gay changes not, as we do
must change with every passing day.
We'll grow old and weary, sometimes
happy, sometimes sad. But he, beyond
the reach of time, will ways be – our lad.

The outcome for Bob Trett and the rest of his crew pals was twelve months in a prisoner of war camp; they were among 131 taken prisoner after the Leipzig operation.

When walking through a village a farmer's wife spotted Bob and shouted out 'Ah English *Fliegerman*', so he thought the better part of valour was to give himself up and did so to a farmer in the area. The farmer took him to the local *Burgomeister*. His son was a schoolboy and spoke quite good English; he told Bob that he was also a part-time anti-aircraft gunner in Berlin. After the war Bob received a letter from the boy's mother asking if Bob could locate a German prisoner of war camp near Aylesbury, as she had not heard from her son for about three months. How the pendulum had swung.

On the whole the German family treated him well, treating his burnt hands, giving him a cup of coffee and later lunch. The villagers kept coming to look at the English flyer. At the time airmen were being collected from all over the area; some having been out all night in the snow. All his belongings were put in a shoe box, wrapped up in brown paper and string and left with the *Burgomeister*. From time to time Bob was asked by the farmer's son if he wanted anything from the box. He was allowed to take anything except the escape kit, which contained £2,000 in Swiss, German and French currency. Certain things that occurred during his time with the family made Bob feel that they had no time for Hitler and his regime. The airmen were then taken to a *Luftwaffe* base, which it turned out was a base for rocket and jet aircraft. By the time it became dark there were some fifty to sixty captured aircrew at the base. The one thing the Germans did not like was the prisoners looking at or paying attention to the various aircraft around. If you did you might be hit with a rifle butt.

From then it was the usual routine. He was taken to the interrogation centre *Dulag Luft* at Frankfurt where Bob was shocked to find the Germans had a file on 102 Squadron, which included crew lists and photographs of officers from the CO down. It was here that he met the rest of his crew apart from one. From there they were marched through the town amidst jeers, boos, spitting and hissing from the locals.

They were transported by railway cattle trucks on a journey of four to five days being fed occasionally by Red Cross workers. Finally they stopped at a town called Heydekrug in Prussia about 8 kilometres from the Lithuanian border and then marched to *Stalag Luft* VI. From there they were taken to *Stalag* 357 in Poland by train to a place renamed by the Germans. After three weeks they were again moved by train to *Thorn Stalag* 355 later renamed 357 at Fallingbostel. It was here that Bob met Ivor Norris from Bristol.

Sergeant Norton or Norval was an army lad from Grimsby and known as the Baron because of his trading qualities. He ended the war at *Stalag* 357, where there were no facilities for cooking but the huts were new and only twenty prisoners per hut. In *Stalag* 357 food and others things were traded daily. One of the guards, Fritz, aged fifty-two, had been in the German Pay Corps since 1912 and was scared of being posted to the Eastern Front. He became Bob and another Ivor's batman. Each day he would light their stove, chopping the wood for the fire with his bayonet. Eventually things caught up with him and he was posted to the Eastern Front when the guards were replaced by resting Alpine troops. The NCO in charge was rather trigger-happy and fired his pistol at the smallest excuse.

All the camp left *Stalag* 357 on 10 April 1945. On 16 April while on the march the column was attacked by British aircraft who thought they were Germans and forty prisoners were killed. On the 19th they encountered a patrol of soldiers whom they at first thought were German *Panzer* troops but turned out to be British men of the 23rd Hussars.

They were then, after a good meal of bacon and eggs, transported to a POW transit camp in Celle. This turned out to be an old *Panzer* barracks, which still had German tanks still in their stalls.

It was a padre from Canada who finally took them to an airstrip near Celle where Dakotas of the 5th Tactical Air Force were delivering stores and petrol. Here in the officers' mess they were given beer, cigarettes and chocolate – all to be charged to the Commanding Officer.

They finally flew to Brussels where they received a fantastic reception.

Here the Salvation Army, British Red Cross and Church Army plied them with razors, toothpaste, towels, and tea and food – all the things you take for granted that are not readily available in a POW camp.

Finally they arrived back in the UK on 23 April 1945, fourteen months after taking off to bomb Leipzig. They had landed in Buckinghamshire where another fantastic reception waited them with a Red Cross nurse on one arm and a WAAF on the other. Here they were given a medical, delousing and finally a meal.

All RAF prisoners were taken to RAF Cosford in the Midlands by coach and train where they were treated like royalty by a staff of over 1,500 airmen and WAAFs who kitted them out with new uniforms after delousing, and sewed badges and medal ribbons on their uniforms. Bob was now a flight sergeant as his time as a prisoner had counted for promotion from sergeant.

He was given fifty-six days' leave, leave coupons and ration coupons equal to a pregnant women who received double and his post office book in which was £300 – quite a fortune in 1945. He also received nine months' back pay. On 25 April he was on leave – the leave he should have taken on 20 February 1944. Sadly, on 8 October 1982, Bob died of cancer.

While in the camp *Stalag* 357 a Russian cook, possibly from a Russian Cossack regiment, painted Bob. The painting (6 inches by 5 inches) is now at the RAF Museum, Hendon.

At 5.30 am Lancaster JB609-F of 12 Squadron flown by Flight Sergeant Bowker crashed near Elspeet. In the wrecked Lancaster were two members of the crew. It is thought they were Sergeants Arthur Corlett and Williams. Their bodies were found at once by the Germans and in the afternoon of 20 February three more bodies were found, making six in all that had been recovered. The Germans thought that the Lancaster had a crew of six and not seven. As a consequence no further search was made for the seventh man, which turned out to be Sergeant Eric Goodridge. He was twenty-four and came from Broad Chalke, Wiltshire. All seven are now buried in Harderwijk Cemetery on the shore of the Ijsselmeer (Zuider Zee). They had been shot down by *Oberleutnant* H.H. Augenstein from a night fighter squadron based at Leeuwarden. After this raid he had forty-two kills under his belt and was promoted to *Hauptman* (Captain). He and his crew were later shot down. At the time of his death he had forty-six kills and was the holder of the Knight's Cross.

Flying Officer Frampton RCAF, flying Lancaster DS788-C, of 408 Squadron was attacked by a fighter over Northern Holland and crashed at Kroswolde. He was killed as were two others in the crew and another two were killed in the fighter attack. One of the crew was taken prisoner and Sergeant Robertson the flight engineer baled out and landed in telephone wires by the side of the railway at Assen at 4 am. Having left his chute and Mae West in the tangled telephone wires Robertson travelled for two days by hiding during the day and moving at night. He was helped by a farmer and then went to Hoogeveen. A Dutch policeman there helped put him in touch with an resistance organisation. After two months at Roermond he was able to cross the Dutch/ Belgium frontiers ending up at Liege. From there he eventually went to a POW camp at Villance, which was in a woods. And then he went on to another camp at La Cornet until he and others were liberated.

Pilot Officer McAlpine of 35 Squadron, flying Halifax LV846-O, was attacked by two *Wilde Sau* German fighters near Magdeburg and he and another member of his crew Flight Sergeant Sinclair were killed in the combat. The port engine caught fire and the aircraft crashed 1 kilometre from Buckow. Flight Sergeant Taylor was shot by the German Home Guard after baling out and landing safely. Flight Sergeant Chant who also baled out and had been wounded in the fighter attack was treated in hospital then taken to a POW camp at Fallingbostel where he died of a coronary attack on 2 December 1944.

Flight Lieutenant Bill McTurk also of 35 Squadron and flying Halifax

LV793-B was attacked by fighters over Stendal. The aircraft was set on fire and the rear gunner Flight Sergeant McCormick was killed in the combat. Bill had set up a regular weaving pattern when the fighter attack came. The overload tanks had been set on fire in the attack. Three of the crew left by the front hatch; the flight engineer for some reason went back to the rear hatch along with the mid upper gunner but neither were seen again. Bill left last and got stuck in the hatch on the way but somehow released himself and ended up landing in a lake at Brandenburg and had to swim ashore – not the easiest thing to do in flying kit. He was soon picked up and taken to *Stalag* III at Sagan where he was placed in Hut 104 and it was from here in March 1944 that the Great Escape took place. Bill, Flying Officer Tricky, and Sergeant Kerr were the only survivors from his crew.

The third crew from 35 Squadron who failed to return was captained by Flight Lieutenant Jones flying Halifax LV834-M. He was also attacked by a night fighter and crashed at Gothre. Only two of his crew survived.

The seven graves today are looked after by the people of Elspeet who have gone so far as to build a memorial in their memory.

Of the 561 Lancasters despatched forty-four failed to return and of the 255 Halifaxes thirty-four went missing – a total 9.5% loss of Lancasters and 13.3% Halifaxes. The Halifax II was withdrawn after this operation.

These were the heaviest losses for Bomber Command so far but on 24/5 March 1944 on a raid to Berlin and on 30/31 March 1944 on an operation to Nuremberg the losses were even higher – seventy-two were lost on the Berlin raid and ninety-five on the Nuremberg raid.

I Am Not There

Do not stand at my grave and weep,
I am not there, I do not sleep,
I am the thousand winds that blow,
I am the diamond glints on snow,
I am the sunlight on ripened grain,
I am the gentle Autumnal rain.

When you wake to the morning thrush,
I am the soft uplifting rush
of quite birds in circled flight
I am the soft stars that shine at night
Do not stand at my grave and cry
I am not there – I did not die.

British Soldier (Northern Ireland)

Chapter 16

The Outcome

—∿∿—

The crews were tinged with excitement on take–off for a raid, particularly if the target was a big German city with its heavy ring of searchlights and anti-aircraft guns. The attack on Leipzig on 19/20 February 1944 was no different.

The attack on the city opened up early, the first primary blind markers going down six minutes before zero hour, thirteen having made it to Leipzig. The blind backers up followed, twelve having reached Leipzig. The individual timing for the primary blind markers with one exception was good but the supporters' timing was very bad and spread from 3.53 to 3.57 am. One supporter bombed the target as early as 2.15 am, one at 3.43 am and another at 3.57 am. The marking tailed off at 3.56 am and then there was a gap from 3.59 to 4.03 am, the indication was that for the most part the main force bombed on Wanganui flares.

The glow of flares was seen through the cloud and smoke, which rose to a great height. The first waves met slight unseen fire from heavy guns putting up a barrage to 23,000 feet, which after fifteen minutes was lowered to 18,000 feet.

No. 1 Group reported an excellent concentration of marking, most crews choosing to bomb on the release point flares although a few were able to see the TIs through the cloud. Some crews arrived too early because of the strong winds and made very large orbits to lose time.

Squadron Leader McLeish of 408 RCAF Squadron arrived sixteen minutes early and made a circuit of the target and then made a second bombing run on H2S.

Flight Sergeant L'Estrange of 12 Squadron was flying Lancaster ND5. On return to base he was presented with a wooden spoon, having brought a 4,000-lb 'Cookie' back.

Photographic evidence after the attack showed the RAF raid on 19 February and the USAAF raid on 20 February had damaged the railway sidings and the roof of the Paunsdorf workshops.

On 22 February evidence showed two of the railway tracks at the Stoteritz station at Leipzig had received direct hits and on 24 February further evidence showed that tracks near Heiterblick station had been damaged by direct hits or near misses.

At ATG Maschinenbau, works 1, 4 and 5 were attacked. In works 1, 100 out of a total of 605 machine tools were damaged. They varied from very small bench shears up to a 2,000-ton hydraulic press. In works 5 fire caused damage to seventy-five of a total of 365 machine tools – those damaged were principally turret and engine lathes. The damage to finished products comprised:

1. Fifty-one fuselages damaged or destroyed on 4 December 1943. This amounted to two weeks' capacity. Damaged material and parts. 130 fuselages amounting to six weeks' potential production.
2. Twenty-five aircraft plus sixty-five fuselages damaged or destroyed on 20 February 1944 – four weeks' potential production.
3. Nine aircraft and eight fuselages damaged on 7 July 1944.

The bombs dropped comprised:

Three cascades
Fifteen flares
Thirteen Target Indicators
Seventeen mines of which seven failed to explode
200 high explosive bombs of which sixty-six failed to explode
70,500 stick incendiaries
1,600 liquid incendiaries of which 154 failed to explode
100 phosphorous canisters

On 20 February 1944, many phosphorous bombs and stick incendiaries, and several HE bombs were found in forest areas without any damage being caused.

The German casualties on 19/20 February were:

336 people were killed, including five soldiers and six Red Cross nurses.
262 people were seriously injured, including six soldiers.
603 people were slightly injured including five soldiers.
539 were buried of whom 164 were rescued alive and 188 dug out dead.
50,000 were bombed out.

Some 700 of all types of buildings were damaged, in particular thirteen public buildings, fifty industrial premises, one traffic installation. Some 107 business premises were destroyed. Various other buildings had heavy, medium or light damage and one bridge had light damage. The newspapers reported that 2,300 tons of high explosive and incendiary bombs had been dropped.

One woman had started work at Leipzig station in 1941. Bombing was frequent, a tunnel was being built that was used for sheltering during the bombing raids. On one occasion she had gone to the tunnel and when she came out she found the station almost totally destroyed. The station was mainly used to relocate people from the Jewish quarter to the concentration camps. It would appear the people in Leipzig knew about this as they saw loaded cattle trucks leaving the station loaded with Jews bound for concentration camps in the east and, for most, death.

The weather was a hazardous. A dense heavy cloud belt with ice, which covered the route to the target area, was reported. Above the cloud the sky was clear.

One navigator said:

> We hadn't been going very long before I discovered that we were ahead of schedule. We slowed down some and I made the necessary adjustments but when crossing the enemy occupied coast I found we were still running too fast.

Bernard Downs believes there had been a security leak and that the German defences were waiting for them and knew the route the bombers were taking. There was a long time lapse from the original pre-briefing and the actual time on target was some fifteen to sixteen hours later, which he feels was ample time for the Germans to make preparations if they got the information on the raid quickly enough.

He argued that defences in the target area were exceptionally heavy, heavier in fact than in Berlin. This was based on experience from his five visits to the German capital.

The anticipated Mosquito diversionary attack on Berlin did not draw off the night fighter force as anticipated. The night fighters had been held back with the sure knowledge of the primary target.

A German report from the *Bundesarchiv* said that 300 aircraft attacked and caused considerable damage to the armaments industry. The south and east of Leipzig were worst hit.

A report was published by the Air Ministry dated 2 March 1944 for the period 1 January to 10 February 1944 entitled 'G.A.F. Night Defensive Activity on the Western Front'.

The report stated that the Germans had for the time being abandoned their previous tactics of assembling the bulk of their fighters over the target area, and were now concentrating their main effort in such a way as to enable them to intercept the bombers on the way into, and out of the target. If the Germans could succeed in these tactics this clearly had advantages over their original method of concentrating their fighters in the target areas. Not only did it mean they did not have to base their plans on a guess as to the identity of the target, and so lay themselves open to be misled by ' dog-legs' and around-about-routes, but also they were able to shoot bombers down before they dropped their load on the target. The important features of this new form of enemy tactic were as follows:

(i) All the Hun requires to know is the general trend of your bombers' direction. This he can usually do at an early stage of the proceedings by means of his long range radar warning system and Observer Corps. Once he determines the general direction he can assemble his fighters in a more or less central position and then feed them progressively into the stream, whatever its ultimate direction. Thus small angle deviation of the bomber route is not likely to upset him to any great degree. In fact if kinks in our routes have the effect of our aircraft spending an appreciably longer time over the more dangerous enemy areas than they would if they went direct, it might well happen, on occasions, that such divergences would be to his advantage since he would have more time in which to perform his infiltration acts.

(ii) The nearer our main bomber stream approaches his main assembly points the easier his task becomes of concentrating his fighters in an area suitable for feeding into the stream.

On 2/3 January and 14/15 January when the bomber raids lay over the Hun's very popular beacon 'M' our loss rate was well above average. On 19/20 February (Leipzig) when our losses were so high, our route again passed very close to 'M'. Our analysis of the enemy's reaction on this particular night, showed that a number of our bombers were intercepted in the vicinity of this beacon and that from 'M' to the route marker near Stendal a very large number of interceptions took place. The traffic overheard on this night does not give a complete story of the movements of the fighters, but instructions were heard sending fighters to beacon 'M' and from there they were in an excellent position to make contact with the stream. Moreover the general trend of fighters would in any event have been from their assembly point at 'M' onwards. This may well account for the large number of interceptions that took place on this occasion during the journey to the target. In this connection it may well also be noteworthy that on our recent attacks routed well to the south (Augsberg and Stuttgart) the stream was well away from the German assembly beacons. The losses on these occasions were well below average.

From 19/20 February 1944 tactics were modified and although the fighter activity did not decrease, the losses for the four operations after Leipzig went down to 2.7% from 6.8%. The modifications included diversions and route marking whose effects varied from night to night. The main reasons for the decrease in fighter success in southern Germany were:

a. The long-range reporting system does not function adequately against routes passing through France and Southern Germany.
b. That the enemy controllers appear unable so far to attempt interception in the stream in these parts. Whether this has been due to lack of special equipment for directing fighters into the stream, to lack of assembly beacons outside German territory, or to inaccurate knowledge of the precise position of the bomber stream, cannot be stated. It is clear, however, that interception at the target has been relied on so far.

The diversionary sweeps and minelaying operations have served a useful purpose on each occasion, firstly by getting the fighters up early, and secondly, by holding a number of them in Northern Germany. 175 mines were laid in Kiel harbour. As well as the attacks on airfields at Venlo, Leouwearden, Twente and Gilze Rijen and Deelen and Volkel sixteen Mosquitoes carried out a diversionary raid on Berlin, of which fourteen were successful and precision attacks were made on Aachen by three Oboe Mosquitoes and military targets in Northern France. Other Mosquitoes patrolled airfields in Germany, shooting down two enemy fighters without loss. One Mosquito was lost on Berlin.

The weather experienced on the route and target 10/10ths cloud with some breaks over the Dutch Coast.

Chapter 17

The Aftermath

—∭—

The German record of production in the aircraft industry showed a lack of foresight and sound planning at the highest levels, which resulted in under utilisation of the tremendous material advantages of this industry until it was too late.

The early attacks by the RAF on the German aircraft factories from 1940 to 1942 produced little reaction beyond some evacuation of factories to the safe areas in the east. The heavier American daylight attacks in 1943 caused serious physical damage to some plants but did not affect their basic production potential and the German defences succeeded in inflicting heavy losses, which caused a temporary suspension of attacks after October 1943.

In 1942, the German Air Ministry produced a plan for the complete dispersal of the industry but due mainly to opposition from the industry itself it was never put into practice.

The total loss of aircraft to the bombing attacks was about 7,500 aircraft between July 1943 and December 1944.

At the end of 1943, in the German industry there was a temporary shortage of aero engines due partly to a shortage of crankshafts for which the bombing attacks were responsible to some extent as well as other factors within the industry.

After a number of attacks on the German aircraft industry Programme No. 225 was drawn up in November 1943, which called for an increase in the overall number of aircraft produced.

On 24 November 1943, the day after a large raid on the German capital, a meeting of the various heads of the aircraft industry in Germany was called by Goring and Milch. Goring was urged to increase the fighter output at the expense of bombers but he refused to accept this radical change of policy at the time.

Up to March 1944, the aircraft industry, unlike other armament industries, was under the control at the *Luftwaffe*. After the main assault on the industry in February 1944 when a series of attacks was made on the plants responsible for 90% of fighter production, and 75% of the plant buildings was damaged or destroyed, control was handed over to the Speer Ministry.

The new organisation was given full responsibility for all future production of single-engine and twin-engine fighters, fighter-bombers, ground attack and reconnaissance aircraft, and types that at that time included the Bf 109, Me 210, Me 410, Fw 190, Ju 88, Ju 388. Its main role was to restore the aircraft industry, which had suffered from air attacks, and to protect it from further attacks.

The formation of the *Jaegerstab* (Committee for Production of Fighter Planes) on 1 March 1944 came under Dr Albert Speer's Ministry and *Generalfieldmarshall* Milch with *Hauptdiensleiter* Otto Saur as its executive head and a staff of twenty-five officials. The formation of the *Jaegerstab* was said to have resulted from a combination of at least three factors, which in the early spring of 1944 were exercising a serious effect on German aircraft production.

The first and probably the most important of these factors was the air attacks on the aircraft factories culminating in the heavy and successful raids of February 1944. As a result of these attacks it was estimated that by the end of February three-quarters of the airframe component assembly plants had received structural damage assessed at up to 75% and damage to equipment and tools up to 30%. Whereas the attacks in 1943 did not affect the armaments and aircraft programmes in 1944 Speer said when interrogated by the Allies after the war that there was a fall in production of 30/40% and if it were not for the air attacks the projected programme would have been achieved.

He also went on to say that the bomber offensive kept a considerable amount of the German armament production inside Germany, and withheld it from the front.

Some 30% of the guns produced consisted of flak guns, while 50 to 55% of the radar and signals equipment was for the defence against bomber attacks. A total of 33% of the optical industry was engaged on the production of aiming devices for flak guns and other anti-aircraft equipment. This effort could have been used on anti-tank weapons and ammunition for the front. Some 50% of the valves produced for the German Air Force were diverted to home defence.

Karl Frydag the German director of the German aircraft industry said that the attacks on aero engine plants should have been earlier to be more effective. He based this view on the vulnerability of the special tools used in the aero engine manufacture and the fact that airframes could be assembled with primitive faculties when needed whereas in the case of aero engines this was impossible.

There is little doubt that in the absence of air attacks against the aircraft industry, the transfer of aircraft production to the Seer Ministry would not have taken place. It was agreed in Germany that no one except Speer had the necessary power to vitalise the industry that had so long been fettered by the policy muddles of the German air industry and the political bosses. When *Jaegerstab* was set up, Saur stated that 70% of the original buildings of the German aircraft industry had been destroyed or damaged.

After March 1944, production rose because the main plan for dispersal was completed.

The production and the use of the United States long-range P-51 Mustang aircraft came as a shock to the German authorities. The introduction of this aircraft heralded a new phase of intense day bombing attacks by the Allies.

After 1 March 1944 fighter production increased. In September 1944 it reached a maximum of 3,375 fighters being produced. Saur and Speer put this down to the combined effects of removing the previously inefficient management of the aircraft industry, a drastic reduction in the number of types produced and the standardisation of production procedure. It was estimated that between the period July 1943 and December 1944 the number of aircraft lost was about 7,500.

Mobile teams under the code name Operation *Hubertus* were sent round instilling a new spirit of drive and efficiency into management and labour by means of a blend of bribes and threats.

Special flying squads were formed, armed with plenary powers and held in readiness to proceed to a bombed factory with the mission to rally the directorate and staff. They supervised the site clearance and emergency rebuilding measures, and organised the restoration of essential services.

It was not until March 1944 that the dangers were spotted and major component manufacturing dispersed. In the summer of 1942, Professor Keinkel had, somewhat to the amusement of his colleagues, moved his development section from Rostock to the Vienna area. Rostock was bombed and heavily damaged in 1942.

There was some criticism by the Air Ministry of attacking airframe production and not engines. The strategy behind this was to reduce the number of aeroplanes available to the *Luftwaffe* in the immediate months ahead. The heavy raids in February 1944 on the final assembly plants were part of the pre-invasion effort to weaken the *Luftwaffe*, and as such it was felt after the war not to be judged on the basis of whether or not they crippled the industry. The facts are that the number of aeroplanes that the *Luftwaffe* had operational in June 1944 was reduced and that the airframe assembly plants were wisely selected as targets.

In Germany certain military and industrial leaders stated that aircraft engine plants rather than airframe plants should have been attacked. Goering commented, 'As between airframes and engine factories, priority should definitely have been given to the latter.'

Speer himself said after the war:

We were surprised for a long time that you attacked the airframe production and not the motor production. We were always worried that you would attack Bayerische Motorenwerke who made Fw 190 engines, and the others. There were only a few big factories. If you had attacked the motor factories at first and not the airframes, we would have been finished.

He said that at the beginning of the war the technical initiative was clearly with Germany, but by the end of the war Germany had lost the lead. He went on to say Britain always had the lead with aero engines, hence it was difficult for Germany to maintain overall aircraft performance. In 1940/41 the *Luftwaffe* had rested on its laurels as regards development. This was a great mistake he commented.

On the other hand, Werner Chairman of the Main Committee for Aircraft engines presented a slightly different point of view. If the Allies could have destroyed the engine industry, according to him, it would have stopped aircraft production more surely than attacks on airframe plants. The 500-lb bombs, however, were too light.

In order to speed up production and to make good the deficit a seventy-two hour week was introduced in the industry. A representative appointed to each factory was invited to meetings of the *Jaegerstab* in Berlin in order to discuss its own particular problems.

Special flying squads were formed and equipped with aircraft, each consisting of five men: an architect, machine tool expert, electrical engineer and an expert in the provision of building materials and one official to take charge of welfare arrangements. They would proceed to a factory that had been bombed and supervise the clearing up and emergency rebuilding measures. It was said that they would take off whilst the Allied bomber formation was still approaching the suspect target. A thorough policy of dispersal was written up to decentralise the activity of major plants.

No single plant handled more than 100 major components for single aircraft and seventy-five for twin-engine aircraft. For bomber factories no more than fifty main components were to be dealt with at one time. Some twenty-seven main aircraft factories were dispersed over 729 smaller works. At the end of 1945 plans were drawn for the occupation of 3,000,000 square metres of underground space by the aircraft industry. In May 1944, 200,000 square metres of cellar space was acquired and mainly used for the accommodation of factories, which had already been attacked from the air. Between May and August 1944, a further 800,000 square metres of underground accommodation was also occupied. However, by autumn half had to be evacuated owing to the advance of the Allied armies.

On 8 July 1944, plan 225 was replaced by plan 226, which called for the production of 6,400 aircraft per month, which later was increased to 7,400. This included 1,000 Me 262s and 100 Me 163s. On 1 August 1944, Speer, the Minister of Armaments and War Production, took over responsibility of all aircraft production and the *Jaegerstab* was dissolved and taken over by Technisches Amt of Speer's Ministry headed by Saur.

At the end of the war 1,308 Me 262s were said to have been built. However, Hitler ordered that this type should be used as a fighter-bomber and so only a small percentage of these became operational owing to the delays caused by the execution of the necessary modifications. The main production for this aircraft was carried out underground where there was enough floor space to produce as many as 2,000 per month.

Frydag, a director of the Henschel concerns from pre-war days onwards, and *Generaldirektor* of Heinkel since the autumn of 1943, gave the following information at the end of the war. In 1942, he was appointed head of the main commission for airframe production, being given a similar position on the body's successor, the main commission for aircraft manufacture, and he was still in office when the war came to an end in Germany. He considered that the most severe blow dealt to the aircraft industry by the area bombardment of towns was the enforced disposal of the electrical and instrument manufacturing industries from Berlin to Silesia, which was recommended after the heavy raids on Berlin in November 1943. With the advance of the Russian armies these industries had to be re-evacuated to Dresden, where further heavy damage was sustained under Bomber Command night raids.

Albert Speer stated that in his opinion in the absence of bombing aircraft production would have followed the programme that came into force on 1 December 1943. He believed that the actual output would not have lagged more than 15% behind the plans laid. Plan No. 255 was scheduled to run until early 1946. He wrote that the strategic bombing was 'The Greatest Lost Battle of all'.'

The German defences deprived the German armies on all fronts of 20,000 guns and 900,000 fit men needed to man them. Railway repairs kept another 80,000 skilled men fully employed in Germany and thousands more were needed for repairs to bomb damage on essential war industries.

Looking at the actual output, calculated as being 15% below the level desired in plan No. 255, it appears that the bombing cost the Germans 2,500 aircraft in the first half of 1944 and 3,000 in the remaining half. Some 205,000 man working hours were lost for the 176,000 industrial workers. The bombing of the aircraft industries took 4% of the total weight of bombs dropped on German targets and totalled 90,671 tons. This included attacks by the 8th and 15th US Army Air Force.

The RAF attacked Leipzig eighteen times during WWII. The cost in aircraft and crews was high, with 124 aircraft failing to return from 2,045 despatched. The sacrifice was high with crews being buried all over Europe in France, Holland, Belgium and Germany. As well as 56,000 making the ultimate sacrifice in training and operations, over 9,000 that survived being shot down became 'guests' of the Germans. The Runnymede Memorial near Windsor has 20,000 names on its walls of airmen/women who have no known graves; many of which served in Bomber Command. They had taken off one dark night from an airfield in Lincoln, East Anglia, or Yorkshire and were never seen again.

Bomb Tonnage Dropped on Aircraft Industry	
RAF	29,000 tons
US 8th Air Force	47,671 tons
US 15th Air Force	14,000 tons
Total	**90,671 tons**

Air Chief Marshal Harris paid tribute to his crews saying:

> There are no words that can do injustice to the aircrew who fought under my command in the RAF. There is no parallel in warfare to such courage and determination which at times was so great that scarcely one man in three could expect to survive his tour of thirty operations.

Lest We Forget

One day a breed of men were born,
from every walk of life,
they came from near and far to fight,
for a certain way of life.

Some were tall and some were short,
and some were dark and lean,
and some spoke different languages,
but all were young and keen.

They all trained hard, and then one day,
a Wing Commander came
and pinned upon their breast, a badge,
Air-Gunners they became.

A squadron was their final goal,
to join an aircraft crew,
on Wimpeys, Lancs and Stirlings,
and some on Blenheims too.

They fought at night and in the day,
their ops increased in number,
some returned – and some did not,
for 'thirty' was the number.

Some surviving to reach this mark,
and some continued flying,
some spent years behind the bars,
with many of them dying.

At last the victory came in sight,
the runways now are silent,
the echoes of the past remain
a conflict, long, and violent.

This breed of men are now but few
but they remember others,
who flew with them so long ago,
their Royal Air Force brothers.

Bunny Austin

Chapter 18

US 8th/15th American Army Air Force

—⚉—

In 1919 when Colonel Mitchell the deputy director of the US Air Service returned to the US from France following WWI he believed that aviation would control future wars.

He prophesied that foot soldiers would be trained to parachute behind enemy lines to wage war. This of course was the role of the parachute regiment troops in WWII. He also prophesied that bombers would be capable of carrying explosives across the ocean (again this was achieved during the bomber offensive of WWII) and that there would be aircraft carriers with 900-foot decks to deploy aircraft. This of course was a major factor in WWII, particularly in the Pacific. He also predicted torpedoes and armour-piercing bombs for aeroplanes to attack at sea.

Yet again, these were used extensively in WWII. He said that air raid protection would also be established.

In 1924 he made a study of predicted future war with Japan who he thought would assume the US were using methods and equipment from WWI. His report was as if he had looked in a crystal ball and could foretell that the Japanese would attack Pearl Harbor. He had gone out to the Philippines and on his return produced a 300-page report outlining in great detail how this attack would be carried out, with targets, numbers of aircraft and height of the attacks. It was if he had had a vision of the future. He then went on to say that the Japanese Air Force would carry out a systematic siege against Corregidor. All this was disregarded by the Navy and Army as if they thought the Air Force had its place but would not play a prominent part in future wars.

Three of his WWI officers, Captain 'Hap' Arnold, his executive officer Captain Carl Spaatz, and 1st Lieutenant Ira Eaker, were to feature prominently in the bomber offensive in WWII.

In 1946 General Mitchell was posthumously awarded the Congressional Gold medal in recognition of his outstanding service and foresight in the field of American military aviation. He had been court-martialled in 1925 but in 1942 was posthumously reinstated with the rank of major general. Only fifty-six days later after his being reinstated the Japanese attacked Pearl Harbor. Just before his death he had said he wanted to be around for the next big show and said he meant the real air power, the real world war.

In 1942, the North American B-25 bomber was nicknamed the 'Mitchell' after Billy Mitchell, the only American military aircraft named after a specific person. This was of course the bomber that General Jimmy Doolittle attacked Tokyo with in 1942. So although not in body Billy Mitchell was around for the real world war in spirit.

In 1941 the United States Army Air Force was formed and 'Hap' Arnold made Chief of the Army Air Force.

In August 1942, Arnold directed the Air War Plans Division (AWPD), which called for 75,000 aircraft and 2.7 million men. The strategic priorities targets were increased from twenty-three to 177, with the German *Luftwaffe* first and submarines second in order of destruction.

In January 1943 and out of the Casablanca Conference came the Combined Operations Offensive Plan Operation *Pointblank*. The primary object was the progressive destruction and dislocation of German military, industrial and economic system and the undermining of the morale of the German people to a point where their capacity for armed resistance was fatally weakened. At the beginning of this offensive in March 1943 the RAF had 669 aircraft and the USAAF 303.

The 15th USAAF were based in Italy and consolidated into the US Strategic Air Forces in February 1944. During this time they were based in Bari, Italy, from December 1943.

On 27 March 1944 the strategic bomber force came under the command of US General Dwight Eisenhower, the Supreme Allied Commander. This only lasted until 1 April 1944 when it passed to SHAEF and with the Normandy invasion taking priority it was September before the strategic bombing campaign again became the priority.

One of the notable figures in the history of the US Air Force was (then) Colonel Billy Mitchell, who in 1918 led the greatest air battle of WWI when 1,476 Allied aircraft attacked St Mihiel. The air forces of France, Italy, Portugal, the UK and the US combined for this operation. The plan for this operation was orchestrated by Colonel Mitchell.

The salient at St Mihiel had been formed in September 1914 and covered an area of 35 miles wide at its base and 15 miles at its apex. This was part of the Germans' attempt to envelope the fortress of Verdun. As well as the Air Force it would also be the first test of the US ground forces. The attack was conducted over fours days from 12 to 16 September 1918. The main priority was to force the Germans out of the salient and then to break the German army in the west.

In August 1918 Mitchell set out the objectives of his plan.

1. Destruction of enemy air forces.
2. Reconnaissance of enemy positions and artillery positions.
3. Destruction of enemy ground forces through bombardment and strafing.

The role of the bombers was to hinder enemy concentration by railroads and the destruction of enemy aviation on its flying fields. The result was a success with the salient being reduced in four days.

But like the RAF at the end of WWI the US Air Service which had comprised 20,000 officers and 150,000 men, was soon reduced to 1,300 officers and 11,000 men.

Between January 1940 and August 1945 the United States produced no fewer than 300,317 aircraft. From 1942 the factories were running twenty-four hours a day, sometimes seven days a week. At one stage 2.1 million people, including many thousands of women, were involved in making aircraft.

In Michigan the Ford Motor Company turned out 5,476 B-24 bombers in 1944/5. In total 12,731 B-17s were built and 16,188 B-24s. Today, only fifty B-17s remain of which twelve are airworthy and only one B-24 is airworthy. They flew 10,631 missions and 4,145 aircraft were lost.

On 4 July 1942, six crews of the 15th Bomb Squadron of the 8th US Air Force were sent to England to train with the RAF on low-level sweeps of German airfields in Holland. They used the Boston, a US aircraft but now being used by the RAF.

The idea was that the 8th Air Force and Bomber Command would combine to sustain night and day bombing over Europe.

'Hap' Arnold was made Chief of the Army Air Forces in June 1941. He had pushed for the US to get into the war before Pearl Harbor and closely supervised the creation of the 8th Air Force in the UK. In 1942 he called for 75,000 aircraft and 2.7 million men and also 8,000 gliders and the production of 8,000 aircraft for use by its Allies.

He named General Spaatz to command the Eighth Air Force and General Eaker to head its Bomber Force. General Carl Spaatz had served in the American Expeditionary Forces in France, shot down three enemy planes and had been awarded the US DSC. After being given command of the 8th Air Force he came with his HQ to the UK in July 1942. When he became commander of the Strategic Air Force he directed the bombing campaign against Germany and directed the 8th Air Force, which was now commanded by Lt General Jimmy Doolittle and the 15th Air Force was now commanded by Lt General Nathan Twining. They were both based in Italy. During his time he insisted on daylight missions despite the RAF insisting that daylight missions they had undertaken previously had produced heavy losses. He also felt that oil production in Germany should be the prime bombing target. And so the US 8th Air Force had arrived and were to become known as the 'Mighty Eighth'.

The RAF had tried daytime bombing early in the war but then went solely to night-time bombing. With the 8th Air Force now in the UK it was decided that the B-17 and the B-24 bombers were more suitable for daytime operations with their 10.50 calibre machine-guns.

In 1942, with the US realising that the Allies were losing the war in Europe, an order was given to Arnold to send as many heavy bombers as he could to England. And so Eaker and his staff had set out for England with seven men and no heavy bombers but by December 1943 the 8th Air Force had 185,000 men and 4,000 aircraft in the UK.

The aircraft to be used by the 8th Air Force was the Flying Fortress, the B-17 made by General Motors in the USA. Later the B-24 Liberator was used, which flew a greater distance and was faster than the B-17. It also carried a heavier bomb load than the B-17.

The first B-17 made its maiden flight in October 1939 and the last B-17 flight was in July 1945. Some 12,700 were built. The idea for a four-engine bomber in the USA was similar to the RAF's in the mid 1930s. The Boeing Company came up with the ideas and in 1935 the Boeing Model 2-99, an all-metal four-engined bomber, came to fruition with the US Army Air Corps. This later became the YB 17 model but as WWII approached there were few B-17s built.

The first model was the B-17E and then the F was produced, which became the first bomber to fly deep into Europe in broad daylight with a fighter escort. It had a range of 2,980 miles and cost $276,000 to build. It was powered by four 930 hp Wright Cyclone engines reaching a maximum speed of 256 mph and at a height of 14,000 feet could drop a bomb load of 2,000-lb bombs.

In East Anglia there were 130 US bases and seventy-five airfields.

The B-17 had a ten-man crew as opposed to the seven in the Lancaster. The pilot was the captain as he usually had the highest rank in the aircraft;

the co-pilot was responsible for the engines, and was overall executive officer and able to take over if the captain was wounded or killed. The British bombers of course had no second pilot.

The B-17's maximum survival was only forty-seven flying days – the rest non-operational or under repair. Of the 12,700 built some 4,000-odd were lost on operations.

The first mission in the UK was on 17 August 1942 – attacks on Rouen and Solterville.

The British and American Air Staffs recognised the threat of the increase of German fighter strength. It was suggested that the whole of the British and American striking forces in the form of fighters and fighter bombers, medium and heavy bombers should be directed against the German fighter resources in Germany and the Occupied Countries.

In April 1943 the combined Bomber Offensive Plan was implemented in a Committee under the auspices of the United States 8th Air Force with representatives of the British Air Staff collaborating. One of the primary objects was to lay down the allocation of American aircraft required to carry this out. The figures agreed were to be used in Washington to ensure that the allocations were adequate and on time, and to avoid diversions to other theatres. It had been calculated that the neutralisation of some sixty targets might paralyse the German war effort. The Committee chose six groups, comprising of seventy-six precision targets. They were the three major elements of the German military machines, its submarine fleet, its air force, and its ground forces, and certain industries vital to their support. The six systems were:

> Submarine constructions yards and bases
> The German aircraft industry
> Ball-bearings
> Oil
> Synthetic rubber and tyres
> Military transport vehicles

It was thought that the effect on these systems would be to reduce construction by 89% by destroying building yards. Attacks on bases would affect the submarine effort at sea. The plan provided for the destruction of 45% of fighter and 65% of bomber capacity. Concentration rendered the ball-bearing industry vulnerable. It was predicted that 78% would be eliminated by the targets specified, with immediate effect upon tanks, aeroplanes, guns, diesel engines, etc.

German fighter strength was growing fast, however, and had increased by 44%, at the expense of bomber strength since the US had entered the war. This was despite heavy casualties and it was essential to arrest this growth quickly.

The target forces were evaluated in four phases. The existing force was too small for deep penetration – a force of 300 aircraft being considered the minimum for this purposes. Such a force would require 800 aircraft in the theatre to maintain it.

The first phases (April to July) would be restricted to reducing the German fighter strength and submarine installations within range of fighter cover. The second (July to October) should achieve an average striking force of 400 aircraft. This it was said should break the German fighter strength by deep penetrations up to 400 miles. In the third phase (October to January 1944), the striking force should be 550 aircraft. This should keep down the German fighter strength and undermine other sources of German strength. The last phase (after January 1944), would prepare for operations on the continent.

The plan would mean the integration of the RAF and US for the offensive. The RAF's task was to 'destroy German material facilities', while the US forces were directed towards the destruction of 'essential industrial targets'. The US 8th Air Force would attack precision targets in daylight complemented by RAF bombing attacks against the remaining industries at night. This plan received 100% backing from the Chief of the Air Staff and was sent to Washington. This in turn was approved by the Combined Chiefs of Staff at the Trident Conference.

On 14 June 1943 the Pointblank Directive was issued, and modified the Casablanca Directive of February 1943. This gave the highest priority to the destruction of the German fighter force and the factories producing fighters. Any invasion of Europe by the Allies could not take place without fighter superiority.

The specific tasks laid down were:

(i) The destruction of German airframe, engine and component factories, and the ball-bearing industry on which the strength of the German fighter force depended.
(ii) The general disorganisation of those industrial areas associated with the above industries.
(iii) The destruction of those aircraft repair depots and storage parks within range.
(iv) The destruction of enemy fighters in the air and on the ground.

The Minister of Economic Warfare's survey of economic developments in German Europe in the six months ending 30 June 1943 had emphasised the increase in German fighter strength. This showed new factories in Austria, Hungary and South Eastern Europe.

In August 1943 the Quebec Conference upheld this change of priorities.

On 17 August 1943 the ball-bearing factory at Schweinfurt was attacked. A total of 217 aircraft took part and sixty were lost. It was a costly trip, which nearly meant the end to such raids deep into Germany. But with a change in tactics as far as protection against fighters (with a pack of thirty-six aircraft instead of the original wedge) the losses were reduced but the danger of collisions flying so close were always there.

In October 1943 Plan Suction was arranged by the USAAF. The main target would be attacked by No. 1 Bomber Force (Heavy) consisting of four Combat Wings of B-17s (Tokyo Tanks). A diversionary attack would be carried out by No. 3 Bomber Force in the area of Hammstede. The main force would be escorted by P-47 fighters up to Aachen then they continue alone to Leipzig. On the return trip they would be again meet a fighter escort at Meepen. The outward journey would be over Felixstowe and the return over Great Yarmouth.

The Tokyo Tanks were internally mounted self-sealing fuel tanks and used on the B-17 bomber. The main wings of the B-17 consisted of an 'inboard wing' mounted to the fuselage and mounting the engines and flaps, and an 'outward wing' joined to the inboard wing and carrying only the ailerons. They were fitted on either side of the joint where the two wing portions were connected. Five cells totalling 270 US gallons sat side-by-side in the outward wing and were joined by a fuel line to the main tank delivering fuel to the outermost engine. The sixth was located in the space where the wing sections joined, with the remaining three cells located side-by-side within the inboard wing. These four delivered another 270 gallons to the feeder tank for the inboard engine. The same thing happened on the other wing. This added 1,080 gallons, which was added to the 1,700 gallons carried on the six regular wing tanks and the 820 gallons that were carried in a tank that could be mounted in the bomb bay giving a maximum of 3,600 gallons.

They were first used in April 1943 and in June were used in great numbers. From July 1943 all replacement B-17s were equipped with the Tokyo Tanks. The one drawback was that although self sealing, vapour build-up in partially-drained tanks made them a hazard in combat.

Another plan was *Buckwheat* when again five combat wings from No. 1 Bomber Force would attack Leipzig. A spoof operation would be carried out to shield the main force from enemy radar. No. 3 using B-24s would be used as a diversion and take off seventy minutes before the main force and appear to be a threat heading towards the Northwest. They would pass over Felixstowe on the way to Leipzig and on return and pass in and out south of Cologne.

A third plan was *Ossify*.

The objective was to send a bomber force to Leipzig and back with the least possible interference and enemy fighters that could oppose the passage of the main force.

No. 1 Bomber Force (Heavy) was escorted by eleven squadrons of P-47 US fighters and two squadrons of Spitfire Mark XIIs of RAF Fighter Command and a further twelve squadrons of Spitfire IX fighters and fourteen squadrons of Spitfire Vs of RAF Fighter Command who would cover the bombers as far as Munster. The outward route would be Felixstowe, Weizenfels and then Leipzig. The return route would be Lubben, Kustrin, Bad Berg and then over Cromer in Norfolk.

The plans for Operation *Argument* were started on 29 November 1943. Ten Combat Wings of B-17s would attack the Bf 109 components and assembly plants, and ball-bearings factories. The escort was twenty-four squadrons of P-47 US Fighters and fourteen squadrons of Spitfire IX RAF fighters. The targets were at Mockau 440 × 1,400 feet (attacked with thirty-five 500-lb bombs) and the assembly plants 1,600 × 2,400 feet (attacked with 240 500-lb bombs).

In February 1944 the aircraft factories in Germany were the prime target in the 'Big Week'. A total of 3,500 B-17s were involved and 244 were lost in a week but the operations were a success as many of the aircraft part shops feeding the *Luftwaffe* were destroyed. This had to be completed by 1 March 1944.

On 17 February General Spaatz told his deputy for operations that he could make plans for an attack on the 20th with the weather forecast good for three or four days but he did expect that with the Germans on full alert he would lose about 250 aircraft. His weather man Dr Krick had given him the forecast over Europe for the next week or so and his decision was that the weather in the UK for take-off would not be good but in Germany there would be similar weather, which would be an advantage as the German fighters would not be able to find them.

However, on the 19th it was reported that in Leipzig it was snowing and General Doolittle cancelled the main strike. But a weather man at the 8th Colonel Hoizman said it would snow during the night but be clear by the time they got there so the operation was on again and take-off time was early on the morning of the 20th.

On 20 February 1944 the USAAF made a daylight attack on Leipzig. It was the beginning of Operation *Argument* and the Big Week. Twelve locations plus targets of opportunity were to be attacked.

It was a cold morning with ice and snow on the airfields in East Anglia with bombers and fighters assembled. But the weather forecast showed an improvement in the area of Germany.

It was the 226th operation by the 8th Air Force and the largest force of heavy bombers (1,003) and fighters (835) ever employed on a daylight bombing operation. On arrival in Germany it was snowing and this continued until about 10 miles from Leipzig. It then cleared so the weather man was correct in his prediction.

The 1st, 2nd and 3rd Bombardment Divisions attacked Leipzig, Bernburg (Ju 88 twin engine fighter production), Gotha (Messerschmitt factory), Brunswick, Tutow, Rostock, Oschersleben (fuselage factory), Halberstadt (wing factory), Oscherleben (fuselage factory) and other targets. It was a seven combat wing formation of more than 1,000 B-17 bombers escorted by seventeen groups of US fighters, P-47s, P-51s, P-38s, and sixteen squadrons of RAF spitfires and Mustangs.

Six other combat wings crossed the Danish coast without a fighter escort to make a co-ordinated attack on the Fw 190 assembly complex at Tutow and two assigned targets east of Berlin.

Targets in the Leipzig area, Brunswick, and Bernburg were hit with excellent results. Over 239 B-17s dropped 1,984 × 500-lb GP bombs and 2,830 × 100-lb bombs from 21,500 feet. Each of the three factory targets at Mockau were saturated with bombs and photographs taken later showed that the Junkers bomb assembly factory was badly damaged, and offices and workshops were gutted from direct hits. Fires were still burning at the time the photographs were taken. The Erla Machinenwerk GMBH fighter assembly factory workshops were severely damaged by direct hits and two flight hangars were also hit. The Allgemeine Transport Bomber Assembly factory had three main assembly workshops that were severely damaged from direct hits and many craters were seen on the runway. The Erla Fighter components factory at Abtnaunddorf was obscured by smoke drifting from heavy fires at Heiterblick but it was possible that the large workshop was damaged. At Heiterblick the main works was covered by smoke.

Five of the ten most important factories in Leipzig suffered severe damage. The western part of the city was seriously affected, especially the industrial area east of the Plagwitz station where the largest wool-spinning factory and dye works in Europe was three-quarters destroyed by fire.

The 1st Bombardment Division lost seven B-17s. The 305th Bomb Group were attacked by a number of enemy fighters.

One German fighter pilot came off second best when *Feldwebel* Johannes de Vhiegher attacked a B-17 but was hit by return fire and his Bf 109 lost control and crashed at Eggstedt on the Kaiser Wilhem Canal. He baled out possibly too low and did not survive the landing. He is now buried at Vetersen.

417 B-17s attacked Leipzig/Mockau Erla assembly plant. Seven B-17s were lost; seven men were killed, seventeen wounded and seventy-two missing in action.

The operation on 20 February was a great success and Leipzig was left in flames. 1,028 bombers, 11,000 men and 832 fighter escort hit major aircraft-making centres.

After further attacks in February the Germans were faced with the problem of reorganising about two thirds of the total production of major Messerschmitt components and about the same proportion of final assembly operations, although the assembly facilities were less badly damaged.

The main plant at Heiterblick and the assembly plant at Mockau who manufactured Bf 109s all suffered heavily. The estimate was forty complete aircraft and an unknown number of component parts were destroyed at these two plants. The bombing also killed 450 workers who were in slit trenches and not well built air raid shelters as at Heiterblick.

The losses were light. Twenty-five bombers and four fighters failed to return but the Germans lost 153 fighters.

The 303rd Bomber Group (H) attacked two targets, the Junkers Aircraft Works at Leipzig and the industrial plants at Hettsedt.

The Junkers Aircraft Works were attacked from 19,000 feet and Hettsedt from 16,000 feet. Each aircraft carried 12 × 500-lb GP bombs and 42 × M-47 incendiary bombs. 34 aircraft were despatched and thirty-two attacked targets in two group formations.

One aircraft crash-landed at Little Staughton and two crewmen had minor injuries. Twenty-five to thirty enemy aircraft were reported but attacks were scattered and not pressed home.

Major Cole flying in 'Ole George' led 'A' Group. Five attacks from twenty enemy aircraft were reported but without any real effect. There was lots of smoke and fire over the targets but this did not prevent very accurate bombing.

The Group Bombardier Lieutenant Charles J. McClain was awarded the Distinguished Flying Cross for extraordinary achievement.

Lieutenant Vern L. Moncure recorded that it was the longest trip to date. 'We were in the air nearly nine hours.' On the outward trip they found 75 mph winds and it seemed they would not make it but on the return it was much faster. He was flying 'Thunderbird'. The majority of the B-17s had names such as 'Bam Bam', 'The Duchess', and 'Miss Bea Haven'.

On 23 February came a commendation from Lt General Spaatz to the 8th US Air Force.

> To be brought to all the attention of all members of your command. Sunday's great air battle was major contribution towards our ultimate victory. The performance of your bombers and fighters was magnificent. To all combat personnel participating in this splendid effort and to all the ground personnel whose help made this great fight possible, I send my hearty congratulations and my deep appreciation for their brilliance and effectiveness of his plan for accomplishing this operation. I desire to commend, particularly, Brigadier General Orville A. Anderson.
>
> Signed Spaatz

> I desire to add my own genuine appreciation for a magnificent job well done.   Signed Doolittle

A message from the Chief of the Air Staff RAF:

> For their magnificent performance during the past few days, please convey my hearty congratulations to all members of the Eight Air Force.

A Commendation received from Brigadier General Williams March 1944:

> 1. A studied interpretation of Strike Attack Photographs taken on the attack against military installations at Leipzig, Germany 20 February 1944, clearly indicates that your organisation distinguished itself by excellent precision bombing.
> 2. Although a deep penetration of Germany under adverse conditions was involved, the bombing run was conducted at proper interval and an excellent slighting operation, on assigned M.P.I. was accomplished.
> An analysis of the bombing results indicates that fifty-nine (59) percent, an exceptionally high percentage of the bombs dropped, struck within five hundred (500) feet of the M.P.I. and that one hundred (100) percent were placed within one thousand (1000) feet of

the M.P.I. These results are directly attributable to good formation flying and proper release of bombs from every aircraft in the Group. 3. I am especially pleased with the remarkable success on this operation, which is due, in large measure, to the untiring devotion to duty exemplified and contributed by all combat personnel of the 303rd Bombardment Group (h). In particular the following personnel, 359th Bombardment Squadron (h); lead aircraft, group formation, are to be commended for the outstanding teamwork which they displayed in assuming the success of this attack.

February 20 will be marked as probably the most important date in the air war of Germany. You and your crews are responsible for the most crushing defeat yet administered to the German Air Force. I can assure you the results of the mission will be felt in future operations. I further wish to commend you and your crews on the excellent air discipline demonstrated on this mission. This was evidenced by an assembly under difficult conditions and by orderly, well flown formations on return to England.

My heartiest congratulations on a difficult mission well done. I am proud to be a part of this command.

Signed Williams

The following is the Endorsement to Commendation received from Colonel D. Stevens:

1. The bombing carried out against Leipzig is a superior example of perfect precision bombing, and is a gratifying reward for long hours of diligent training and untiring devotion to duty.
2. It is indeed a pleasure to forward the above commendation for an outstanding performance. My hearty congratulations to all personnel of the 359th Bombardment Squadron (H), both ground and air, who made such an outstanding operation possible.

Signed Kermit D. Stevens,
Colonel, AC, Commanding.

2/Lt Carroll Ted Binder flew as a navigator in 'Pugnacious Peter', a brand new B-17 on 20 February. This was his first operation. The aircraft was flown by 2/Lt Jim Gorman who had flown on fourteen missions; the RAF would break a new pilot in by flying him with an experienced crew as a 'second dickie' and the US obviously did the same with new crewmen. 2/Lt

Ray Hofman would be second pilot to Gorman. Even though he was a navigator Ted still was, when required, an air gunner and had to clean and make sure his guns were working correctly. They had cleaned them the night before so it was only a last-minute check.

After take-off the order was given by Ted to test the guns but to be careful as there were so many aircraft around.

Fresh streams of smoke poured out from every part of the southern part of Leipzig. This was the good evidence of the fires started in the previous night's RAF raid. The last two minutes seemed to last for ever before the bombs were dropped on Leipzig.

All went well on the return trip and after half an hour they were again picked up by the fighter escort. It was a comforting sight when at least a dozen fighters were near at hand and three miles below the Spitfires. By the time he got to bed after interrogation, a meal and stripping and cleaning the guns it was 22.00 hours. They had taken off at 7.30 am.

On the six-day Big Week campaign 137 bombers were lost and 2,600 aircrew. There were 2,548 fighter support missions of which 712 aircraft were from the 9th and 413 from the 15th Air Forces with losses of twenty-eight.

On 29 February 1944 'Cabin in the Sky' was piloted by 1st Lt William Lawley Jr (Later Colonel) of the 364th Bomber Squadron, part of the 305th Bomber Group. As he left the target area over Leipzig because he could not release his bombs he was attacked by no fewer than twenty German fighters. In the initial attack the co-pilot was killed and eight of the crew wounded; he himself had deep wounds to his face, neck and hands. The aircraft had one engine on fire and a damaged wing that sent the aircraft into a vertical dive. Lawley was bleeding heavily but having got the dead co-pilot off the control column he managed to level out the aircraft at 12,000 feet and gave the order to bale out. Two of the crew could not bale out owing to their wounds and not being able to use their chutes. Despite losing the flight engineer who had baled out he decided to make for the UK. It was a five-hour flight but with badly wounded men in his crew he felt he had no choice. The fire was extinguished and the bombardier helped Lawley with the damaged controls. Over occupied France Lawley passed out through loss of blood and exposure from the smashed windscreen but after being revived he was able to release his bombs as he approached the English Channel. But as he approached the English shores an engine caught fire, then a second ran out of petrol then a third engine caught fire. He was now flying on one engine. Suddenly he saw an airfield that turned out to Redhill (a fighter strip) and he made a successful crash-landing.

The crew were unhurt in the landing and the flight engineer who had baled out over Germany was taken prisoner but survived the war. It turned out that the bomb racks were frozen hence the bombs had not released.

William Lawley Jr was awarded the highest decoration in the USA, the Medal of Honor, and served in the US Air Force until 1972. He died in 1999.

S/Sgt Archibald Mathies, his pilot Lt C. Nelson and navigator 2/Lt Walter E. Truemper were flying in a B-17 called 'Ten Horsepower' of the 510th Bomber Squadron of the 351st Bomber Group on 20 February 1944. Mathies was flying as flight engineer and ball turret gunner. The aircraft was attacked by enemy fighters and the co-pilot Bartley was killed.

Nelson was wounded and unconscious, the radio operator wounded and the B-17 badly damaged. Truemper managed to fly the aircraft back to base at Polebrook and to the Control Tower he volunteered with Mathies to try and land the damaged bomber. The other members of the crew were ordered to bale out but having seen from another aircraft the damage to the bomber Truemper was ordered by his commanding officer to bale out too. But he replied that the pilot was still alive but could not be moved and said he was going to try and land the B-17. He crashed in an open field on the third attempt. All three aboard including Mathies were killed.

He and Truemper were later awarded the Medal of Honor and also the Purple Heart, awarded to all US personnel wounded in action. He was twenty-five and had been born in Stonehouse, Scotland. One of the crew who had baled out over Germany was Lt Joseph R. Martin who was made a prisoner of war.

On 20 February Lt Warren O. Van Winkle was killed on an operation to Boehlen synthetic works near Leipzig. He was a pilot with the 409th Bomb Squadron of the 93rd Bomb Group. The flak was intense around Leipzig and Lt Winkle's aircraft was hit and badly damage by flak over the target and then attacked by fighters. Seven of the crew baled out and the aircraft crashed near Craula and he was killed in the crash.

He was awarded the US DFC, having completed twenty-five missions. This was presented to his wife posthumously along with the Purple Heart and Air Medal with three oak leaf clusters. He left a widow and a daughter who was only three months old and whom he never met.

Jimmy Stewart the famous Hollywood actor was a major and a pilot flying with the 8th Air Force in the UK. On 20 February he was Deputy Leader of a Combat Wing. When they reached Leipzig it was obvious that visual bombing was possible and so as per the briefing he took over on the lead position.

In spite of fighter attacks and later heavy anti-aircraft fire he held the formation together and directed bombing run over the target in such a manner that they were able to release their bombs with great accuracy.

Stewart was awarded the US DFC for this operation, his citation signed by Lt General Jimmy Doolittle. He was at the time flying with 703 Squadron of the 445th Bomb Group based at Tibenham, near Norwich.

The 401st Bomb Group (H) led by Colonel (later Brigadier General) Harold Bowman was later given a Distinguished Unit Citation and Colonel Bowman the Silver Star. Colonel Bowman was cited in the name of the President of the United States for his gallantry, tenacity of purpose and brilliant leadership while leading a heavy Bombardment Division and giving a crushing blow to the enemy's war effort.

General Jimmy Doolittle's orders were 'Win the Air War and isolate the battlefield'.

In other words, destroy the *Luftwaffe* and cut off the beaches of Normandy for the invasion.

The attacks were said to have only caused a two-month delay in aircraft production and it was predicted that German fighter production would peak in the summer of 1944. Speer explained to the author in 1980 a year before his death that because of the attacks production was far lower than his estimates. It is calculated that the loss was 15 to 20%. The loss in military aircraft was 31%.

Between 1 November 1943, and 1 April 1944, the number of single-engine Bf 109 and Fw 190 fighters that the German aircraft industry actually produced fell short of the figure planned by 4,115 aircraft. The number of twin-engine fighters and bombers produced fell short of the planned numbers by 700 aircraft. During that period the *Luftwaffe* was deprived of some 4,000 aircraft, which would have been available for the air war had this Anglo-American bombing assault on German aircraft industries not been launched.

On 2 November 1943 312 tons of bombs were dropped on the Wiener Neustadt Messerschmitt Bf 109 airframe works in Austria.

According to Giulio Douhet the only really effective aerial defence cannot be indirect. The 15th Air Force lost ten B-17s and in February 1944 in attacks on Austrian and Germany aircraft plants some eighty-nine of the 15th Air Force bombers were lost. This worked out as five times as many as those of the escort aircraft. Of course, Douhet would not have known about radar and the development of flak since his death.

It was estimated that between 30 February and 10 May 1944 about 2,000 to 2,500 aircraft were lost.

On 25 May 1944, 550 B-17s and 443 B-24s of the 8th Air Force attacked two German aircraft and component plants, and Mockau and Heiterblick factories. Fair to good results were recorded.

On 29 May the target was again Heiterblick and Erla the aircraft components factory and main works. They were manufacturing fuselages and wings etc for Bf 109s.

The greatest damage was in the north of the target where three large component-erecting shops had been hit. One suffered a heavily buckled roof. Other severe damage was seen in the south where the boiler house had been destroyed. Many other buildings in the west and south of the works were damage or destroyed. A small hutted camp on the opposite side of the road from Taugha Leipzig had suffered severe damage.

On the 29 May Mockau in Leipzig was also attacked. The weight of the attacks fell across the Allgemeine Transport bomber assembly factory, damaging the flight hangar and an assembly shop, and across the south-west corner of the landing ground.

T/Sgt William P. Mitchell Jnr flew with the 447th Bomb Group. 'Paper Doll II', a B-17 of 710 Squadron, had twenty-five yellow bombs painted on it to represent twenty-five missions and five Swastikas indicated the crew had shot down five German fighters. It had been with the 447th since 3 October 1944.

The US flew in formation and the less turbulence there was the tighter the formation could fly. The rear or fourth plane in each squadron became known as 'Tail End Charlie' although the crews themselves often called it 'Coffin Corner' as they would be the first to be attacked by fighters. The expression 'Flying Coffin' came from the German *Luftwaffe* pilots. In the early days they were not protected by Allied fighters and so were easy prey for the enemy fighters.

Each division had four wings and 447 led the 4th Wing. On 29 May the first aircraft of 447 took off at 8 am and a further twenty-five aircraft took off at thirty-second intervals. In total 993 B-17 and B-24s took off from the UK.

After five hours' flying the bomb doors were opened when they neared Leipzig, about 30 miles from the target. Bert Moran, William Mitchell's pilot, then checked each member of the crew and the navigator Rudolph Jacob reported to the bombardier Raymond Maguire that the Messerschmitt aircraft factory was 10 miles ahead. These members of the crew were not the original members and had only been in the crew since the 20th, the original members having been killed by friendly fire.

All was well until suddenly and just before the order 'bombs gone' came from Maguire they were hit by flak on the No. 3 engine, on the right side and close to the co-pilot John Higgs. The aircraft did a half roll onto its back and broke up. It crashed on the outskirts of eastern Seegerritz about 8 km from Leipzig. The site of the crash was over half a mile – the indication was that it had exploded before hitting the ground. The gunners managed to get out in time. But William being the radio operator/gunner was in the front part of the aircraft. Because of the angle of the aircraft and not being able to get to their chutes, all five in the front of the aircraft were killed and buried in Seegerritz on 30 May. But it would appear John Higgs, the sixth man to be killed, was not buried until 31 May as he was found under the aircraft.

William Mitchell Jnr was twenty and had joined the US Army Air Corps in January 1942. In 1949 his remains were returned to the USA and he is now buried in Tennessee, which means his grave can be visited by family and friends.

On 8 June 1944, two days after D-Day General Carl Spaatz commanding the US Strategic Air Forces in Europe issued orders that henceforth the primary aim of his forces would be to attack the enemy's oil supplies.

Near Munich a newly formed fourth *Gruppe* of JG3 was training hard with the new *Sturmbock* Fw 190 fighter, which was to be employed in the *Luftwaffe Sturmgruppe* tactics against the American formations when they attacked Germany. Each *Gruppe* of the *Sturmbock* Fw 190s was to be escorted into action by two *Gruppen* of Messerschmitt Bf 109s who were fitted with updated engines and reduced armament. They would deliver short sharp attacks en masse. It was thought that with so many aircraft and the length of the force it would be difficult for the fighters. A force of 1,000 bombers was divided into groups of thirty-six aircraft flying 4 miles apart. They were strung over 120 miles and far too large for the escort to completely cover.

An attack was made on 29 June 1944 when 1,150 aircraft (559 B-17s and 591 B-24s) were despatched. They were divided into three forces that would target one synthetic oil plant, aero engine works and aircraft assembly and components plants in Central Germany. The force was escorted by sixteen fighter groups. There were twelve assigned primary targets. Some 705 aircraft dropped 1,775 tons on nine primaries and other targets. Haze and high cloud in the UK made it difficult and caused some groups to abandon the mission. Many of the groups encountered intense flak. The second and third forces suffered enemy aircraft attacks at Leipzig and Boehlen.

The first force of 179 aircraft attacked a synthetic oil plant at Boehlen, of which 142 were able to drop their bombs on Boehlen and the secondary target Wittenburg.

The second force of 380 B-17s was despatched to attack an aero engine works, a ball-bearing works, a aircraft assembly works and two aircraft component plants in the Leipzig area. Because of cloud at 27,000 feet and contrail from 15,000 feet up group and combat wing assembly was hindered, which caused four wings to abandon the mission on the Mockau aircraft assembly and Abtnaundorf aircraft component factories. In total 129 aircraft attacked, dropping 242 tons of heavy bombs and fifty-eight tons of incendiary bombs on three primaries and other targets. The flak was intense to moderate and accurate at Leipzig. Thirty enemy aircraft attacked one wing in the Leipzig area and the damage was three aircraft lost, two to flak, and one crash-landed. In addition fourteen aircraft suffered major damage and sixty-two minor.

Forty-one aircraft attacked the Heiterblick aircraft component factory, nineteen the Leipzig ball-bearing works and thirty the Taueha aero engine works. The results were said to be poor. Damage was seen at Taueha-Mitteldeutsche Motorenwerke. One aero engine test shed had a large hole in the centre of the building caused by a direct hit and another suffered minor blast damage. At Heiterblick workshops and erecting shops were destroyed or damaged. At Abtnaundorf-erle Maschinonwerk no damage was observed.

The third force of 591 B-24s targeted one aircraft assembly plant, three aircraft components and two aero engine works in Aschersleben, Megdeburg, Oschewrsleben and Bernburg in the area of Leipzig.

This attack did not please Air Chief Marshal Lee-Mallory. General Spaatz was attacking oil and the German aircraft industry but Lee-Mallory in his diary entry of 29 June 1944 said that the US had chosen to go Leipzig to bomb aircraft factories whereas he wanted them to attack the big rail movement east of Paris to stem troop movement in the area of west and south-west of Paris. He thought the German army was the threat and not the *Luftwaffe*. He felt that if the German army was allowed to build up, the break out of the beach head would be difficult and another Anzio would be created. He went on to say that the Americans had no idea of balance and that they wanted to attack aircraft factories, come what may. He went on to say that the *Luftwaffe* was no sort of menace but the German army was. He wanted attacks to be made on rail yards with the idea of disrupting movement to the battle front.

Perhaps he was right but the attacks on the German Air Force and its source of aircraft meant there was less opposition in the air particularly at the time of the Normandy landings.

In Big Week thirteen major assaults on at least fifteen aircraft centres were made, the Allies dropping 18,000 tons of bombs. The Allies lost 387 bombers and thirty-seven fighters but forty-four German planes were shot down, which was more than they lost during the Battle of Britain.

Photo reconnaissance showed that 80% of German's twin-engined fighter production had been knocked out; 60% of Germany's single-engined production was completely destroyed. In addition these operations destroyed 25% of the *Reich*'s heavy bomber building capacity and 60% of transport production.

Further attacks by the US Air force were made on 7, 20 July, 28 July, and in 1945 on 27 February and 6 April.

On 7 July 1,129 Fortresses and Liberators set out to bomb aircraft factories in the Leipzig area and the synthetic oil plants at Boehlen. The AGO Focke Wulf works in Oschersleben was a particular target. Early in the morning of 7 July radar in Germany picked up air movement over East Anglia. The alarm went out as the force made its way to Germany and the warning was given to all flak batteries. Smoke pots on the ground were set off to generate smoke screens over potential targets. The German fighters were given the order over Magdeberg. The plan was for thirty aircraft of IV/JG3 escorted by sixty Bf 109s to attack the 100-mile long bomber stream at its mid-point. In one attack eleven B-24s were destroyed within a minute. The US 2nd Air Division lost twenty-eight Liberators that day. The majority were destroyed by the *Sturmgruppe*. They lost nine fighters shot down and three were damaged but it had been a very successful day for the *Luftwaffe*.

The damage from the three raids on 20 July 1944, 27 February 1945 and 6 April 1945 was distributed over the whole town. Business and residential damage was heaviest in the immediate vicinity of the main station, particularly to the north-west and in the south-west part of the town. Three priority industries, the town gas works and the Leipzig World Fair grounds reported to be carrying out war activities, had been moderately to severely damaged. The main station itself received only slight fresh damage but the railway facilities, goods depots, and loco depots had suffered more heavily.

On 6 April 321 bombers with fighter escort were despatched and bombs were dropped but no bursts were visible due to 10/10 cloud cover. The weight of the attack was across the junction of the three main lines north-east of the main passenger station. Although tracks were blocked, by the time photographs were taken one line each on the tracks to Halle and Riesa appeared to have been made serviceable. Sidings and sheds in the goods yards and storage sidings had been destroyed as were two of the locomotive depots. There was also damage to the probable post office station, but not to the main passenger station.

On railway bridges over roads on the lines to Halle and Dessau a number of small diggings were seen. It was thought that these may have been preparations for demolition.

The attack on 27 February was carried out by thirty-nine aircraft. The main attack was on the aircraft factories in Leipzig, and the secondary target was the marshalling yards.

On 7 July 1944 a force of 1,129 B-17s and B-24s set out to bomb aircraft factories in the Leipzig area plus synthetic oil plants at Boehlen, Leuna-Merseburg and Lutzkendorf. The Focke-Wulf works in Aschersleben was a prime target for the bombers and the Junkers plants at Bernburg. The force was led by Brigadier General William M. Gross, the commander of the 1st Bombing Division, in an aircraft of 600 Squadron.

The intense flak barrage towards Leipzig was bypassed but German fighters under Major Walther Dahl were in the air and heading towards the bomber force.

His force attacked a group of B-24s of the 492nd Bomb Group, which at the time lacked fighter cover. Just two rounds from the German Bf 109 fighter could take off the tail of a B-24, which was not as sturdy as the B-17.

The *Luftwaffe* were well organised but the US Liberators (B-24s) equipment could pick up the enemy fighter frequencies and heard the German pilots being ordered to attack the third formation as the first formation was too well protected for them to attack.

The 1st Division was assigned to attack the aircraft factories of the Erla complex and the 492nd Wing was briefed to attack the Junkers plants at Bernburg and Aschersleben. Each attacking division, 1, 2 and 3, were to depart the coast at separate points. The courses of the 1st and 3rd Divisions would converge, with the latter leading on a common penetration route to a point approximately 100 miles due west of Berlin. They would then fly to a point 40 miles south-west of the capital, feint towards Berlin to provoke a fight, and then turn sharply west and south to their respective targets in the Boehlen/Merseburg/Leipzig areas. It was felt that the 3rd and 1st Divisions, sweeping closest to Berlin, would evoke the most serious reactions, and the bulk of the available escort was assigned to these two forces.

Between April and August 1944 attacks were thought to have caused a loss of about 4,000 new aero engines, about four months' production and about 600 engines in for overhaul of used engines. One of the factories was at Leipzig/Taucha and one of two of the most important factories. In March its output should have been 450/500 engines per month but it was estimated that this was down to 300.

On 15 February 1945 the primary target was Bohlen an oil plant near Leipzig, but as it was obscured by cloud the secondary target Dresden was attacked instead. A total of 211 aircraft set out and 465.6 tons of bombs were dropped on the marshalling yards at Dresden.

The last operation by the 15th Air Force was on 25 April 1945 when the Skoda factory at Pilzen in Czechoslovakia was bombed. They were de-activated in Italy on the 15 September 1945.

The losses to the US 8th and 15th Air Forces in WWII were 30,000 men killed and 30,000 taken prisoner, which exceeded the total losses of the US Marine Corps and the US Navy. In addition, 14,000 were wounded. During WWII 135,000 aircrew flew with the 8th Air Force. They flew 687,462 sorties and dropped 1,307,117 tons of bombs. Those that survived became members of the 'Lucky Bastards Club'.

By September 1944 Germany had lost 75% of its fuel production and of the 1.5 million tons of bombs dropped on Germany 500,000 tons were dropped by B-17s. At the end of the war what remained of the German aircraft industry was sent to the USA, Britain, France and Russia.

In Speer's book *Inside the Third Reich* he mentions the bombing of the airframe plants of the aircraft industry in February 1944 rather than the engine factories. Destruction of them would have, Speer said, blocked any increase in aircraft manufacture, particularly as engine factories could not be dispersed among forests and caves.

The Death of the Ball Turret Gunner

From my mother's sleep I fell into the state,
And I hindered in its belly,
Till my wet fur froze,
Six miles from the earth,
Looked from its dream of life,
I woke to black flak and the nightmare fighters,
When I die they wash me out of the turret with a hose.

Randal Jarrell

Chapter 19

The Last Operations

—ᴍ—

The last operations to Leipzig or the area of the Leipzig were carried out in February, March and finally April 1945.

On 13/14 February an attack was carried out on the synthetic oil plant at Boehlen south of Leipzig. Owing to cloud conditions, the master bomber instructed the illuminators to retain their flares and directed two main forces to bomb the near edge of the green target indicators' glow and later its centre. The markers appeared to have been rather scattered and bombing was considered to have dispersed over the marked area. For this operation 211 Halifaxes of 4 Group, 115 Halifaxes of 6 Group, and thirty-four Lancasters and eight Mosquitoes of 8 Pathfinder Group were despatched. Of this force 186 of the 211 despatched, 107 of the 115 despatched and twenty-eight of the forty-two despatched of 8 Group attacked the target.

It was again attacked on 19/20 February. This time 237 out of 254 Lancasters despatched attacked and three out of six Mosquitoes despatched of 5 Group. It was not a success owing, it was thought, to the Master Bomber Wing Commander Benjamin DFC and Bar of 627 Squadron being shot down by flak over the target. There was no evidence of where any of the main bombing fell but reconnaissance showed that only superficial damage was made. The flak was moderate and decreased as the attack developed. Fighter opposition was slight.

On 22 February came Operation *Clarion* when 10,000 Allied planes were airborne for targets all over Europe, one being the Baumsef marshalling yards near Leipzig, attacked by the US 9th Air Force. This meant the end of movement for the German army.

On 5/6 March Boehlen was again attacked by 248 Lancasters and ten Mosquitoes of 5 Group. But because the area was covered by cloud only limited damage was done to the oil refinery.

On 20/21 March came another attack on Bohlen, this time by 224

Lancasters and eleven Mosquitoes of 5 Group. This time the operation was a success and the bombing accurate. The plant was still out of action when the Americans captured the area in April 1945.

On 10 April there was a daytime attack by Bomber Command. The targets in Leipzig were the Engedof and Mockau marshalling yards. The former attack was carried out by 110 Lancasters of 6 Group and eighteen Lancasters and six Mosquitoes of 8 Pathfinder Force. The latter raid at Mockau was carried out by ninety Halifaxes of 6 Group and 8 Pathfinder Group.

The two forces flew throughout in three compact boxes presenting a formation one mile wide and 3,000 feet deep with a fighter escort. Skirting north of the Ruhr they made a rendezvous with six Mustang squadrons south of Osnabruck and with a further seven squadrons later. The whole force turned south-east on to a leg of nearly 70 nautical miles to the targets. En route there were some signs of Me 262 jet-propelled fighters. The weather was excellent and the visibility clear. The crews were able to map read to the target and a good concentration of bombing was reported around the aiming point with smoke and dust rising up to 10,000 feet. Two explosions were seen, one emitting black oily smoke. Only two aircraft were reported missing.

The daylight attack was followed by a night attack on the marshalling yards at Wahren. This was carried out by seventy-six Lancasters and eleven Mosquitoes of 5 Group and three from 8 Pathfinder Group. It was a clear night and the marking was on time and accurate.

But because the fuses of the bombs had a long delay no results were observed apart from one violent explosion 100 yards west of the marking point. The flak defence accuracy was negligible despite there still being (even at this later stage in the war) over a 100 guns in Leipzig, and 100 to 2,150 searchlights reported in a wide belt in the Leipzig area. But the fighter attacks were considerable. Two Fw 190s and one Ju 88 fighter were claimed as a destroyed. Six aircraft of Bomber Command were reported missing.

Photographs taken on 11 April showed heavy damage, and some of the wagons were still burning.

F/O Cameron RAAF flying Lancaster HE739-T of 630 Squadron was on his bombing run when the rear gunner F/Sgt Gerald Bourner, aged twenty-two and from Bournemouth, heard two loud bangs followed by a fire in the fuselage. They had been hit by a fighter. The order to bale out was given and Bourner jumped out and landed in a ploughed field about six miles north of Leipzig.

He hid his parachute and harness etc in a ditch and made his way down a road in a westerly direction but had not gone very far when he met his bomb aimer F/Sgt Grenville Gould, aged twenty-two and from Leamington Spa. They continued on together but when daylight came they hid in a haystack where they were discovered by two Poles who gave them food. As there was little cover in the area they decided about midday to move on. In between Leipzig and Halle in the area of Landsberg they were met by two British Army POWs from a nearby working camp. There had been an air attack in the neighbourhood and the working party had scattered. They then arranged to join the working party and that night they met up again with the army POWs who provided army clothing and boots. On the morning of 13 April at about 1000 hours the Germans evacuated the camp and they joined in the march towards a farm at Mutzclena where they stayed along with their guards until liberated by American troops on 19 April 1945.

They had both been in the RAF for two years. F/Sgt Bourner had been a draftsman and Gould an engineer in civilian life. F/O Cameron was a POW as were three other members of the crew; the final member of the crew was killed.

Chapter 20

Post-war

—ᴍ—

Between September 1939 and 2/3 May 1945 when the last operation by Bomber Command was carried out, they had mounted 391,137 bomber sorties against German targets. They had dropped 47,250 mines, sinking or damaging 1,000 ships, which was more than any other branch of the RAF and more than sunk by the Royal Navy. The cost was heavy with 47,293 men lost on operations and in training of which 37,637 were lost over Germany.

The results from Bomber Command operations were impressive. The Germans' shortage of aircraft, guns, tanks, ammunition, locomotives, rolling stock, lorries and clothing was down to the bombing operations. At the Ardennes the Allied bombers meant the downfall of the offensive in December 1944. A lack of petrol and oil, and the destruction of the railways paralysed the movement of German troops.

The destruction of industrial towns prevented the production of arms and ammunition.

Field Marshal Kesselring gave three reasons for Germany's defeat:

1. Allied strategic bombing behind the German lines.
2. Attacks by low-flying Allied aircraft.
3. Terror raids against the German civilian.

General Karl Koller, Chief of the German Staff and the head of *Luftwaffe* operations, said the Germans lost the war because they did not attain air supremacy. Everything else must take second place. The man who loads or fires a field gun is a military target; so is the gun and the ammunition for it. The driver who transports the ammunition to the base or the ammunition dump, the men who make the weapons in the factories, the gas and electricity that kept the factory going – were they not targets?

In 1945, Churchill put Harris up for a peerage but Clement Attlee who was now the new Prime Minister refused the recommendation and also a campaign medal for Bomber Command.

It was thought that a John Strachey, whom Harris had some reservations about when he joined the RAF and then transferred to the Air Ministry as an air commentator, had a hand in Harris's rejection. Harris's reservations about Strachey in the RAF stemmed from the fact that in 1929–31 he was Parliamentary Private Secretary to Oswald Mosley. He broke away from the Fascists in 1940 when he joined the RAF. Harris had made a request to have Strachey removed from within the Directorate of Bombing Operations; this is said to be due to his changeable political persuasions. In 1945 Strachey was now Under-Secretary of State for Air and is credited for Harris being left out of the Victory Honours List.

All other commanders such as Montgomery, Alexander, Fraser and Tedder were made either viscounts or barons. Harris received nothing although in 1946 he was and delighted to become a Marshal of the Royal Air Force.

For over sixty years moves have been made for a medal to be awarded to the men of Bomber Command, ground crew as well as aircrew. All attempts so far have failed.

In 1945 Churchill wrote to Harris, the AOC of Bomber Command.

All your operations were planned with great care and skill. They were executed in the face of desperate opposition and appalling hazards, they made a decisive contribution to Germany's final defeat. The conduct of the operations demonstrated the fiery gallant spirit which animated your aircrews, and the high sense of duty of all ranks under your command. I believe that the massive achievements of Bomber Command will long be remembered as an example of duty nobly done.

The raid on Dresden in February 1945 was chaired by Attlee, then the deputy prime minister, who approved the operation. Churchill was in Yalta at the time.

In January 1946, Churchill wrote to Attlee:

No C-in-C in the RAF after Lord Dowding bore so heavy burden as he and none contributed more distinguished qualities to the discharge of his duty. As Minister of Defence, I had the opportunity and the duty of watching his work very closely and I greatly admired the manner in which he bore the altogether peculiar stresses of planning and approving these repeated, dangerous and costly raids far into the heart of the enemy's country.

For nearly four years, he bore the most painful responsibilities and never lost the confidence or loyalty of Bomber Command, in spite of the fact that it endured losses equalled only, in severity, by those of our submarines in the Mediterranean.

Unmoved by Churchill's reasoning, Attlee would not reverse his decision. It is widely known that although approving and going along with the bombing campaign he disliked Harris and his decisions.

Germany began the war with great numerical superiority in aircraft, and succeeded against little opposition. As a consequence the Germans delayed making necessary changes and moving forward. When they finally make changes it is thought they then went too far and made too many.

It is a widely held view that many of these changes were due to parts shortage caused by bombardment. The Daimler-Benz 603 engine was unreliable because modifications for sleeve bearings led to engine malfunction and caused many accidents.

General Werner Kreipe who was in command of flying training stated that Hitler, Goering and the General Staff never understood the significance of the power they were against because of the early conquests in Europe.

And it was not until 1 March 1944 and only after effective attacks on the German fighter aircraft industry that fighters were given priority over tanks, U-Boats, flak guns, and V-weapons. Kreipe went on to say the German army general staffs became loaded down with Nazi Party fanatics whose belief was that a quick victory could be had on the ground and who thwarted a pre-war *Luftwaffe* plan for a strategic air force.

In April 1944 after the attacks on the fighter industry they then decided to go all out on defensive fighter production. General Adolph Galland who commanded the fighter arm of the German air force urged the production of 5,000 fighters a month to take on the UK's bomber offensive and regain command of the air.

But Goering opposed this and wanted a bomber force as well as a fighter force. The problem was a lack of manpower and training facilities, and importantly a shortage of aviation fuel. Goering wanted an amended plan of reduced fighter production and an increase in bomber production, which Galland termed 'entirely unrealistic'.

Hitler's thought that the Me 262 jet aircraft, which he named *Blitzbomber*, should be used as a bomber. To support this desire Messerschmitt promised him that it could carry a 1,000 kg bomb. In theory it never ever carried anything more than a 500 kg bomb. But along with Hitler the Nazi Party was fully behind a bombing policy. Hitler's opinion about the Galland and Goering plan was that the Me 262 should be used as a fighter-bomber. He maintained this idea until October 1944 in which time the Me 262 had achieved nothing as a fighter-bomber. It was only then that

Hitler relented to Galland and a few Me 262s were released to the fighter arm of the *Luftwaffe*.

Speer said that but for the bombing of the fighter industry he could have produced 30 to 50% more fighter planes. Much of his labour force was used in the repair and reconstruction of bomb damage, and defence measures such as dispersing industry at Normandy again because of the bombing and underground factories. He estimated 250,000 and 300,000 were employed in this work. He was never able to stop the use of men and materials for expansion of basic production.

Speer said at the end of the war 'One cannot win aerial warfare through cement and tunnels.'

In 1960, Attlee said that he thought Harris not frightfully good as a leader of Bomber Command and insisted that all attacks on cities did not achieve as much as he would have done if he had made more effective use of his bombs. Harris replied that targets and strategy was decided by the government of the time in which Attlee was a prominent member. Also, the decision to bomb industrial cities for morale effect was made, and in force, before he became CinC Bomber Command.

Over the years from time to time Bomber Command, and in its particular attacks against Dresden and Hamburg, has come under attack. However, over the last four or five years people have been able to read and see documentaries of the contribution Bomber Command made and there has been a much more balanced discussion about what had to be done if we were to win WWII.

But in 1953 when Churchill again came to power he made up for his actions in April 1945, when he did not support Harris as much as he should have done, and made him a baronet.

The official history of *The Strategic Air Offensive Against Germany* did not help but rather over many years put fuel on the fire of the actions of Bomber Command. It made direct attacks on Harris's actions and stated that much of the bombing effort was wasted. One of the authors of this history, Sir Charles Webster, was clearly opposed to the bombing offensive. Although he spoke to Harris, he was clearly going through the motions of giving a balanced overview of the offensive and already knew what he was going to write. Even the former Chief of the Air Staff Sir Charles Portal refused to have any part of the history but did intercede when certain offensive passages were brought to his notice and insisted they were withdrawn. The strangest thing is there is no evidence that the authors interviewed Dr Albert Speer who one would have thought would have been at the top of the list to be interviewed. Perhaps he would have brought things to their notice that they did not want to hear and would have had to include. Harris was always to the time he died a great admirer of the Bomber Command ground crews.

In 1983, the Bomber Command Museum was opened by the Queen Mother and Sir Arthur Harris.

A monument to Bomber Command is now on the cards to be erected in London.

Bomber County

The skies are empty now as darkness falls,
The bare deserted runways scarred with weeds
Across the lonely fen a night bird calls,
The wind sighs softly in the whispering reeds.

A fitful moon rides through the cloudy blue,
A bomber's moon, remembered now no more,
Where once the very air vibrated to
The mighty Merlin engines' throbbing roar.

Dispersal huts stand crumbling and forlorn,
Their broken windows open to the rain,
The taxi track is fringed with waving corn,
The echoing hangars used for storing grain.

Upon the cracking tarmac wander sheep,
A derelict crew-room door creaks in the breeze,
The silent world around is lost in sleep
And stars are twinkling far above the trees.

Those very stars which were a friendly aid
To those who flew upon the wings of night,
The crews who never grudged the price they paid
To keep aglow the flam of freedom's right.

There is no flare path now to show the way,
And guide the homing bombers to the ground
The old control tower stands in gaunt decay,
In silence and in darkness wrapped around.

Remember those who flew, across the years,
Those bright young lives they gave so long ago,
No looking back with bitterness or tears,
But thankfulness – for they would wish it so.

Audrey Grealy

Appendix

Losses at Leipzig

—◊◊◊—

20/21 October 1943

Squadron and Aircraft	*Crew*
7 Squadron Lancaster JB175-A Hit by a night fighter flown by Oblt Heinz-Wolfgang Schnaufer IV/NJG1	F/S D.M. Watson killed Sgt F.E. White killed Sgt E. Carter killed Sgt D.S. Wilson killed Sgt E.C. Pocknell killed Sgt L.W. Searle killed F/S K. Gore killed Buried at Gieten, Holland
7 Squadron Lancaster JA907-U Hit by a night fighter and crashed at Oudleusen, Holland then burst into flames. Sgt Lashford baled out at low level	F/O J.W. Leitch DFC RAAF killed F/Lt A.G. MacLeod DFC killed Sgt J. Hardy killed Sgt F.W. Lashford POW F/S C.B. Jolliffe DFM killed F/S F.E. Noble killed F/S F. Simmonds killed Those killed buried at Dalfsen
57 Squadron Lancaster JB234-E	P/O F.E.S. Parker killed F/O P.S. Porteus killed Sgt J. O'Leary killed Sgt R.A. Chumbley killed Sgt C.T. Halston killed F/S J.K. Read RAAF killed

| | Sgt C. Wharton killed |
| | Crew buried in Berlin |

83 Squadron Lancaster JA701-E	W/O S.G.W. Hall killed
	Sgt E.J. Boardman killed
	F/S I.L. Richards killed
	Sgt J. Manderson killed
	P/O S.J. Bell killed
	F/S T.A. Martin killed
	Sgt H.J. Bird killed
	Names on the Runneymede Memorial

83 Squadron Lancaster JB154-A	S/L R.J. Manton RCAF killed
Hit by a night fighter and crashed at	Sgt A.E. Evans killed
Assen	S/L A.G.A. Cochrane DFC killed
	F/S A.C. Branch DFM killed
	F/S R.L. Taylor killed
	Sgt F. Earnshaw killed
	F/S C.W. Foster killed
	Crew buried in the Southern General Cemetery

97 Squadron Lancaster JB275-H	P/O K. Painter killed
Crashed at Falkenburg	Sgt R.C. Saunders POW *Stalag* 4B
	Sgt T. Andrews POW *Stalag* 4B
	Sgt M. Deacon killed
	Sgt J.E. Bacon killed
	Sgt S.F. Hone killed
	Sgt D.W. Angell killed
	Those killed buried in Berlin

100 Squadron Lancaster ED555-A	P/O T.L. Simpson killed
Crashed at Elderwolde	Sgt L. Cohen killed
	Sgt A.W. Lower killed
	Sgt P.R. Cowling killed
	Sgt C.W. Gibb killed
	F/S D. Storey RCAF killed
	Crew buried at Elde

103 Squadron Lancaster ED881-S	W/O A.H. Pargeter RNAF killed Sgt H.E. Thompson killed Sgt H. Sykes killed Sgt W.G. Cave killed Sgt L. Cross killed Sgt J.C. MacLean killed Sgt J.P. Neville killed F/S E.H. Willcocks killed 2/Pilot Names on the Runneymede Memorial
106 Squadron Lancaster ED358-T	P/O P. Hanavan killed F/O S. Smith killed A/F/Lt R.W. Moore killed Sgt D.E. Day killed F/O A.W. Porter RCAF killed Sgt E.J. Plumridge killed Sgt F.G. Smith killed F/Lt G.C Cooper killed 2/Pilot Crew buried in Berlin
115 Squadron Lancaster DS725-F Crashed at Gross Engersen	F/Lt J.T. Anderson killed Sgt D.L.W. Horn killed F/O D.J. Boston killed Sgt G.H.M. Batten killed F/O F.G. Andrews killed Sgt C.W. Gibb killed F/S F. Cowrie killed F/O R.S. Clements killed 2/Pilot Crew buried in Berlin
166 Squadron Lancaster LM341-B Went out of control after icing up Crew ordered to bale out when starboard wing broke off. Sgt Hutchins sucked out	Sgt S.T. Athey killed F/S H. Millard killed Sgt G.D. Hutchins POW *Stalag* 4B Sgt T.K. Wardley killed Sgt L.J. Lawrence killed Sgt L.R. Hall killed

	Sgt R.E. Scott killed
	Those killed buried in Berlin
166 Squadron Lancaster LM312-K	Sgt D. Bartley killed Sgt C.A. Maskell killed Sgt E.F.M. Barham killed Sgt L.A. Steele killed F/S C.R.A. Walker RCAF killed Sgt G. Read killed Sgt J.I. Wilson RCAF killed
	Crew buried in Berlin
405 Squadron Lancaster JB348-R Crashed at Harrenstate where the crew that were killed were originally buried	P/O K.R. Wood RAAF F/O J.N.R. Redpath RCAF F/S W.H. Hedley killed Sgt J.H. Lovelock killed Sgt F.W. Bundy killed W/O 1 D.O. Johnson RCAF POW *Stalag* 4B F/S E.C. Brunet RCAF killed later WOII
	Those killed buried in the Reichswald War Cemetery
619 Squadron Lancaster EE114-B Crashed at Longweld nr Hannover	P/O C. Firth killed F/S C.M.D. Wright RCAF killed Sgt G.W. Dillnut killed Sgt G.M. Weighell killed Sgt D. Demaine killed Sgt M. Jones killed Sgt A.G. Osborne killed
	Crew buried in Hannover
625 Squadron Lancaster JA714-R Crashed in the sea at Waddensee after being hit by flak over the Dutch coast	F/O W.P.Cameron RCAF killed Sgt L.N. Wild killed Sgt J.H. Hawkins killed Sgt J.W. Diggle killed P/O V.A. Snook RCAF killed

Washed up 26/11/43
P/O C.W. McFarlane RCAF
killed
Sgt F.A. Porter killed

P/O Snook buried in
Westersschilling
The remainder of the crew
names on the Runneymede
Memorial

Crashed in the sea

3/4 December 1943

7 Squadron Lancaster JA685-Z Crashed at Meppel	Sgt C.H. Phillips POW *Stalag* 357 Sgt J.H.F. Cochrane killed Sgt G.W. Hewitt killed Sgt B. Cooper POW *Stalag* 4B Sgt W.R.J. Craze POW *Stalag* 4B Sgt R.V.D. Smith killed Sgt A.H. Bale killed Those killed buried in Cransberge
10 Squadron Halifax HX191-J	P/O F.J.T. Walker killed Sgt W. Brock POW *Stalag* L1 Sgt J. McNeil POW *Stalag* L6 and 357 Sgt D. Hudson killed Sgt G. Slaughter killed Sgt R. Miles killed Sgt F.G. Selby killed Sgt Redbourne killed 2/Pilot
35 Squadron Halifax LW343-U	F/O D.J.H. Cheal POW *Stalag* L1 P/O J.C. Bonet RCAF POW *Stalag* L1

Sgt H.H. Smith POW *Stalag* 4B
Sgt K. Holt killed
P/O E.A. Alliston killed
Shy J.A.N. McKenzie killed
Sgt F.J. Diamond killed

Those killed buried in Bergen-
op-Zoom

51 Squadron Halifax HR782– Hit by flak	Sgt S. Ainsworth killed Sgt R.D. Brown POW *Stalag* 4B Sgt M. Cotten POW Sgt H.G. Tarrant killed Sgt A.H. Ashley POW *Stalag* 4B Sgt H.J. Bondett POW *Stalag* 4B Sgt K.D. Wheeler POW Those killed buried in Rheinberg
51 Squadron Halifax HR732–	P/O A.J. Salvage killed P/O F.J. Baker killed F/S M. Hampson killed Sgt W.W.B. Hamilton killed F/S I.G. Davies killed Sgt R.J. Edwards killed F/S D.W. Milliken RCAF killed All on Runnymede Memorial
76 Squadron Halifax LV902–H	F/S I.M. Lowe RCAF killed later WOII F/S W.R.K. Boles RCAF killed Sgt L. Newey killed Sgt S. Jones killed F/O J. Stott killed Sgt J.R.W. Kerner killed Sgt J.R.E. Nadeau RCAF killed Crew names on Runneymede Memorial

77 Squadron Halifax DT730-B	F/O R.J. Casley killed F/S C.R. Boyd killed P/O J. Miller killed Sgt F.E. Ryder killed F/S W.J.H. Webb killed F/S W.R. Farrell killed F/S K.E. Lees RCAF POW *Stalag* 4B F/S R.M. Holingworth RAAF killed 2/Pilot Those killed buried at Becklingen War Cemetery
78 Squadron Halifax LW313-0 Crashed Bad Muenster am Stein	F/Sgt G. Cunningham killed Sgt H. Hiley POW *Stalag* 4B and L3 Sgt G.A. Kennaby POW *Stalag* 4B Sgt K. Hughes POW *Stalag* 4B F/S H. Wright RCAF killed Sgt P.J. Regan RCAF died as a POW in hospital Sgt E. Evans killed Those killed buried at Rheinberg Cemetery
97 Squadron Lancaster JD232-U	P/O A.J. Coleman RAAF killed F/S L.G.K. Lock killed F/S C.P. Matthews killed Sgt D. Moore killed F/S V.N. Turner RNAF killed Sgt C.R.W. Jones killed Sgt J.E. Marchant RCAF killed Names on the Runneymede Memorial
100 Squadron Lancaster JB291– Crashed nr Leipzig	F/O C.E.J. Plumridge POW later F/Lt repatriated 2.2.45 Leittia F/O A.C. Petley-Jones RCAF POW Sgt F.A.W. Palmer POW *Stalag* 4B/344

Sgt A. Hamilton POW *Stalag* 4B
Sgt A.J. Kirby killed
Sgt W. Mason killed
Sgt D.P. Lawrence killed

Those killed buried in Berlin

---

102 Squadron Halifax JD303–S	F/O E.L.J. Key killed F/O T.H. Jackson killed Sgt G.W. Guy POW *Stalag* 4B Sgt W.R. Cox killed F/O J.A. Tippins POW *Stalag* L1 F/S R.J. Argent killed Sgt C.W. Phillips killed All killed buried in Berlin

---

115 Squadron Lancaster DS765–A	F/Sgt S.P. Clark DFM killed Sgt A.E. Watkins killed Sgt R.C. Rigg killed Sgt K.R. Butcher killed F/O A.E. Busby killed Sgt A.W. Dowsett DFM killed Sgt F.F. Scott killed F/Sgt Clark, F/O Busby, and Sgt Dowset are buried in Berlin. The remainder are on the Runneymede Memorial.

---

405 Squadron Lancaster JB222–M	F/O N.H. Bowring killed F/Lt G. Belcher killed WOII G.W. Acorn RCAF killed P/O G.C. Holland killed P/O J. Anderson killed F/S G.A. Davis DFM killed F/S C.M. Holder killed Crew buried in Berlin

---

426 Squadron Lancaster DS733–L Crashed at Espel	F/S R.G. Sturley RCAF, died as a POW 4.12.43 P/O D.A. Clark RCAF POW *Stalag* L1 P/O W.P. Neale RCAF killed Sgt H.W. Booth POW *Stalag* 4B

P/O D.T. Cooper RCAF POW
Stalag L1
Sgt A. Wolkowski RCAF died
of wounds 4.12.43
Sgt J.B.L. Legault RCAF killed

Sgt Wolkowski and Sgt Legault
are buried in the Reichswald
War Cemetery, the remainder
that were killed are on the
Runneymede Memorial

429 Squadron Halifax JD374-M	P/O S.R. Kelso RCAF killed F/S H.M. Shade RCAF killed F/S C.H. Schofield POW *Stalag* 4B Sgt R.H.McD. Grant RCAF POW *Stalag* 4B F/S F.F. Norro RCAF killed Sgt K.H. Bucholtz RCAF POW *Stalag* 4B F/S L.E. Cabana RCAF killed Those killed buried at Sage War Cemetery
429 Squadron Halifax JD361-Y	P/O B.G. Hingston RCAF killed F/S H.M. Brown RCAF POW *Stalag* L1 Sgt J.R. Williams killed F/S J.C. Lochead killed Sgt G.R. Hooper RCAF killed F/S D.G. Hamilton RCAF killed F/O W.E. Hampton RCAF killed 2/Pilot Those killed buried in Berlin
431 Squadron Halifax LY968-K Crashed at Gross Hehlen/Celle	F/O A.W. Edgar RCAF killed F/S R.J. Henry RCAF POW *Stalag* L7 W/O M.O. Dechambean RCAF POW *Stalag* 4B Sgt N.T. Anderson RCAF killed

P/O A.E. Freeman RCAF
POW *Stalag* L1
Sgt J.C. Arsenault RCAF POW
Stalag 4B
Sgt M.V. Phillips killed

Those killed buried in Hannover

431 Squadron Halifax LK685–C Shot down over Bremen	F/S R.W. Ritchie RCAF killed later WOII, buried in Becklingen F/O J.B Shannon RCAF POW *Stalag* L1 Sgt V. Jenkins POW *Stalag* 4B F/S S.J.S. Fulham RCAF POW *Stalag* L1 Sgt B.R. Horning RCAF POW *Stalag* 357 Sgt J.D. MacMillan POW *Stalag* 4B Sgt D. Lynford-Pike POW
431 Squadron Halifax LK898–	S/L R.G. Cook DFC RCAF killed P/O M.V. Snow RCAF killed Sgt H.J.R. Brookman killed Sgt G Wood killed F/Lt E.L. Lister killed Sgt W.J. Rattiran RCAF killed Sgt J. Williamson RCAF killed All buried in Becklingen
431 Squadron Halifax EB137–N	F/S F.A. Long killed F/S R.R. Steven killed F/S W.C. Burley killed Sgt G. Heider RCAF killed F/S G.F. Brown killed P/O G.H. Armstrong RCAF killed Sgt J.G. L'Argent killed All buried in Bergen War Cemetery

576 Squadron Lancaster JB550-J

F/S R.B. Mathews killed
F/O R.S. Bowden killed
Sgt C.H. Bryram killed
Sgt A.D. Roulson killed
F/S R.H. Sinclair RNZAF
killed
Sgt D.J. Bealey killed
Sgt D.W. Blackman killed

All buried in Berlin

---

625 Squadron Lancaster ED392-Q
Exploded in the air throwing the
survivors clear

Sqn Ldr E.Q. Moody POW
Stalag L1
P/O E.L. Jacobs POW *Stalag*
L1
Sgt R.A. Boothman killed
Sgt M. Boylan killed
Sgt J. Earle killed
Sgt O.V. Kent killed
W/O R. Reid killed

Those killed buried in Hannover

---

630 Squadron Lancaster ED920-D
Crashed at Volgfelde

P/O J. Syme RAAF killed
Sgt E. Hubbert killed
Sgt J.D. Cattley POW *Stalag* 4B
Sgt G. Leggott killed
F/O J.C. Doherty killed
Sgt K. Swinchatt killed
Sgt J. Heron killed

P/O Syme, Sgts Hubbert, and
Leggott on the Runneymede
Memorial
The remainder are buried in
Berlin

19/20 February 1944

---

7 Squadron Lancaster ND470-S
Crashed Tollwitz, Germany
Aircraft blew up
Hit by a night fighter and exploded –

S/L F.B. Curtis POW
F/Lt C. Bush DFC killed
F/S E.A. Howe killed
Sgt K.F. Scammell killed

two survivors blown clear
S/L Nixon awarded DFM in 1941
with 51 Squadron

F/Sgt R.F. Jordon POW *Stalag* 357
P/O A.D. Johnson killed
WO II H.R. McKay RCAF killed
S/L T.R. Nixon DFC DFM killed
(2/Pilot Bombing Leader 7 Squadron)

Those killed buried in Berlin

---

7 Squadron Lancaster JB468-U
Crashed Jessen/Elster, Germany
Shot down by a night fighter from below
and it is believed that S/L Davis tried
to crash-land the aircraft

S/L K.G. Davis killed
F/O R.F.B. Powell POW *Stalag* 357
F/Lt F. Stephenson POW *Stalag* III
F/O K. Marriott DFM killed in combat
Sgt J.S. Woolston POW *Stalag* 357
F/Sgt A. Grange DFM POW Died a POW 21.2.44
Sgt R. Child POW *Stalag* VI

Those killed buried in Berlin

---

9 Squadron Lancaster W5010-Z
Crashed Luderitz-Dolle, Germany
Crew were originally buried here

F/Sgt D.P.J. Froud killed
Sgt F. Harman killed
Sgt D.B. Carlick killed
F/Sgt L.T. Fairclough killed
Sgt W.H. Shirley killed
Sgt S.L. Jones killed
P/O R.L. Biers killed RCAF

Crew buried in Berlin

---

10 Squadron Halifax LW324-J
Crashed nr Wesendorf
Shot down by Oblt Brinkhaus
in a Ju 88 of NJG2

F/Sgt J.L. Walker POW
Sgt R. McArthur POW
Sgt T. Stewart POW
Sgt J. Thorpe POW
Sgt D.H. Thomas POW
Sgt P. Croal POW
Sgt H. Hopkinson POW

All POW at *Stalag* L6/357

12 Squadron Lancaster ND410-Y Crashed in the sea off Holland	P/O P.D. Wright killed P/O E. Travers-Clarke killed (Son of Lt Gen Sir Travers-Clarke) P/O A.J. Gillis killed RCAF, washed up 30.4.44 F/Sgt B.A. Stratton killed Sgt B.G. White killed Sgt T. White killed, washed up 27.4.44 Sgt T.E. Roe killed, washed up 7.5.44 Ouddorp P/O Gillis and Sgt White buried in Bergen-op-Zoom Sgt Roe buried in Duddorp The names of the remainder of the crew are on the Runneymede Memorial
12 Squadron Lancaster JB609-F Crashed Elspeet nr Appledoorn Shot down by a night fighter flown by Oblt Hans-Henry Augenstein of III/NJG1	F/Sgt N.C. Bowker killed Sgt A.I. Corlett killed Sgt E. Gedge killed Sgt H.G. Williams killed Sgt F.W. Burdett killed W/O J. May killed Sgt E.S. Goodridge killed Crew buried Harderwijk
15 SquadronSquadron Lancaster R5739-K Crashed Gertzberg nr Eisenberg	P/O M.J. Hurley RAAF killed F/Sgt C.S. Benson RNZAF killed F/O J. Fenley killed F/Sgt A.Mc. Woodford killed F/O L. Chalmers RCAF killed Sgt H.F. Moroni killed F/Sgt G. McMaster RAAF killed Sgt D.F. Frame POW *Stalag* 357 F/Sgt A .M. Woodford RAAF killed Those killed buried in Berlin

35 Squadron Halifax HX325-J Crashed Berenbostel Attacked by a Ju 88 flown by Fw Frank NJG5 Sale on his 50th operation	S/L J. Sale RCAF DSO* DFC Died while a POW in hospital, buried in Choloy S/L G.H.F. Carter DFC* POW *Stalag* L3 F/Lt B.O. Bodnar DFC POW *Stalag* 357 F/Lt H.J. Rogers POW *Stalag* 357 F/Lt R.L. Lamb POW *Stalag* 357 F/Sgt K.K. Knight killed in combat, buried in Hannover W/O B.H. Cross DFC DFM POW
35 Squadron Halifax LV793-B Crashed nr Alast, Brandenberg Shot down by Oblt Schulte NJG5	F/Lt W. McTurk POW *Stalag* L3 Sgt T.C. Kerr POW *Stalag* L6/357 F/O E.J. Trickey POW *Stalag* L3 W/O R. Wright killed, buried in Berlin F/Sgt W.H. McCormick killed, on Runnymede Memorial F/Sgt G. Forman killed, buried in Berlin F/Sgt A.F. Poynton killed, on Runnymede Memorial
35 Squadron Halifax LV834-M Crashed Gohre shot down by Fw Bahr NJG6	F/Lt R.V. Jones killed P/O H.D.S. White DFM POW *Stalag* L3 Sgt R. Booth killed, buried in Berlin F/Sgt T.D. Henderson killed, buried in Berlin F/Lt J.W. Warren DFC killed, buried in Berlin F/Sgt G. Carrell killed, buried in Berlin Sgt W.A. Jefferies POW/ wounded, *Stalag* L6/357
35 Squadron Halifax LV864-O Crashed nr Buckow	P/O K.G. McAlpine killed in combat, buried in Berlin

Sgt Traylor shot by the German Home
Guard after baling out
Sgt Chant died of a coronary attack
2 December 1944.

F/Sgt G.W. Traylor killed,
buried in Berlin
Sgt L. Chant died while a
POW/wounded, buried in
Becklingen
F/Sgt A.A.J. Meyers POW
Stalag L6/357
P/O A.G.S. McCulloch POW
Stalag L3
F/Sgt D. Sinclair killed in
combat, buried in Berlin
Sgt R.J. Twine POW *Stalag* L6/357

---

49 Squadron Lancaster JB469-B
Crashed Brockelkuslche
in the Hannover area
Shot down by a night fighter flown
by Oblt Martin Becker of 1/NJG6

F/Sgt E. White killed
Sgt J.R. Ward killed
Sgt G. Compton killed
Sgt.J.E. Ellis killed
Sgt D. Stevens killed
Sgt J. Loveland killed
Sgt H. Thomas killed

Sgt Ellis is remembered on the
Runneymede Memorial
The remainder are buried in
Hannover

---

49 Squadron Lancaster ND516-N
Crashed nr Karow
Shot down by a night fighter

P/O A.J. MacKenzie POW
Stalag III
Sgt W.S. Purdie killed
Sgt G.T. Critchley POW *Stalag*
357
Sgt G. Hobby killed
Sgt A.C. Grems killed
Sgt T.A. Stevens POW
Sgt K.A. Archer killed

Those killed are buried in Berlin

---

51 Squadron Halifax LW481-X
Crashed nr Bucknitz
Shot down after three attacks by a
night fighter

P/O R.E. Carder POW *Stalag* L3
F/Sgt J.R. Everett 2/Pilot killed
P/O E.S. Storey POW *Stalag* L3
P/O C.A. King POW *Stalag* L3
P/O G. Kettley POW *Stalag* L3
Sgt C. Berdsall POW

F/Sgt W.H.T. Alexander POW
Stalag L6/357
Sgt A.R. Albone killed

Those killed buried in Berlin

---

57 Squadron Lancaster ND503-E Crashed at Volksen Hit by flak and a night fighter	P/O W.G. Davies killed Sgt R.W. Ridsdale POW *Stalag* 357 F/O K.J. Tubbs killed F/Sgt J.A. Wheeler RCAF killed Sgt C.V. Clarke killed Sgt J. Dixon RCAF killed Sgt W. Rees killed Those killed buried in Hannover

---

61 Squadron Lancaster ME591-Z Crashed at Essen	P/O J.W. Golightly killed Sgt W. Rees killed Sgt R.S.J. Betteridge killed F/Sgt J.F. Allen RCAF killed F/O M. Yowney RCAF killed Sgt T.J. Hynes killed Sgt H.J. Newey killed Sgt J. Cairns killed Crew buried in the Rheinberg War Cemetery

---

61 Squadron HK538-F Shot down nr Gifhorn	F/O H Wallis killed Sgt T Preston POW *Stalag* IV F/Sgt L Tozer POW *Stalag* 357 F/Sgt A A Pardoe killed F/Sgt K Simms killed Sgt D J Brewer killed P/O E Bremner killed Those killed buried in Hannover

---

77 Squadron Halifax LL184-K Crashed in the sea and sank	W/O J. Dunlop killed Sgt W. Neil killed Sgt T.R. Swinton killed F/Sgt D.J. Dawson killed Sgt C.S. Foster killed Sgt C.E. Jones killed

Sgt B.R. Garfield washed up,
19.5.44 west of Texel, buried
Bergen op Zoom

All others on Runnymede Memorial

77 Squadron Halifax LL143-J	F/Lt H.A.L. Ellis DFC RAAF killed Sgt J.N. Schofield killed Sgt P.H.J. Mackie killed F/O R.D. Sullivan killed Sgt H.F. Payne killed P/O C.W.G. Graham killed P/O D. Fletcher killed All on Runnymede Memorial
77 Squadron Halifax LL239-A Crashed Reetzer Hutton District of Dresden	F/Sgt J.C. Dalzell killed Sgt F.L. Bones killed F/Sgt R.A. East POW Sgt A.P. Burch POW *Stalag* L6/357 Sgt J. Taylor killed Sgt J. Mclvor killed Sgt L. Huggett POW *Stalag* L6/357 All killed buried in Berlin
77 Squadron Halifax HR949-H Crashed Viel Hesdin	F/Lt D.A. Thomas POW *Stalag* L3 Sgt A. Smith POW *Stalag* L6/357 F/Sgt D.K. Measures POW *Stalag* L3 F/O D.L. Thorman evaded Sgt A.L.E. Roberston POW *Stalag* L6/357 Sgt A.L. Slater evaded Sgt D.A.Di-Goacca evaded
78 Squadron Halifax LW367-Q Crashed Kalleukote, Holland	P/O T.H. Smith killed P/O G.G. Bunn killed P/O D. Riach killed F/Sgt A. Hamilton killed Sgt W.E. Webb killed

	Sgt R. Chaplin killed
	Sgt H. Hemmings killed
	All buried at Steenwijkerwold

78 Squadron Halifax LK763-K	Sgt V. Smith killed
	F/Sgt R. Coulter killed
	F/O I.R.M. Douglas-Pulleyne killed
	Sgt G.P. Reynolds killed
	Sgt G. Beal killed
	Sgt R.G. O'Neil killed
	Sgt L.E. Mears RAAF killed
	All on Runnymede Memorial

78 Squadron Halifax LV816-N	F/Lt B. Denman killed
Crashed Gohrau nr Wittenburg	F/Sgt W.A. Lea POW *Stalag* L6/357
Shot down by Oblt Becker NJG6	F/O E.M. Wells POW *Stalag* L3
	F/O J. Wilson killed
	P/O R. Messer killed
	Sgt E.H. Glibbery killed
	W/O E.F. McAneeley killed
	All killed buried in Berlin

83 Squadron Lancaster ND448-S	F/O T B Field killed
Crashed Niemegk	F/Sgt M. Kelter killed
	Sgt C. Howes killed
	F/O M.J. Reid RCAF killed
	Sgt R.A.J. Rudge killed
	Sgt G. Wheeler killed
	F/Sgt G. Daley RAAF killed
	Sgt G.I. Patterson killed
	Crew buried in Berlin

83 Squadron Lancaster ND585-T	P/O V.A.R. Langford killed
Crashed Kats (Nord Beveland)	Sgt E.W. Curzon killed
Hit by a night fighter flown by Lt Heninz	F/Sgt W.D.L. Lloyd killed
of I/NGJG1	Sgt W.S. Crockford killed
	F/O R.F.D. Perkins killed
	Sgt G.J.T. Davies killed
	F/Sgt W.R. Sutton killed
	Crew buried Vlissingen

100 Squadron Lancaster ND571-N
Crashed nr Stendhal attacked by a
night fighter

F/O G.R. Sidebottom POW
Stalag III
Sgt V.R. Mendelski POW *Stalag*
Koppernikus
F/Sgt R.H.E. Dray POW*Stalag*
IV
P/O J.M. Mason POW *Stalag* III
Sgt S. Ambrose POW *Stalag* 357
P/O D.G. Parry POW *Stalag* III
Sgt C.G.R. Pope POW *Stalag* 357

101 Squadron Lancaster DV267-K
Crashed Leek Tolbert, Groningen
nr Halbertstadt

W/O J. Laurens DFM killed
Sgt W.A.G. Kibble POW *Stalag* 357
F/Sgt L. Burton POW *Stalag* 357
Sgt C.H. Waight killed after
baling out
Sgt R.V. Aitken POW *Stalag*
Bankau-Kreulberg
Sgt L.E. Royston POW *Stalag*
357
Sgt W.F.D. Bolt killed after
baling out
Sgt J.A. Davies POW *Stalag*
Bankau-Kreulberg

Sgt Bolt and WO Laurens
buried in Leek (Tobert)
Waight buried Noordijk

102 Squadron Halifax JN972-H
Crashed Scharringhausen

F/Sgt K.G. Cummings RCAF
killed, buried in Hannover, later
P/O
F/O O.P.J. McInerney RCAF
POW *Stalag* 9C/L3
Sgt N.F. Lingley killed, buried in
Hannover
Sgt R.P. Rees killed, buried in
Hannover
Sgt J. Torrance killed, buried in
Hannover
Sgt L.G.K. Giddings POW
Stalag L6/357
F/Sgt J.C. Clarke killed

102 Squadron Halifax HY185-B
Crashed nr Leipzig
Shot down by Oblt Becker
over Brandenberg

Did not bomb the target

F/O W.B. Dean POW *Stalag* L3
Sgt R.C. Trett POW *Stalag* L6/357
Sgt A.J. Milner POW *Stalag* L3
P/O W.W. Stenning POW
Stalag L3
Sgt W.C. Loosemore RAAF
POW *Stalag* L6/357
Sgt M.A. Clarke POW *Stalag*
L6/357
W/O I.M. Dryden RCAF POW
Stalag L6/357

---

103 Squadron Lan ND408-T
Crashed Paderborn area

W/O F. Law killed
Sgt D.C. Bell POW *Stalag* 357
F/Sgt K.W. Flowers killed
Sgt A.H. Daines killed
Sgt C.J.D. Baldwin POW *Stalag*
357
Sgt R.S. Johnstone killed
Sgt A.J. Bristow killed

Those killed buried in Hannover
War Cemetery

---

103 Squadron Lancaster JB745-J
Crashed Dueshorn-Celle

Sgt W.L. Bradley killed
Sgt F.J. Taylor killed
F/Sgt T.F. Johnstone killed
Sgt F.G.F. Osborne killed
F/Sgt J. Luck killed
Sgt E.W. Hamilton killed
P/O A. Stevens killed

Crew buried in Hannover

---

106 Squadron Lancaster ME630-P
Crashed at Layet
Shot down by a night fighter

F/O E.R.F. Leggett killed
Sgt E.F. Windeatt POW
F/O N.C.F. Bloy POW *Stalag* III
F/O F.B. Chubb POW *Stalag* III
Sgt T.H. Jones PCW *Stalag* 357
P/O S.W. Payne RAAF POW
Sgt J.C. Harrison POW *Stalag* 357

F/O Leggett buried in Berlin

156 Squadron Lancaster ND358–T
Crashed Zasenbach
Shot down by a night fighter

S/L A.D. Saunders DFC RCAF
killed
F/Lt W.M. Sterns DFC RCAF
killed
W/O J.W. Gibb DFC killed
F/Sgt J. Taylor killed
F/O C.D. Gough DFC killed
F/O W.J. Donner DFC Late
F/Lt RAAF killed
F/O R.L. Reeves killed

Crew buried in Hannover

---

156 Squadron Lancaster JA921–Q
Crashed Eemnes, Holland
Hit by a shell under the aircraft, which
went up 700 feet. Then over Holland a
fire started on the port side but after the
decision to bale out came the tail of the
aircraft snapped off and the aircraft
went upside down. Five bodies were
recovered but Hughes's body was never
found. Hughes's brother was also killed
on 24 December 1943 with 576 Sqn
A memorial has been erected at Eemnes
to this crew

W/O R. Stanners killed
Sgt E. Hopcraft killed
Sgt H.W. Hughes killed
F/O E.J.C. Kryskow RCAF
died of his wounds
Sgt R. Prankett killed
Sgt A.C.G. Merces killed
Sgt T.J. Brewer killed
F/O J. Kingston RCAF POW
Stalag III
Sgt Hughes's name on the
Runneymede Memorial
Remainder of the
crew buried in Amersfoort

---

158 Squadron Halifax LV786–P
Crashed Lingen

F/Sgt K.G. Williams POW
Sgt G. Bailey killed
Sgt B.C. Aldis POW
Sgt J.A. Cooper POW
Sgt L.J. Terrett POW
Sgt S. Bennion POW
Sgt E.M. Stephens POW

Sgt Bailey buried in the
Reichswald War Cemetery

---

158 Squadron Halifax LW501–M
Crashed Beedenbostel
Shot down by a night fighter

F/Lt S.W. Holmes killed
Sgt J.A. Filby killed
F/Sgt L.A. Horton killed
Sgt A. Rogerson killed
Sgt W. Wakefield killed

Sgt T. Nelson killed
Sgt G.J. Barrett POW *Stalag* L6/357

Those killed buried in Beedenbostel

166 Squadron Lancaster DV220-J Crashed Krahne shot down by a Fw 190 Manuel's DFM gazetted 9/7/1943	F/Sgt F.F.G. Allan RCAF killed Sgt T.H. Lee POW *Stalag* LVI F/Sgt F.J. Hughes RCAF POW *Stalag* 357 W/O2 J.J. Yelland RCAF killed Sgt W.A. Dykes killed F/Sgt J. Manuel DFM POW *Stalag* 357 Sgt A. Rose POW *Stalag* 357 F/Sgt Allan buried in Berlin WOII Yelland and Sgt Dykes are on the Runneymede Memorial
166 Squadron Lancaster ME627-Z Crashed at Mkranstaed	F/Sgt R.A. Kingston RAAF killed Sgt R.V. Mercer killed Sgt G.M.C. Campbell killed F/Sgt M.H. Foster RAAF killed Sgt S. R.G. Gardiner killed Sgt A.R. Bailey killed Sgt D.J. Dennehy killed Crew buried in Berlin
166 Squadron Lancaster ME637-F Crashed in the sea	S/L R. Bows killed Sgt F.G. Brooks killed F/Sgt H. Gregg killed F/O W.F. Hughes RNZAF killed Sgt A.K. Barlow killed Sgt E.L. Morton killed Sgt D.B. Asquith killed Names on the Runneymede Memorial

207 Squadron Lancaster EE126-O
Crashed at Pestinghausen
Shot down by three night fighters

P/O W.D. Jarvis POW *Stalag* III
F/Sgt S.T. Pearson POW *Stalag* 357
Sgt M. Askew POW *Stalag* 357
Sgt J.T. Morey killed
Sgt L.T. Linton RCAF killed
Sgt P.L. Paddook POW/ wounded *Stalag* 357
Sgt J.J.R. Rogers killed

Sgt Linton buried in Becklingen
Sgt's Morey and Rogers buried in Sage

---

207 Squadron Lancaster ME633-Y
Crashed in the sea

P/O J.J.R. Clark killed
Sgt N. Doherty killed
F/Sgt C.H. Maxted killed
Sgt B.H.J. Baldwin killed
Sgt D.C. Everett killed
F/Sgt T.J. Moran RCAF killed
Sgt H.C. Parker killed

Names on the Runneymede Memorial

---

408 Squadron Lancaster DS788-C
Crashed Kropswolde
Shot down by a night fighter
Salvaged in 1973

F/O J.A. Frampton RCAF killed
F/Sgt J.J. Astles killed
F/C G.W. Reynolds POW *Stalag* III
Sgt K.W. Tindall killed in combat
Sgt K.H. Bennett RCAF killed
Sgt K. Smith RCAF killed in combat
Sgt F.W.C. Robertson evaded capture

F/O Frampton, F/Sgt Astles, Sgt Tindall, Sgt Bennett, Sgt Smith buried in Hoogezand-Sappemeer, Holland

---

408 Squadron Lancaster DS632-G
Crashed nr Jerchel
Shot down by a night fighter

F/Sgt B.V. Griep RCAF POW
F/Sgt J.S James RCAF POW
F/O R.T. Wall RCAF POW

Sgt J.B. McKinnon RCAF POW
Sgt W. Plunkett RCAF killed in
combat
Sgt C.A. Hughes killed in
combat
Sgt J. Meikle POW

Sgt's Plunkett and Hughes
buried in Berlin

---

408 Squadron Lancaster LL720-R
Crashed at Hulst
Shot down by Hptm von Bonin NJG1
aircraft fell in the Westersahelde River

F/Lt E.S. Winn RCAF killed
F/O J R Leaman RCAF killed
P/O J.R. Bonneville RCAF
killed
F/Sgt R.H. Wade RCAF killed
Sgt E. Driamnitski RCAF killed,
body recovered 14.3.44 in
Baalock
Tech/Sgt N. Hanbury Brown
USAAF killed
Sgt E.W. Bolt killed

F/Lt Winn, Sgt Bolt, F/O
Leaman, and F/Sgt Wade
buried in Schoonselhof,
Antwerp
T/Sgt Hanbury Brown buried
in US Neuville-en-Condroz

---

408 Squadron Lancaster LL719-V
Crashed between Machern and
Puechau

F/O G.W.Mc. Richter RCAF
killed
F/Sgt D.I. Bowden killed
Sgt G.N. Bennett RCAF killed
WOII S.L. Roach RCAF killed
Sgt R.G. Kelly RCAF killed
Sgt F.G. Skeet killed
Sgt C.W.G. Roberts killed

F/O Richter buried in Berlin
Sgt Bennett buried in Berlin
WOII Roach buried in Berlin
Sgt Roberts, Sgt Kelly, Sgt Skeet,
F/Sgt Bowden buried in Choloy
War Cemetery

419 Squadron Halifax LW327-A Crashed Gorzke	F/O L.T. Lucas POW *Stalag* L3 F/O G.P. Davies killed F/Sgt J.P. Hairsine RCAF POW *Stalag* L6/357 F/Sgt J. Pluta RCAF POW *Stalag* L6/357 Sgt G.R. Herriet RCAF POW L6/357 Sgt P. Newberry killed Sgt J.F.G.R. Dehoux killed Those killed buried in Berlin
419 Squadron Halifax JD114-V	F/Sgt D.K. MacLeod killed F/O J.R. Piper killed Sgt J.L. Beattie killed Sgt G. Gettings killed Sgt M.B. Leboldus killed Sgt D.C. Lewthwaite killed Sgt A.H. Hackbart killed All named on Runnymede Memorial
426 Squadron Lancaster DS776-A Crashed at Valkenswaard Noord Brabant Attacked by a night fighter	F/Sgt M.A. MacKenzie RCAF killed F/O H.A. Hancock RCAF killed F/O P.C. Cox RCAF killed WOI F.R. Alleyn killed Sgt J V. Gwynne killed Sgt G. Whalen RCAF killed Sgt E.A. Dowe RCAF killed All buried in Woensel
427 Squadron Halifax LV829-D Crashed Gohrau	F/O D.C. Olsvik RCAF killed P/O J.P. McKenzie RCAF killed P/O R.L. Warren RCAF killed P/O D.H. Jonasson RCAF killed F/Sgt A.G. Taillon RCAF killed F/Sgt J.G. Burke RCAF killed F/Sgt W.R. Tobin RCAF killed All buried in Berlin

428 Squadron Haliax JD271-M Crashed in the sea nr Ijsselmeer	F/O C.W. Woolverton RCAF killed, washed up 17.6.44 Audyk F/O G.A. Smith RCAF killed F/Sgt H.S. Lister RCAF killed Sgt A.W. Gotham killed Sgt C.W. Sherratt killed Sgt E.C. Webb RCAF killed Sgt N.M. Stewart RCAF killed, washed up 11.5.44 All buried in Andijk
429 Squadron Halifax LK662-Q Crashed Andisleben	F/O L.B. Fincham RCAF killed WCII O.L. Morrison RCAF killed F/O M.F. Meech RCAF killed Sgt W.H. Cotterill killed WOII S.L. Mingle RCAF POW *Stalag* L6/357 Sgt L.R. Martin RCAF POW *Stalag* L6/357 Sgt V.A. Barton RCAF PCW *Stalag* L6/357 Those killed buried in Berlin
429 Squadron Halifax LK993-J Crashed nr Gardelegen	F/Lt J. Bowen killed F/O H.F. Blackman killed WOII A.C. Forsyth killed F/Sgt M.E. Bridewell killed Sgt T.A. Brown killed Sgt M.R. Smoke killed F/Sgt P.A. Gilfeather killed F/Sgt C.B. Murray killed All buried in Berlin
429 Squadron Halifax LK974-Z Crashed at Wahrburg Shot down by a night fighter Oblt Becker NGJ6	F/Lt J.J. Stephens RCAF killed WOII J.W. Gibbons RCAF killed WOII P.A. McIntyre RCAF killed Sgt R.F. Hawker killed Sgt J.R. Hamilton killed Sgt V.E. Reed RCAF killed WOII W.H. Ostlund RCAF POW *Stalag* L6/357 Those killed buried in Berlin

431 Squadron Halifax LK905-D
Crashed nr Epse

F/O M. Sonshine killed
WOII A.G. Harvey RCAF POW
Stalag L6/357
F/O J.A. Houston killed
P/O D.A. McKerry killed
Sgt R.H. Gillander killed
Sgt A.C. Twitchett killed
F/O E.J. Kee killed

Those killed buried in Berlin

431 Squadron Halifax LK964-T
Crashed at Boedorf, suburb of Leipzig

F/Sgt J. Howell killed
F/O J.H. Cunningham killed
F/Sgt E.H. Cutler killed
WOII L.G. Howell killed
F/Sgt S.J. Vernon killed
Sgt J.D. Bates killed
Sgt D.J. Rawlinson killed

All buried in Berlin

433 Squadron Halifax HX230-Q
Crashed at Jueterbog
Shot down by Lt Niklas NJG3

F/Sgt R.J. McKay killed
Sgt J.E. Davidson killed
Sgt F.W. Daplyn killed
Sgt J. Oliver killed
Sgt J. Hein RCAF killed
Sgt J.J. Murphy killed
Sgt J.B. Fraser killed

Crew buried in Berlin

434 Squadron Halifax HX230-Q
Crashed Gohre

F/O C.L. Murray RCAF killed
F/O W. Hayter killed
P/O C. Broadfoot killed
WOII J. Donnelly killed
Sgt J. McGregor killed
Sgt A. Pearae killed
Sgt J. Dove killed

Crew buried in Berlin

434 Squadron Halifax LK945-O
Crashed nr Grimma
Shot down by Oblt Becker

F/Lt L.H. Cameron RCAF killed
F/Sgt J. Gilman POW
F/Sgt G. Raymond POW

F/O D. Rioux POW/wounded
Sgt J. Holder killed
Sgt E. Davies killed
Sgt G.N. Ferrier POW

Those killed buried in Berlin

---

434 Squadron Halifax LL257-Z
Crashed at Barber
Shot down by a night fighter
at Celle

P/O H.D. Beames RCAF killed
F/O W. Gallagher POW
F/Sgt D.L. Temple POW
Sgt G. Hand POW
Sgt R. Jennings killed
Sgt G. Hatch POW
Sgt W. Oliver killed

Those killed buried in Hannover

---

460 Squadron Lancaster ND569-E
Crashed Troglitz

F/Sgt S.V. Mackrell RAAF killed
Sgt G.A. Fidler RAAF killed
F/Sgt I.A. Thomson RAAF
killed
F/Sgt H.E. Tappenden RAAF
POW *Stalag* 357
F/Sgt K.K. Groves RAAF
POW *Stalag* 357
Sgt L.H.G. Weller RAAF killed
F/Sgt N.J. Randell RAAF POW

Names of those killed on the
Runneymede Memorial

---

460 Squadron Lancaster JB610-H
Crashed at Steinhudermeer Lake
nr Wunstorf

W/O K.J. Goodwin RAAF killed
Sgt C.C. Wood killed
F/Sgt V.W. Dellit RAAF POW
F/Sgt M.D. Wiggin POW
Stalag 357
F/Sgt F.A. Hennessey RAAF
killed
F/O J.N. Morris RAAF killed
Sgt F. Clarkson killed

W/O Goodwin, Sgt Wood, are
on the Runneymede Memorial
the remainder killed are buried
in Hannover

463 Squadron Lancaster DV338-C	P/O E.A. Fayle RAAF killed Sgt C.T. Baker killed F/O L. Chappell killed Sgt L.K. Topham killed Sgt R.J. Farrell killed Sgt A.L.N. Vickery killed F/Sgt B.P. Bennett RAAF killed Names on the Runneymede Memorial
466 Squadron Halifax LV781-H Crashed in the sea at Harlingen, Holland	W/O J.F. Moran killed F/O M.G. Pepper killed W/O A.N.D. McPhee killed F/Sgt L.A. Laver killed Sgt E.F. Harper killed, washed up 29.7.44, Harlingen Oyke, buried Harlingen Sgt G.E. Brown killed, buried Harlingen Sgt R.F. Banks killed Remainder on Runnymede Memorial
514 Squadron Lancaster DS736-D2	F/Sgt N. Hall killed Sgt K.L. Cragg killed Sgt J.R. Williams killed Sgt F.R. Lewis killed Sgt W.K. Watkins killed Sgt T.S. Woodford killed Sgt A. Hodson killed Names on the Runneymede Memorial
514 Squadron Lancaster LL661-J	F/Lt L.J. Kingwell killed Sgt W.A. Bates killed Sgt G.E. Knight killed Sgt H.M. Whichelow killed Sgt H. Taylor killed W/O H.S. Fidge RAAF killed Sgt D.W.Newbury killed W/O1 J.D. Dodding RCAF killed Names on the Runneymede Memorial

514 Squadron Lancaster DS823-M Crashed at Essern after attack by a night fighter	F/Sgt W. Henry killed, later P/O F/Sgt W.S. Ball RCAF killed Sgt S.W. Ricketts killed Sgt F.B. Vallance killed Sgt D. Kenny killed Sgt W. Lannigan killed Sgt A.E. Bennett killed Crew buried in the Rheinberg War Cemetery.
550 Squadron Lancaster LM461-U Crashed at Kiefernwald Shot down by a fighter at Elberfield	W/O J.I. Miller killed Sgt R.E. White POW *Stalag* 357 Sgt D.V.H. Evans POW *Stalag* LVI Sgt G.E. Brown POW *Stalag* 357 Sgt P.H. Hurst POW *Stalag* LVI Sgt T.K. Williams killed F/Sgt J.P. Harrison POW Sgt F C Thomas killed Those killed buried in Berlin
576 Squadron Lancaster DV386-E2	F/Sgt A.J. Kirk killed Sgt W. Moores killed Sgt E.M. Howard killed F/Sgt R.L. Smith killed F/Sgt W. Kitson killed F/Sgt M. Churchman killed Sgt T. Finnerty killed Names on the Runneymede Memorial
625 Squadron Lancaster LM384-X Crashed Bledeln	F/Sgt C.E. Pearson killed Sgt A.A.T. Sinclair killed Sgt G.A. Paterson POW *Stalag* 357 F/O J.V. Pearl RAAF killed Sgt G.A. Cartwright killed Sgt A.R. Trivett killed Sgt T.R. Evans. killed Those killed buried in Hannover

625 Squadron Lancaster JA862-T
Crashed in a swamp nr
Kaltenweide, 6 miles north of
Hannover

S/L B.N. Douetil POW
Sgt J. Gill killed
Sgt N. McMillan killed
F/Sgt F.T. Price
POW/wounded *Stalag* 357
while a POW after attack by
Typhoons while on a route
march and died eleven days later
P/O B.V. Cude killed
Sgt B.K. Sparkes killed
F/O F.L. Hale killed

Those killed buried in Hannover

---

625 Squadron Lancaster ME588-A
Crashed at Almke Brunswick
Aspin awarded immediate DFM after
the raid on Leipizg in October 1943,
London Gazette 23/11/1943

P/O J.D. Aspin DFM killed
Sgt P.R. Wheeldon killed
Sgt J.C. Landon killed
Sgt W.E. Riley killed
Sgt G.H. Eastwood killed
Sgt R.S. Watson killed
Sgt P.S. Skebo RCAF killed

Crew buried Hotton, Luxemburg

---

626 Squadron Lancaster ME589-D2
killed
Crashed into the sea off
Schiermonkoog

F/Sgt   A.M.Mc.   Matheson

Sgt H. Cook killed
Sgt M. Latham killed
Sgt A.W. Mitton killed
Sgt H. Dunn POW
Sgt G.H. Bodycott killed
Sgt J.J. Pullman killed

Sgt Mitton buried in Nes
General Cemetery
Sgt Bodycott buried in Vredenhof
Remainder of the crew are on
the Runneymede Memorial

---

630 Squadron Lancaster ND532-N
Crashed at Leipzig having been shot
down by three fighters, one Oblt
Kraft NJG1

P/O W. Yates DFC killed
Sgt W.A. Isaacs POW/wounded
Stalag 357
Sgt A. Spence killed
F/Sgt R. Findow RCAF POW
Stalag 357

Sgt D. Scott POW
F/Lt E. Stead MID killed
F/Lt D. Dawson killed

P/O Yates, Sgt Spence, F/Lt
Stead and F/Sgt Dawson buried
Berlin

---

630 Squadron Lancaster JB710-W

F/Lt C. Armour killed
Sgt J. Byars killed
P/O H. Kidd killed
F/O J. Cross killed
Sgt R. Giles killed
Sgt L.A. Young killed
Sgt G. Griffiths killed

All the names are on the
Runneymede Memorial

---

640 Squadron Halifax LW422-R
Crashed at Gohrau shot down by
Fw Bahr NJG6

F/O W. Waugh killed
F/O J.S. Cant killed
F/Sgt I.D.J. May killed
F/Sgt J. Briggs killed
Sgt C. Morrice killed
F/O A.S. Barclay RCAF killed
F/O W.H. Murray RCAF killed
Sgt C.A. Hilton killed

All buried in Berlin

---

640 Squadron Halifax LW55O-U

Crashed at Trebbin having been hit
by flak over Leipzig

W/O B.S. Woodham POW
Stalag L6/357
F/Sgt P. Wilson RCAF killed
F/O W. Hodgkins POW
Stalag L3
Sgt H.G. Coker POW *Stalag* L6/357
Sgt M. Godfrey killed
Sgt R. Goldsbrough POW *Stalag* L3
Sgt W.R. Anderson POW *Stalag* L3

Those killed buried in Berlin

---

692 Squadron Mosquito DZ612-N
Crashed St Sever, France

F/Lt W. Thomas killed
F/C J.L. Munby DFC killed

Aircraft that Crashed in the UK

103 Squadron Lancaster JD530-F Collided in mid air with Lancaster ND334 on approach to landing	F/Sgt H.W. Gumbrell, pilot Crew uninjured
103 Squadron Lancaster ND334 Collided with JD530 while preparing to land.	W/O J.C. Warnes, pilot inj Sgt D.H.J. Cunningham killed F/O R.H. Fuller killed Sgt S. Clapham inj F/Sgt C. Bagshaw killed F/Sgt H.S. Gunn killed Sgt A.O. Haines killed Sgt Cunningham buried in Brigg F/O Fuller buried in Cambridge City Cemetery F/Sgt Bagshaw buried in Urmston, Lancs F/Sgt Gunn buried in Glasgow Sgt Haines buried in Brigg
158 Squadron Halifax HZ351-S Crashed at Catfoss after take-off	P/O P.M. Jennings killed, buried Little Milton P/O N. Caffery killed, buried Kimblesworth F/Sgt H.E. Jones killed, buried Penmaenmawr Sgt G.F. Gillings killed, buried Wandsworth Sgt S.P. Morris killed, buried Llanfechain F/Sgt G.R. Fitzsimmons RCAF killed, buried Harrogate P/O C.J. Seymour killed, buried Rolvenden
166 Lancaster LM382-Q Crash-landed at Manston airfield 6.05 am Hit by a night fighter on the outward trip	P/O J. Catlin inj Sgt H.C. Wright inj P/O A.W. Pragnell inj P/O F.C. Simm inj Sgt T.P.F. Hall inj Sgt T. Powers inj Sgt W. Birch inj

10 April 1945

44 Squadron Lancaster ND631-B F/O Jones liberated by Soviet forces	F/O P.W. Kennedy RCAF killed WOII A.F.D. Turner RCAF killed F/S J.E. Short killed Sgt E.P.P. Olson killed F/O W.J. Jones POW F/S C. McBurney killed F/S G.E. Bull killed P/O G.C.R. Woodhouse killed 2/Pilot Crew buried in Berlin
83 Squadron Lancaster ME423-C Hit by flak and abandoned in the air Crashed in the area of Fulda	F/Lt D.W.R. Shand survived F/Lt W.W. Simpson survived W/O E.M. Annear RAAF survived F/S W.J. Newling survived F/O A. McDonald slightly injured F/O F.J. Naylor killed found dead in his open chute. Buried Nederweert, Limburg F/S P. McHale survived P/O W.J. Ryekman RCAF POW
207 Squadron Lancaster NE472-0 Crashed at Burg Rohl, Belgium Hit by heavy flak crashed Burg Rohl, Belgium Baled out at 4,000 feet	F/O P.M. Anderson DFC RCAF killed, found by the US F/O P.M. Anderson DFC RCAF killed, found by the US forces Buried Brussels Town Cemetery F/O C.M. Hewelleon survived Sgt C.F. Collins survived Sgt E. Nichols survived F/O K.A. Larcombe survived Sgt E.J. Mattherson survived Sgt J.R. Pearl survived
415 Squadron Halifax NA185- Crashed at Leipzig	F/O R.S. Evans RCAF killed, on Runnymede Memorial

F/O L.M. Spry RCAF killed,
buried in Berlin
F/S M.K. Burns RCAF killed
Sgt J.M. Andrews killed, buried
in Berlin
P/O D.L. Lorenz RCAF killed,
buried in Berlin
F/S D.R. Teevin RCAF killed
F/O L.E. Veitch RCAF killed,
buried in Berlin

---

433 Squadron Lancaster PB903-F
Hit by flak short of the aiming point fire
in the starboard engine. Aircraft turned
on its back and dived steeply into the
ground and exploded
Crashed at Lutschen village

P/O R.J. Grisdale RCAF killed
F/O I.B. Zierler RCAF killed
F/S J.M. Hirak RCAF killed
Sgt W.A.J. Thurston killed
F/O W.G. McLeod RCAF killed
later P/O
F/O I.B. Zierler RCAF killed
F/S J.M. Hirak RCAF killed
Sgt W.A.J. Thurston killed
F/O W.G. McLeod RCAF killed
later P/O
F/S F.G. Seeley RCAF killed
later P/O
F/S D.W. Roberts ECAF killed

Crew buried in Berlin

---

462 Squadron Halifax NA240-
Those killed buried in Berlin

P/O A.D.J. Ball RAAF killed
F/S N.V. Evans RAAF killed
W/O R.E. Taylor RAAF killed
Sgt F.B. Brookes killed
F/O P. Murray RAAF killed
F/S J.A. Tait RAAF killed
F/S K.J. Hibberd RAAF
survived

---

619 Squadron Lancaster SW254-S
Crashed at Loberitz

F/Lt A.E. McMorran RCAF
killed
F/Lt B.A. Williamson RCAF
killed
F/O R.H. Jackson RCAF killed
F/Lt F. Jackson RAAF killed

	F/S H.J. Burke survived POW P/O J.W. Chambers killed in action P/O C.T.W Perring killed in action Those killed buried in Berlin
630 Squadron Lancaster HE739-T	F/O A.V. Cameron RAAF survived POW Sgt G.S.W. Hooper survived POW F/S J.E. Hogan RAAF survived POW F/S R.W. Beardwell survived POW F/S G. Gould evaded F/S J.R. Dickens killed found dead after baling out Sgt C. G. E. Bourner evaded F/S Dickens buried in Choloy
630 Squadron Lancaster RF122-S Crashed at Glebitz, 21 miles west of Leipzig	F/O R. Sasson killed F/O J. Hopwood killed F/S M.S. Munro killed Sgt S.C. Walton killed F/O P.F. Fleming survived POW Sgt W.H. Jenkins killed F/S I.L. Lynn survived POW Those killed buried in Berlin

Bibliography

—⚋—

Jimmy Stewart: Bomber Pilot, Starr Smith
Eighth Air Force, Donald L. Miller
Inside the Third Reich, Albert Speer
Uncommon Valour, A.G. Goulding
'We Act With One Accord' 35 Squadron, Alan Cooper
Bomber Command War Diaries, Martin Middlebrook and Chris Everitt
RAF Bomber Command Losses, W.R. Chorley
The Poems We Wrote – An Anthology of Air Force Poems, Edited by Eddy A.
   Coward
German Aircraft Industry and Production 1933–1945, Ferenc A. Vajda &
   Peter Dancey
Fortress of the Big Triangle, Cliff T. Bishop
Arming the Luftwaffe, Edward L. Homze
'Bomber' Harris, Dudley Saward
The Bomber's Eye, Gp Captain Dudley Saward OBE

Sources
ACM Lee-Mallory's diary at the National Archives Air37-784
Gary Moncur US 303rd Bomb Group (BG.com)
National Archives
A Brief Service Account of T/Sgt William P. Mitchell USAAF by Joseph W.
   Campbell

Index

—⁂—

Adams, W/C 119
Aitkin, R. Sgt 131
Arnold, Capt later General 152, 153, 154, 155
Atcheson, S. P/O 121
Attlee, C. 176, 177, 178
Augenstein, H.H. Oblt 138

Bach, J.S. 81
Bancer, P/O 87
Barron, J.F. S/L 126
Bartlett, Capt 18
Bartlett, L. 118
Beetham, M. F/O later Marshal of the RAF 95, 96
Bednall, C. 96, 97
Benjamin, W/C 173
Binder, C.T. 2/Lt 163
Birch, W. Sgt 114
Blake, W. F/O 108, 110, 111, 115, 116, 121, 124, 125
Bodgers, P/O 121
Bolt, B. Sgt 130, 131
Bottrell, Sgt 103
Bourner, G. F/Sgt 174, 175
Bowman, H. Col later Brig/Gen 166
Bradburn, P/O 105
Brady, Sgt 122
Bulman, Major 19
Burton, L. F/Sgt 130, 131
Butt, Mr 22
Byford, F/O 111

Cameron, F/O 174, 175
Carter, J. Sgt 112, 122
Carter, G, S/L 128, 129
Cartlin, J. P/O 114
Caunt, F/Lt 121
Chamberlian, Neville 28
Chant, F/Sgt 138
Child, R. 118,132, 133
Churchill, Winston 24, 26, 29, 30, 31, 35, 36, 176, 177, 178
Cole, Major 161
Compton, 1st Lt 103
Corlett, A. Sgt 138
Coryton, AVM 41
Cowman, Sgt 117, 118
Crawford, F/Lt 110
Cross, W/O 129

Dahl, W. Major 171
Davis, J. Sgt 131, 132
Davis, S/L 133, 135
Dawson, B. 106
Dean, F/O 108
Denman, F/Lt 102
Doolittle, J. General 153, 155, 159, 166
Donk, A. van der, Mr 130
Douhet, Giulio 11, 12, 16, 166
Dowding, Lord 177
Downs, B. 99, 100, 101, 102, 104, 106, 110, 118, 119, 123, 124, 129, 142
Dugay, Sgt 111

Edwards, H. Gp Capt 96 ,97
Eisenhower, General 50, 77
Eaker, I. 1st Lt Later General
    152, 154
Ewens, P/O 121

Farant, F/Sgt 126
Fedden, Alfred H.R. Mr 18, 19
Fitch, F/Lt 122
Forbes, Col 24
Forsyth, Sgt 112
Frampton, F/O 138
Fraser, Sgt 111
Frydag, K. 146, 149

Galland, A. Gen 178,
Garget, B. 106
Gavotti, Lt 12
Goddard, W/C 19
Goodridge, E. Sgt 138
Goebbels, Dr 94
Goering, Herman 66, 74, 77,178
Gorman, J. 2/Lt 163
Gould, G. F/Sgt 175
Grange, A. F/Sgt 133
Griffiths, Sgt 120
Gross. W.M. Brig/Gen 171
Gumbrell, F/Sgt 125

Haigh, S/L 104, 111, 125
Hall, T. Sgt 114, 115
Harris, S/L later C in C 23, 24,
    25, 27, 38, 39, 40, 41, 46, 47, 49,
    77, 98, 150, 176, 177, 178, 179,
    180
Harrision, J. 132
Hart, F/Lt 103, 126
Harvey, D.C. F/O 105
Healey, F/O 109, 110
Hemmings, F/Sgt 112, 134

Hendry, B. 106, 118, 119
Her Majesty, the Queen Mother
    180
Herrman, H. 97
Higgs, J. 168
Hitler, Adolph 17, 21, 28, 30, 66,
    77, 80, 84, 178
Hofman, R. 2/Lt 164
Hoizman, Col 159
Horley, F/Sgt 111, 112
Houston, J. W/O 111, 124, 125
Hughes, Sgt 115

Jay, Sgt 122
Jennings, P/O 105
Joiner, P. 106
Jones, Sgt 125
Jones, F/Lt 139
Junkers, Hugo 65, 67
Jupp, G. 106, 123, 124

Keinkel, Professor 147
Kerr, Sgt 139
Kingston, F/O 115
Koller, Gen 176
Knauss, Dr 66, 67
Knilans, N. 93, 94
Krampe, F/O 103
Kreipe, Gen 178
Kryskow, F/O 115

Laing, J.R. F/O 105
Laurens, J. 130, 131
Lawley Jnr, W. 1st Lt Later Col
    164, 165
Lawrence, W/C 134
Lees, J, F/Lt 96
Leggett, F/O 131, 132
Leipizig, Erla 75
Lennard, F/O 125

Ludlow-Hewitt, Edgar, Sir ACM 27
L'Estrange, F/Sgt 140
Lunn, F/Sgt 110
Luther, M. 81
Lloyd, F/Sgt 105

Maguire, R. 167
Mallory-Lee, ACM 169
Marshall, P/O 120 125
Mathies, A. S/Sgt 165
McAlpine, P/O 138
McCelland, F/Lt 89, 90
McClain, C.J. Lt 161
McCormick, F/Sgt 139
McLeish, S/L 121,140
McPherson, A. F/O 29
McTurk, B. 104, 138, 139
Marriott, K. F/O 132, 133
Martin, J.R. Lt 165
Mattock, R.D. F/O 100
Measures, W/O 133
Mendelsson F. 81
Merrill, P/O 126
Messerschmitt, Professor 74
Milch, General 18, 69, 72, 74, 77, 78, 146
Mimms, W/O 120
Mitchell Jnr , W.P. T/Sgt 167, 168
Mitchell , W. Lt/Col 15, 16, 152, 153
Moncure, V.L. Lt 162
Montague, Lord 11
Moorhouse, Rhodes. Lt 26
Moran, B. 167
Morgan, A, Sgt 120
Mosley, O. 177
Mulch, Erhard 66, 74
Mussolini, Benito 12

Nelson, C. Lt 165
Nettleton, John, W/C 46
Newton, F/Lt 103, 126
Norris, I. 136

Parker, C. F/O 102, 130
Parkinson, Sgt 109
Peirse, Richard, Sir AM, 38
Pelletier, S/L 103, 117, 118
Phillips, Captain 24
Pickard, G/Capt 98
Portal, Charles, Sir, ACM 35, 38, 179
Powers, T. Sgt 114, 115
Pragnell, T. P/O 114, 115

Rance, P/O 126
Raymond, F/Lt 120
Reddish, P/O 111, 119
Reed, P/O 87
Richardson, Sgt 117
Ritchie, G. 103, 107, 112, 119, 122, 123
Roberts, G.W. F/Lt 100
Robertson, Sgt 138
Rollins, W/O 125, 126
Roosevelt, President 21
Ropp, De, Baron 18
Royston, B. Sgt 130

Sale, J, S/L 128, 129
Saundby, Robert, AM 40, 41
Saur, Karl-Otto 72, 79, 146, 147, 149
Schnaufer, Major 59
Schneider, Hugo 82
Sherwin, T. 106, 119
Sim, F. 115
Sinclair, F/Sgt 138
Singleton, J. Mr 39

Smith, T. 99, 100, 101, 102, 129, 130, 134
Smuts, Jan General 14
Soper, F/Sgt 109
Southwell, V. 120
Spaatz, General 48, 152, 154, 155, 159, 168, 169
Speer, Albert. Dr 47, 48, 55, 63, 78, 79, 146, 147, 149, 172, 179
Stahler, Sgt 112
Stanners, W/O 115
Stevens, K.D. Col 163
Stewart, J. Major 165, 166
Storey, N. 126, 127
Strachey, J. 177
Stuart, F. F/Sgt 91
Symonds, D.S. F/Lt 105

Tank, Dr 70
Taylor, F/O 103, 126
Taylor, F/Sgt 138
Tedder, ACM 50
Toovey, F/O 110
Townsend, W/O 104
Trenchard, Lord 14, 27
Trett, R. Sgt 107, 108, 128, 135, 136, 137
Tricky, F/O 139
Truemper, W.E. 2/Lt 165
Turner, P. 119

Twinning, N. Lt Gen 155

Utz, F/Lt 97

Wadsworth, Sgt 122
Walker, W. S/L 104, 105
Wagner, R. 81
Warner, W/O 125
Watkins, K. 121
Webster, C. Sir 179
Weir, Lord 18, 19
Weller, S/L 120, 125
Wever, Walther. General 21, 24
White, C. W/O 91
Whitehead, Sgt 122
Williams, F/O 110
Williams, Sgt 138
Williams, Brig/Gen 162, 163
Windeatt, E. 118
Winkle, W.O. Van Lt 165
Wilson, F/Sgt 112
Windeatt, E. 107, 131
Wright, A. Sgt 111
Wright, B. Sgt 114, 115
Wright, C. P/O 130,131

Young, L. 104, 107

Zorner, Paul 59, 112, 113